SALON CONFIDENTIAL

Susan Michael

This book is dedicated to every hairstylist who has made the profession look easy. Thank you for always putting your client's best interests first. You are greatly appreciated.

Acknowledgments

Thank you, Lord, for giving me the focus I needed to complete this book.

To every stylist I interviewed (you know who you are), I can never thank you enough. You trusted me, a total stranger, with your stories, making Salon Confidential possible. I could not have done this without you.

To my husband, Mark, my encourager, supporter, and best friend. Love you more!

Table of Contents

Hairstylist, hair·styl·ist, [ˈherˌstīləst] (n):

A special person who touches

more hearts than hair.

Introduction

No doubt hairstylists and bartenders hear the deepest, darkest secrets that lead to the wildest, craziest, and sometimes scariest of stories. A specific code of ethics comes with any profession involving client confidentiality. Sometimes, professionals desire to break that code and reveal what is too good to keep to themselves. Knowing the significance of confidentiality from working in the emergency department (i.e., HIPAA) and most professions, it was enticing and motivational for me to open that door so stylists could break that code of silence in a non-threatening way. I contacted stylists nationwide, thanks to friends who knew of stylists who would want to share their stories. Some stylists interviewed connected me to others they knew would be interested in being interviewed. Most stylists would initially start the interview by saying they didn't know if they had any interesting stories. Once I planted the seed, "Tell about a time when a client..." my book grew into the most amazing stories.

The stylists interviewed for this book were remarkable, talented, funny, and dedicated individuals to the profession. They came from various backgrounds and different parts of the country. I never expected the response that I received from these stylists with such enthusiasm. Some went as far as to say it was an honor to be interviewed. Truth be known, it was an honor for me to interview all of them.

The common thread among them when interviewing was, "I always said that we should write a book." Salon

Confidential allowed stylists to release those pent-up stories safely, with the understanding all names would be changed, protecting the innocent and not-so-innocent. They even shared personal stories of unique situations between them and their clients.

Actual events inspired this fiction set in a fictitious town and studio out west. Throughout the book, the reader will experience a wide range of emotions regarding scandalous, humorous, poignant, embarrassing, and horrific stories, keeping the reader engaged from the beginning to the end. Given the number of stories selected for this book, 107 in all, I decided to share them from the perspective of six hairstylists.

Matthew is a graduate of Paul Mitchell School and the manager and lead stylist. He is very organized and an innovator. With 30 years in the profession, he is known as Lockston's top stylist. He's originally from Arizona.

Lexi had been a stylist for 20 years, owning her salon in Doylestown, Pa. She always vacationed in Lockston, with the goal that someday it would be her forever home. She is known around the studio for her upbeat and energetic attitude.

Isabella left the sunshine state of Florida after 24 years as a hairstylist. An avid hiker, she felt the mountains of Colorado calling. She came to Lockston with a dual license in cosmetology and massage therapy.

Celeste wanted to be closer to her daughter, leaving Grand Island, NE, and bringing with her 28 years of experience. She was known as the "voice of reason in the salon."

Gabby came by her name rightly. With 23 years under her belt, she had her fill of the hustle and bustle of New York City life. She brought cutting-edge techniques and artistry, having studied under José Eber in Beverly Hills years earlier.

Arianna was the youngest of the six stylists, with 14 years in the business. She was a real go-getter who wanted to be Matthew's assistant manager someday. Arianna always had a soft spot for those with disabilities and believed everyone was good until proven otherwise. She grew up in Lockston.

On June 9, 2000, My Preference Hair Studio in Lockston, Colorado, opened its doors, offering Lockston the A-Team of stylists. It wasn't long before the studio became well-known for its manicures, pedicures, facials, makeup, massages, and tanning beds. It was the first in Lockston to offer a full-service salon. Reflecting on their clients' conversations throughout the years, past and present, this collection of stories has closely been guarded, knowing it would be professional suicide if ever disclosed.

Readers can only hope the conversations were about someone they knew and not themselves.

Salon Confidential opened the door for all to wonder.

1. Beautician and the Beast

Isabella

Bodies mutilated, brutally murdered. Having sex with the victims after they were killed, decapitating their heads, and positioning them in a way that would shockingly greet the first person who entered the room.

I love to read, especially a good thriller. Gabby and I were on a much-needed thirty-minute break, exchanging titles of must-read books. We discussed several suspense novels when the conversation disturbingly shifted to the most unusual clients. My mind immediately went back eight years earlier to a phone conversation with a former coworker, Cierra, who had moved to Georgia. She had called me to tell me about the strangest client. I will always remember that phone call. The story is told from her perspective.

***

As I drove home, trying to forget about the day, I couldn't help but think about my new client, Mike. He was of average build, looking business-like in his suit, as he caught my attention while entering the salon. His soft brown eyes locked onto mine as we exchanged glances. My first impressions were impressive, but I was not interested; I was already seeing someone.

"I want HER to cut my hair," he announced as he walked up to the counter, pointing to me. It was a stark contrast from the standard greeting when customers walked into the salon, but who was I to turn down a paying customer? I did not recognize him, yet my mind raced. Have I cut his hair before? Maybe someone told him to ask for me. He is nice-looking.

Finishing my client, the receptionist came over and quietly announced with a smile, "Cierra, Mike is waiting for you when you finish with Simone."

"Okay, I'll just be a few minutes."

"Hmm, looks like somebody's in demand." Simone waited for my reaction.

"I guess so," is all I could say, trying to determine if Mike knew me. It was Mike's turn. As he sat down, he smiled at me. I put the cape on him and asked how he wanted his hair cut.

"Just trim it up."

Talking was kept to a minimum, with responses even shorter.

Mike was quiet and not much of a conversationalist. I just chalked it up to him being shy. Thinking back, I realized now that his quietness didn't match up with his entrance into the salon. While cutting his hair, he commented, "You know you're the first woman to cut my hair." Curious but not enough to have him elaborate, I did not respond. My lack of interest in why I was his "first" only prompted Mike to repeat that statement, hoping I would give in. That never happened.

My first impression of Mike drastically changed. This guy was strange, but I couldn't quite put my finger on it. As I started to blow dry his hair, he said something else to me that I couldn't quite make out.

"I'm sorry, I couldn't hear what you were saying with this blow dryer running."

"I said you must have a sick sense of humor."

"Why?"

"Because you like holding a gun to someone's head!"

He was referring to the blow dryer I was using that was in the shape of a 45 Magnum. When you pulled back the hammer, it turned on. I purchased it because it was cool-looking and fun and would be a conversation piece. It never crossed my mind that it would appear I was holding a gun to someone's head. I finished drying his hair, and he paid me (tip included). It was the last time I used that blow dryer.

Mike came in two more times after that. I was able to cut his hair the second time, but the third time, I had a client who was going to take a while, so he went to Tiffany, the stylist who had the station next to mine. Passing my station, we exchanged glances, both saying "Hi" as I apologized, unable to take him. He didn't seem upset. After he left, Tiffany and I discussed how Mike was weird but nice-looking. There was something about him that didn't seem right, but we were clueless as to what it could be.

***

It had been about two years since I had seen Mike. I wasn't complaining, but I often wondered what had happened to him. Driving home on this particular night, I thought it would be the perfect time to read a good book and relax. The combination of a beautiful evening with a gentle breeze blowing made it inviting to sit on the patio with an iced tea and a good suspense novel. I was in the mood for a thriller, non-fiction, so I selected the book I had recently purchased about the students brutally murdered in Georgia. It was all over the news and piqued my interest. While flipping through the book, I looked at the pictures, and my heart skipped a beat.

"Oh my gosh, it's Mike! I know it's him. I can't believe I used to cut his hair!"

What threw me was the name of this serial killer did not match up with the name and person I knew. Yet, the picture strongly resembled Mike. I was confident it was him, but I still needed that confirmation. As I searched the internet, my fears became a reality. Revealing that the killer went by his birth name and the pseudo name "Mike," my stomach vacillated between turning into knots and throwing up. I couldn't believe it was the same guy. I knew something was strange about him, but I never thought he could be a murderer, not to mention a serial killer.

I couldn't sleep that night knowing I could have been one of his victims. Unbeknownst to me, I fit the description: petite in size and a brunette.

I thought about the day he walked into the salon, singling me out. The statement he had made while getting his hair cut played repeatedly in my mind. What if I had asked him why I was the only woman to cut his hair? Would he have tried to lure me in, using the old pick-up line, "I feel like I can trust you." He cleaned up nicely and was decent in the looks department, making it easy to pull women into his web of deception.

Thank God I never fell for his pick-up line. Yes, I like a good thriller as much as the next person. I just don't like it when it involves a previous client who was a serial killer. Something is unsettling about cutting someone's hair who took pleasure in brutally mutilating and murdering his victims, making the hair stand on the back of my neck.

While lying in bed, my thoughts wavered that evening between the victims and their loved ones. That uncomfortable feeling I had while cutting this monster's hair was nothing compared to what these victims and their families had experienced.

The only thing that brought me comfort that night and the days and weeks to follow was that Mike had been executed by lethal injection for all five murders.

2. Gawd, I'm Screwed

Gabby

Though it's been twenty-one years since my husband and I exchanged vows, we are in love with each other more than ever. We each learned mistakes from our first marriage, ensuring we didn't make the same mistakes twice. According to statistics on second marriages, we've been very blessed, with the divorce rate for second marriages at 67%.

Unfortunately, that wasn't the case for my client, Valerie. She was 42, 5 feet 5 inches tall, tanned, with brown shoulder-length hair with a few highlights. She enjoyed jogging. I would see her jogging in the mornings as I drove to work. I never saw her in the same jogging outfit twice. She and her husband, Vinnie, had been married for 17 years. He enjoyed lifting weights and was significantly buffed. It was a second marriage for both. I thought things were going well with them until her most recent appointment. Scheduled for a cut and blowout at noon, Valerie had something else in mind.

"I don't want this brown hair anymore. I want to be blonde. Make it short."

"Whoa. First of all, you're not scheduled for a color. Second, we need to talk about this. Maybe add more highlights instead? Why the drastic change?"

"No, I want to be blonde. I want a different look. I want everything new. I found out this morning that Vinnie has been cheating on me for years. I took all his stuff and threw it out on the front lawn. I don't want him in my house or his things. I'm leaving him today!"

"Valerie, it's too soon to make such a dramatic change in your appearance. You just found out this morning. Let's gradually build up to your new look. I have some ideas I think you will like. Okay?"

"I guess so. I'm just so mad at the SOB. I've given him everything in this marriage so it wouldn't fail. I didn't want to go through another divorce."

"If you don't mind me asking, how did you find out?"

"He had been distant from me for months. He's been sleeping in the guest bedroom for the past five months. Vinnie claims it's for my benefit due to his snoring, tossing, and turning. I told him he might want to add flatulence to the list. He has spent a lot of time on his phone and more time with his friends, whom I've never met. Vinnie is smart, but I'm smarter because I never told him to sign out of his email. We share a joint account with separate emails. Call it woman's intuition, but I had this feeling to check his email."

"I can't believe he never signed out of his email after all this time, Valerie."

"Nope. He is also clueless about me accessing his phone location without him knowing it through a shared location app. I could also check out his location history via his email. When he said he was going out with Tom for a beer after work, I was able to get the address. This app also gave me names and phone numbers saved in his phone."

"Wow! It sounds like you opened up a can of worms."

"I sure did. I came across an address last night after he left the house to go out with Tom again, supposedly for drinks at the Blue Pine Bar 'n Grille. I drove by the bar, and his SUV wasn't there. So I drove over to the address I found on his phone. There was Vinnie's SUV. I wanted to bust out his headlights. Instead, I keyed the driver-side door. I was tempted to carve a heart on it with our initials inside, like you'd see on a tree." We both laughed, but she wasn't even close to being done telling me everything.

"This morning, I drove by the whore's place, and she was walking her dog towards the park nearby. I had a brainstorm of an idea. I parked my car, got out, and started jogging in the park, in the opposite direction towards her. I waited till she got closer before I said anything.

"What a cute dog. Is that a Yorkie?"

"Yes, it is."

"He is so cute."

"Thank you."

"Did I see you the other day with Vinnie DeGallo?"

"Yes, do you know him?"

"I went to school with him. I wasn't sure if that was him. It's been a while. He's a really nice guy. He was very popular in school. How long have you two been dating?"

"It's been about two years. I'm sorry, but I didn't catch your name."

"Oh, my name is Diana Corinci. It used to be Davis. Tell him I said, 'Hi.' It was nice meeting you."

"You too."

"Oh Valerie, this is unbelievable. That was a brilliant move, and you were so smooth. I don't know if I could have stayed that calm."

"The hardest part, next to hearing her say it's been two years with him, was the word vomit coming out of my mouth that he was a nice guy."

When Valerie confronted Vinnie, he denied it, unlike his

mistress. Valerie had contacted a lawyer and had started divorce proceedings. Vinnie had this revelation that they could work it out. He kept coming around for months, acting like he truly loved Valerie. He was crying and begging her to take him back. Maybe Valerie's new look, eventually going blonde, changed his mind. Whatever the reason, he was like a boomerang husband, always returning.

I could see Valerie torn over her decision to divorce Vinnie. She kept saying there was something different about him since she kicked him out. "The Vinnie I see now is the one I knew when we were first married. It's been nice to see this side of him again." *Don't do it, Valerie. His track record has disaster written all over it.*

Not long after she told me this, she welcomed him back home. He had been out of the house for a year. Valerie stopped the divorce proceedings, and they were "in love" again. For months, Valerie would talk about how she got the old Vinnie back and how good it felt. They were even going on little getaways that they had never done before. Okay, I'll admit when I'm wrong. Maybe I misjudged Vinnie. I was happy for Valerie. She was thankful she never went through with the divorce.

About 16 months later, I was taking the trash out at work when I noticed a car that had backed into the area, parking close to the dumpster. We usually don't have cars parked there. As I tossed the trash bag into the dumpster, my hand slipped off the metal lid, slamming it down and making a loud noise. Popping up from the back seat of this car were two heads. I did not recognize the girl, but I knew without a shadow of a doubt it was Vinnie. I looked at him in shock as he returned the look of, "Gawd, I'm screwed, literally and figuratively."

"What the hell, Vinnie!" I shouted, throwing my hands in the air. I just shook my head and walked back into the studio.

He must have said something to Valerie because she canceled her next appointment and never returned to the studio, probably out of embarrassment.

I knew I was right!

3. Guess What I'm Doing

Arianna

Since I was little, I wanted to be a hairstylist. I'm not sure how I arrived at the decision. It could have been from all those times I watched my mother standing in front of the bathroom mirror, styling her long, thick hair. Sometimes, she let me brush her hair, adding a few curlers, just for fun. On the other hand, I always had a plethora of ribbons and bows at my disposal to be creative, carefully selecting the one that would match the day's outfit.

My barbies always wore new hairstyles daily. It wasn't hard convincing the neighborhood girls to play beauty shop at least once a week. Being the eldest of two children and the only girl, I suckered my brother into allowing me to "fix" his hair several times. To this day, he denies it.

Being the youngest on staff, the "walk-in" station on the studio's first floor was my station. Since I was single, I volunteered to work the evening hours on our slow days (usually Tuesdays). My clientele list continued to grow every year. I still cherish those moments when customers requested me. Aside from walk-ins, I had a client who was becoming a "regular." Three times Brent had requested me. He always requested the last appointment of the day, usually Tuesday evenings, four weeks apart.

Brent was a construction worker. Standing shy of 5´11´´, he weighed close to 200 pounds. His sandy brown hair was curly, hitting the base of his neck. Although it was fine, there was a lot of it. When he smiled, his dimpled cheeks only added to that mischievous boyish grin, leaving you to think: He has been caught with his hand in the cookie jar! Sometimes, he wore glasses. Other times, I assumed he was wearing contacts. I couldn't tell you the color of his eyes. It didn't matter.

It's common knowledge among hairstylists that you never close the studio in the evening by yourself. I didn't think twice about that rule when Isabella said she was too sick to stay and finish working. I'll never know why she showed up, but I finally convinced her to go home. Lexi was on the second level with her clients, so I wasn't concerned about being the only one on the main floor. It wasn't like people were coming in droves to get their hair cut that night.

The last two hours dragged on. Brent would be in shortly for his appointment, so I decided to prepare everything for closing. It was a bitterly cold January evening. Streetlights showcased the snow that had been falling since early afternoon. The constant wind blowing was a stinging reminder that winter was far from over. The thought of going out there at the end of the day gave me chills. Hearing the front door open, Brent entered, stomping his feet on the long runner in front of the door as large clumps of snow fell to the floor.

"Phew, it sure is cold out there, Arianna!"

"Yeah, I know. I'm dreading getting in a cold car. I think I'll invest in one of those remote starters. Come on over and have a seat." Even though I knew the answer, I still asked him how he wanted his hair cut.

"The usual. A little longer on the top, shorter on the sides."

I placed the cape on him and asked how he was doing working out in this weather. There wasn't much to talk about at the end of the day. I just wanted to get out of there and go home. The music was playing through the speakers in the studio, yet silence filled the air. I didn't care to get into a lengthy conversation, and I could tell Brent seemed a little preoccupied with his thoughts, so I did my job quickly without appearing eager to be done.

While standing on Brent's left side, trimming his hair, I noticed something moving out of the corner of my eye. I saw subtle movements taking place under the cape. At first, I didn't think anything of it. Then I noticed movement, causing the cape to "pop up" in the middle of his lap. No way. He is not doing what I think he's doing. I glanced at Brent in the mirror, and he was staring back at me with that boyish grin for God knows how long. I quickly turned my attention to cutting his hair.

The cape moved faster and faster, flapping as his hand hit it. My heart started to pound out of my chest, and I could feel the palms of my hands starting to sweat. I kept telling myself to stay focused. *Just breathe and stay focused, Arianna.* To no avail, I discretely looked around for anyone to help me or at least witness what I witnessed, even though I knew I was the only one on the floor.

As I slowly moved around to the back of the chair and Brent's right side, the movement became quicker and louder. That's it. I couldn't take it any longer. I was trembling in my shoes and ready to burst into tears out of fear. Before I knew it, Brent slumped over the left side of the chair. The flapping motion under the cape had ceased. I had hit him with the blow dryer as hard as possible, knocking him out briefly. "Lexi, get down here! Call 911!" She could hear the fear in my voice as she ran down the steps, clueless about what had happened.

"What happened?"

"Call 911! This perv was beating off while I was cutting

his hair, so I hit him with the blow dryer.”

“WHAT?”

“Yeah, and he was grinning the whole time. Jerk.”

Lexi placed the call, her voice anxious and tense the entire time she talked to the 911 operator. What seemed like an eternity was only a few minutes before we heard the sirens getting closer. It was a race against time. Would the cops arrive before Brent was conscious, or would I have to knock him out again for my protection? As the two cops ran into the studio, Brent was waking up. I no sooner told them what had happened when I heard, “Sir, get your hands out from under the cape where we can see them.” While moaning, he slowly reached up to rub his head with his right hand, “Oh, what happened? My head is killing me.”

“Sir, get both hands above your head NOW!”

Raising his arms slowly, Brent looked dazed, confused, and in pain. I didn’t care-he deserved it. One of the officers unsnapped the cape and removed it as we waited for the “act of confirmation” to be revealed. We all stood there in shock.

Brent had been cleaning his eyeglasses.

4. A Bittersweet Thank You

Matthew

It's the beginning of summer. School is out, and the highways are filled with travelers embarking on long, anticipated vacations. Yet, we stay busy at the studio. This is an excellent problem from a manager's point of view. I must keep reminding myself that I created this "nice" problem by employing quality staff.

It was a Monday; we were closed, but I had paperwork. As I looked at the schedule for the upcoming week, I had already counted the days until the weekend. For the first time in a long time, it looked like we would get out of here early on Saturday. One of my regulars had canceled, and I had nothing on the books after two o'clock. The much-needed R&R was coming early that weekend.

While in the office, the phone rang. I can't believe Cami (the newly hired receptionist) forgot to turn on the answering machine before she left on Saturday. If I don't answer, it'll just keep ringing.

"My Preference Hair Studio. How can I help you?"

"Yes, I'd like to schedule an appointment for this Saturday." *Insert eye roll while silently cussing, and take a slow, deep breath.* I wanted desperately to say we were booked, but in good conscience, I couldn't do it, or could I? While stalling to decide if I should lie out of this one, I told her to let me check that day and asked what she needed to be done.

"I need a haircut, facial, makeup, nails and toes done. The works!" Oh, how I wanted to end the conversation. *Don't do it, Matthew. Your staff will hate you for it. She can go elsewhere. Tell her you have no openings.*

"I have a two o'clock opening. Would that work?"

"Yes. Thank you so much. I appreciate it." I took Layla's name and told her I looked forward to her coming in. Not really, but it sounded professional. Who knows, she could turn into a regular after Saturday. Now, I had to break the news to the girls. Yes, a lot of money would be made with this client, but I felt the need to schedule her for some reason. It looks like the R&R will be on hold till later in the day.

Saturday arrived, and I had ordered lunch consisting of sandwiches, pasta salad, and dessert for the staff, especially those putting in the extra time for Layla this afternoon. It was more like an apology lunch.

Layla arrived on time. Her slender build made her look taller than her actual height of about 5 feet 8 inches. She had layered medium brown shoulder-length hair with highlights and bangs. She looked like she was in her late 40s, but once we started talking, I found out she was only 31. Life had not been kind to Layla from the sound of it. Or should I say from what she wasn't telling me? I didn't want to pry, so I kept the conversation light. I did most of the talking. She was very polite but quiet throughout our time together, preoccupied with her thoughts. The girls did an excellent job on her makeup, manicure, and pedicure. I knew they would. Layla looked great when it was all said and done. She seemed pleased. As she paid me, tip included, I asked if she wanted to schedule another appointment.

"Not at this time. Thank you so much for getting me in today. It meant a lot to me."

"It was my pleasure. Take my card and call me if you decide to schedule another appointment." She left, and after cleaning everything up and thanking the girls again for staying to do Layla, we could not leave the studio fast enough to enjoy what was left of a beautiful Saturday.

The following week was going to be crazier than the previous one. I had meetings with reps and appointments with some of my more challenging clients. The challenge was with their hair rather than their personalities. It was Wednesday, and I was already feeling the pressure of my schedule for the rest of the week, ending with a bridal party. Given the bride, eight bridesmaids, mother of the bride, and mother-in-law, it would be all hands on deck. Oh, and the flower girl.

I was finishing up a client when Cami approached me. "Matthew, you have a phone call."

"Okay, give me about two minutes; if they don't want to wait, I'll call them back." The person on the phone decided to wait. I asked Cami to finish cashing out my client and scheduling her four weeks out, handing her my appointment book while I took the call.

"Hello, this is Matthew."

"Hi Matthew, this is Layla. You did my hair last Saturday."

"Yes. Hi Layla, how are you?"

"I'm okay. I just wanted to thank you again for taking me on Saturday."

"It was my pleasure."

"You and the staff made me feel so special and beautiful. I came to you to have everything taken care of because..."

Layla's voice trailed off. I couldn't quite make out what she had said.

"I'm sorry, Layla, I didn't quite catch what you said."

"I said I wanted everything taken care of because I had decided when I returned home to kill myself. When I looked in the mirror, I saw a different person I had never seen before, someone who looked beautiful. It was at that moment I decided not to take my life." Her voice was choking up. I was tearing up, not sure what else to say. I was in shock. I couldn't believe what I had just heard. I never had a client tell me that before. How do you respond to something like that? I cleared my throat and came up with the best response I could think of.

"Layla, I'm so glad I could do your hair. It was an honor. I'm even happier that you made the right choice. Have you thought about talking to someone?"

"Yes, I scheduled my appointment yesterday. I feel a burden lifted off of my shoulders. I had been thinking about killing myself for the past month. It's complicated. You and your staff made me feel special and beautiful. I hadn't felt like that in a long time."

"Layla, you are a beautiful, special person, and I am very proud that you have scheduled that appointment. I appreciate your call. You have made my day. Thank you for taking the time to call."

"You're welcome, but I wanted to make sure I thanked you. You saved my life." I could tell she was holding back the tears. Her voice was shaking. Wow! I never thought this would be the result in a million years when I took Layla's call that Monday. Thank God I didn't turn her away. The outcome could have been different.

Layla, you have touched my life forever.

***

If you or anyone you know is experiencing suicidal thoughts, the Suicide and Crisis Hotline is available 24/7. Dial or Text 988.

Lifeline Options for Deaf/Hard of Hearing ASL Users call 988. TTY Users: Use your preferred relay service or dial 711 then 988.

5. I'd Rather Take My Chances with Godzilla

Lexi

As hairstylists, we have a lot on our plate on any given day, including our days off. We show up looking presentable but also need time to get our hair done. That said, my client, Tessa, was also a hairstylist. I've been doing her hair for years. We always share the stories of our clients when we are together. This particular story regarding a bridal party stood out, which she shared with me on one appointment. The story I'm sharing with you was told from Tessa's perspective.

***

A bride's wedding day is one of the most memorable days of her life, filled with excitement and nerves while wanting to look her best. The focus is always on the gown first, with the hair a close second. That said, I had met with Victoria and her mother, Sylvia, six months earlier to schedule their appointment. First impression: Victoria was going to make a beautiful bride. She had blonde hair and blue eyes, was of medium height, had a slender build, and was tanned. Her mother was the spitting image of Victoria, just stockier. Victoria had an air about her, accompanied by a sense of entitlement. It was undeniable her mother had passed those traits on to her, unfortunately. They both were enjoyable during the consult, which put my mind at ease. Victoria's two sisters, her aunt and future mother-in-law, and seven bridesmaids were all scheduled on this day. I had a total of 13 in all. I was nervous about doing all of them within a given time frame. Inquiring about the length of hair for each and the style, I made it clear they must have their hair washed before the appointment since I will not have time to wash hair, blow dry, etc. Both understood and agreed to the terms.

June 12, 2010, was not only Victoria's big day but also the day that changed my life professionally. The entire entourage arrived on time. I had heard that Victoria was marrying into money and the groom's parents were paying for most of the wedding. I could not see her settling for anything less. Tension filled the air as Victoria and her mother walked into the salon. You could tell Victoria was not in the mood for her mother's help, which involved critiquing Victoria and her decisions. This led to arguments throughout their time with me. After listening to them engage in conversation, I realized I was spending the day with Bridezilla and Momzilla!

While I was styling Victoria's hair, she inquired if her mother remembered to bring the shoes. "No, I forgot them." Even if Sylvia wanted to apologize sincerely, she never had time before Victoria reamed her out.

"Are you kidding me? I can't believe you forgot them. You need to go get them now!" Yelling between the two as f-bombs were dropped was excruciating until Sylvia left.

In the meantime, I noticed only one sister in the salon, who was very compliant with her mother. When I inquired about the other sister, I was told, "Oh, she's out in the car getting high." This day just kept getting better and better. The bridesmaids were the saving grace in all of this. Being quiet and polite, they knew their place, unlike the aunt who had her fill of the future mother-in-law's attitude. Auntzilla walked over and slapped her in the face.

"Just because you have money, b**ch, doesn't mean you dictate what's happening here. She is MY niece!"

The future brother-in-law, who just happened to stop by, immediately grabbed his mother, holding her back from retaliating. Auntzilla needed to be held back, permitting distance between the two.

After the one-hour round-trip drive to retrieve the shoes, Momzilla returned. Could it get any worse? It was starting to look more like a Jerry Springer episode. As Sylvia handed the shoes to Victoria, Bridezilla responded, "I thought we were going with the other shoes? I can't believe this."

"We discussed this. These were the shoes we decided on, Victoria." At this point, it didn't matter what her mother said. Victoria had had enough, throwing the shoes back at her mother.

"That's not helping, Victoria. Just put these on."

"Fine!" It was the first time Victoria conceded with her mother.

I had finished up the last bridesmaid, breathing a sigh of relief. I was emotionally exhausted. Finally, it was over, and so was the drama. Well, I thought it was over. As Momzilla approached me, she announced boisterously, "This is all adding up...I have been here for hours. I could have done this myself," tossing $350 at me.

Yes, June 12, 2010, changed my professional life forever. I am now a successful nail technician.

6. Nico's Intuition

Isabella

You're lucky if you have one good friend in this world. Someone who is there in the good times and bad. Someone who likes you for you and doesn't put on a façade for years. Those friends are hard to come by. Makenzie and Mallory were those friends. They were both in their mid-30s. They did everything together. Makenzie was heavy set, given her short stature. She was a Christian and had met her husband, Noah, through the church. He was a great husband by all outward appearances. Their marriage appeared beautiful, almost perfect.

Mallory was the cute little, petite, redheaded, hot-looking best friend who was married to Mason. She was very materialistic and seemed happy in her marriage. They didn't do as much as a couple, like Makenzie and Noah, but that didn't bother Mallory too much. She would tell Makenzie, "I appreciate the time Mason and I have together. You know, our date nights are twice a month. But you and Noah always seem to do stuff together. I'm a little jealous."

Is Mallory jealous of Makenzie? Not a chance. These two were complete opposites in the looks department. Plus, money was no object for Mallory. Mason made a very good living as a dentist, affording Mallory the luxuries she had become accustomed to.

On the other hand, Noah was in construction and doing very well financially. He and Makenzie lived more conservative lives. Both of their husbands were nice-looking. To hear these girls talk, their husbands were "a great catch."

Makenzie and Mallory would always schedule their appointments in the studio for the same day, at the same time, or as close to the same time as they could. I would have Makenzie and Celeste, whose station was next to mine, would have Mallory. This way, they could still chat with each other when they weren't talking to us. And boy, did they chat about everything. Sometimes, Celeste and I would listen for entertainment purposes.

However, this particular visit was different. Makenzie shared that Noah had been acting differently towards her the past month. He seemed to be more distant.

"When Mason and I ran into you two at the store last week, I didn't notice anything off about him," as Mallory tried to reassure Makenzie, everything appeared fine between them.

"I know, he acted like everything was fine, but I could sense it wasn't. I don't want to get too personal, but even the intimacy has dropped off between us. It's been over a month and a half since he wanted to be with me. I know he works hard during the day and is tired when he comes home, but that never deterred him before." I found myself searching for the right words to comfort her.

"You know, Makenzie, sometimes guys go through that quiet phase. They don't want to talk; most men aren't talkers. They also don't want to be asked, 'What are you thinking?' five times a day. They want to be left alone. Does he kiss you goodbye when he leaves for work?"

"Not like he used to. There used to be passion in his kisses. It's almost like it pains him to kiss me."

"Does he tell you he loves you?"

"He'd tell me, but the tone in his voice says otherwise. And it's not until I say it first that he'll repeat it. I honestly think he's seeing someone."

We were all shocked. Mallory chimed in, "Oh my gosh! He would never cheat on you." You could see the hurt in Makenzie's eyes and hear the pain in her voice as she described what was becoming painfully apparent to all of us. Noah was seeing someone, but who? Makenzie started detailing all of Noah's indiscretions. "He's on his phone more than usual, texting. If he's not texting, he's quietly talking to someone in another part of the house. I tried to listen but couldn't pick up what he was saying. He's not staying home as much after working all day. Instead of date night with me, it's been with the guys. We haven't had a date night in over two months."

"OMG, it just came to me. I have a brilliant idea," Mallory said, beaming with excitement and eager to share. Pausing to cut Mallory's hair, Celeste jumped in. "Well, don't keep us in suspense."

"Why don't we set Noah up?" Makenzie's mouth dropped open as if to mouth, "What?"

"How do you propose we do that?" Makenzie was intrigued by the idea but felt guilty at the same time. "I don't know that I'm comfortable doing that. I feel like I'm sneaking behind Noah's back, and that's not me."

"Makenzie, are you serious? He's sneaking behind your back, which doesn't bother him!" Mallory was not holding back, and I had to agree with her. I could tell Makenzie was at a crossroads between denial and acceptance, which was understandable.

"I never said that he's cheating. I don't know if that's how I want to find out. I wouldn't know where to begin." Mallory was usually very persuasive, so it was only a matter of time before Makenzie gave in.

The following month, the girls were back in the studio

discussing how they tried to set up Noah, to no avail. "Looks like we need to go to Plan B," Mallory said confidently. "The next time he says he's going out with the guys, find out where, and I'll drive by to see if his truck is there." We all agreed that sounded like a plan. Celeste and I were even trying to come up with some other ideas. Unbeknownst to us, they had already tried them the previous month.

"Do you think Mason would help out?" At this point, Makenzie was getting desperate. Mallory felt including Mason would be too risky, so they dropped that idea.

The following month, Makenzie showed up early for her appointment. It was right after lunch. I had just finished my spinach salad with grilled chicken. "Hey, you're early. I just finished my lunch."

"Can I talk to you?" Oh no. Makenzie's concern prompted my mind to go in a hundred directions with what it could be.

"Sure. Is everything okay?"

"I wanted to tell you what happened a couple of weeks ago. First of all, when Noah said he was going out with the guys, Mallory had driven over to the Blue Pine Bar 'n Grill but did not see his truck. Then Noah told me his boss had asked him to help build a deck. It was going to take two weekends. I told Mallory about it, and she asked if I knew where the boss lived. I had an idea. Plus, all I had to do was look for Noah's truck. Well, I drove over there and did not see his truck. So I drove over to Mallory's to tell her. As I approached her house, her garage door was closing. I saw her car in the garage. I also saw the bottom half of a truck parked next to hers."

"What! She's cheating on Mason. With whom?"

"Well, wait till you hear this one. It looked like Noah's truck, but I wasn't close enough to see the license plate. I couldn't breathe. My chest tightened up, thinking it could be his truck."

"What did you do?"

"I did what any wife would do at the moment. I knocked on the door. Twice. There was no answer. Then I rang the doorbell. I could hear Nico, Mallory's Pomeranian dog, barking his head off. I was used to him greeting me at the door. Finally, after about three minutes, Mallory opened the door."

"Hey, what's going on?" Nico continued to bark excessively in the background but not at me.

"I was stopping by to tell you I didn't see Noah's truck at his boss's house. However, I did see a truck in your garage."

"Oh, Mason is at a golf outing, and one of his buddies left his truck here. He rode with Mason."

"By now, Nico's barking became more intense. I couldn't take it anymore and invited myself in. I could see Nico in the hallway, barking at the coat closet. As I pushed past Mallory and got closer to the closet, I could smell cologne. A men's cologne, as in Stetson Cologne. I'd know that scent anywhere. That was the only cologne Noah would wear. I reached for the doorknob, silently praying. *God, please don't let Noah be on the other side of this door.* I opened the closet door to find my husband standing there with a look of surprise. How I had hoped it wasn't him. I did not give him a chance to respond as I slammed the door in his face. I couldn't speak. Running out of the house, I got in my car as fast as possible, crying all the way home."

Listening to Makenzie, I couldn't believe what I was hearing. I was trying to process this as fast as Makenzie was telling me the story. Mallory was the other woman. She acted like such a good friend this whole time. She devised the plan to set Noah up—ironically, she set herself up.

"Isabella, I'm not going to get into all the details, but it got ugly between Noah, me, and Mallory. She should be coming in any minute for her appointment, right?"

"Celeste said something about her calling and asking for a later appointment today. I figured something came up, and that's why she changed it. Now I understand. I'm so sorry, Makenzie."

"Yeah, me too." Makenzie left that day looking defeated and hurt. I felt so bad for her. Mallory showed up an hour later. As she entered the studio, Makenzie walked through the doors behind her. She had been waiting out in the parking lot the entire time.

"It's about time you showed up, whore!" Mallory turned around, surprised that Makenzie was standing inches from her face. But that did not deter Mallory from speaking her mind. "Maybe you should have taken better care of your man. I had to pick up the pieces. You should have known." There was screaming and fighting, literally. Matthew intervened at this point.

"That's enough!" he said as he separated them. You don't bring your dirty laundry into my studio and act like this. I won't have it. You two need to leave. You can call for your next appointment. From this day forward, it WILL be separate appointments." They both left, never to return to the studio.

***

Update: Both couples got divorced. Noah married Mallory, and to this day, they are still married. Noah ended up with cancer, which affected his physical appearance. If I didn't know better, I'd say that was their karma.

Makenzie is happily remarried. She and her husband have a successful small business.

7. Fame, Fortune, and Ugliness

Matthew

What a week at work. Being the lead stylist at the studio had its perks as well as its drawbacks. The drawbacks, although few and far between, were challenging when both the client and stylist were disappointed with each other, and my goal was to find a solution that satisfied both. In this case, communication could have been stronger with this client, instead leaving Celeste second-guessing what the client wanted on more than one occasion. This client did not sing any accolades when it was over. That's all right. We knew, unfortunately, she'd be back. She couldn't argue the fact that Celeste was good at her job.

There were many perks, but this next one was beyond my expectations. One of my clients, Teresa, was the senior editor at the Lockston Times. She had been covering the story about the upcoming charity event for breast cancer at the Lockston Cultural Center. Sponsored by the two local hospitals in town and the radio station WLOX 92.9, famous names were on the list to fly in for the event. It was the talk of the town. Of course, with the big names also came a list of demands that needed to be in place before these celebrities entered the Center.

One of the demands was for Lockston's top hairstylist

backstage to style hair- no cutting!

So, yours truly was selected. I couldn't believe it. I was going to have access to these distinguished guests. I would joke around with Teresa when she came in for her appointment, thanking her for giving me enough time to make all my mistakes on her before I had contact with "real clients." She laughed, "I still have time to change my mind, Matthew. You better make me look good."

Naturally, I won't say who these high-profile clients were for obvious reasons. However, they were both females, in their sixties, and very well known. "Sheila" was in the movie industry, and "Crystal" was in the political realm.

The day of the event finally arrived. I could hardly sleep the night before. I was the talk around the studio. I had told my coworkers I was taking the limo to work but decided against it. Instead, I thought I would be like them and drive my car. Through all the "shut ups" and "yeah, you wish," I knew they were jealous, but they were also very happy for me.

I had to be at the Cultural Center by 5:30 p.m., so I made sure my last appointment of the day was finished by 4:30. Taking a quick inventory of my bag, I had several brushes, combs, flat iron, and curling irons along with two blow dryers and a plethora of gels, mousses, and hairsprays. Throwing the bag on the front seat of my jeep, off I went to what would become a memorable night on so many levels.

Teresa met me at the main doors, whisking me to the dressing room. By all outward appearances, I was calm, relaxed, and collected. Internally, I had a range of emotions from nervousness to excitement, knowing I was about to meet a movie icon. Preoccupied with getting everything on the table, I heard a sarcastic tone, "So this is the person who is going to make me look as good as I already do?" Looking up, I smiled and extended my hand. "Hello, Miss Sheila, I'm

Matthew. It's a pleasure to meet you."

"Nice to meet you. Let's get to work."

Her no-nonsense demeanor set the boundaries, keeping conversations to a minimum as she reviewed the evening's agenda. Looking at me expressionless, Sheila made her request.

"Matthew, do you have a pair of scissors on you?"

"No, I'm sorry."

"What kind of hairstylist are you that you don't have a pair of scissors on you? How do you do any work?"

"I was told I would be styling your hair only. I know you have your stylist to cut your hair and would never want anyone else touching it." Looking at me in disgust, she continued to voice her disappointment.

"I can't believe you don't have a pair of scissors on you! What kind of hairstylist wouldn't carry scissors with him when they're going to do someone's hair? You amaze me, Matthew."

"Miss Sheila, I had no intentions of cutting your hair and was given strict orders that you only wanted it styled, so I prepared my bag accordingly. I apologize that I'm unable to help you with your request."

The disgust on her face was an unfavorable look, conflicting with the hairstyle I was giving her. Conversations were nonexistent the remaining time we were together. Teresa stopped by to see how things were going. I mentioned Miss Sheila needed scissors, but I didn't have any. Teresa reassured me she would see what she could do and not worry about it.

Forty-five minutes before the event started, Teresa located scissors. Sheila was very appreciative of the effort put forth to fulfill her request. Realizing why she needed them, I found myself appalled and disgusted. I was also relieved that I never included my $450 scissors in my bag.

She needed to cut the dead skin off her foot.

***

Well, so much for working with a movie icon. Now, my focus was on Crystal, who was arriving any moment. I pondered asking her when her last pedicure was, but I changed my mind.

Crystal's assistant entered the room. I said hello, only to be ignored. That was fine. I was there to do Crystal's hair, not his. Crystal appeared in the doorway, smiling as she greeted me softly with a hello.

"Hello, Miss Crystal, I'm Matthew. How are you today?"

"Fine, thank you." She was quiet, reserved, and respectful.

"You can sit here, and we'll get started. How would you like your hair styled?" Her assistant abruptly chimed in, cutting Crystal off.

"Did you see *The Oprah Show* when Crystal was on and had an extreme makeover? That is how she wants her hair done."

"No, I did not see that show. I'm not sure what you're talking about."

As the assistant explained what they had done on Oprah, I tried to picture it, but it wasn't matching up. Wanting to show him on Crystal what it sounded like he was describing, the assistant became blatantly frustrated with me, raising his voice.

"Why can't you hear what I'm telling you? This isn't rocket science!" Crystal sat there quietly, never saying a word. Finally, I directed my questions to Crystal, asking if she was comfortable with a particular style.

She replied softly, "That would be fine." I felt terrible for her having to travel with an assistant with the ugliest attitude I'd ever seen. Yet, I was just as shocked that she would allow him to talk to people that way. In some ways, she contributed to his abusive personality by allowing him to be obnoxious toward others.

Just when I thought I had seen and heard it all, it was time to attend the meet and greet backstage. It was for those who had made contributions ($500 and up). Crystal's assistant announced before Crystal walked in that there would be no pictures or autographs. People were upset. Some contributed $1000 or more and couldn't get a picture with her.

A woman with her fifteen-year-old daughter walked in after the announcement. Noticing the girl had special needs, it looked like she possibly had Down syndrome. No sooner did the flash go off on her camera, and Crystal's lovely assistant was in this girl's face.

"What do you think you're doing? I said NO PICTURES! What part of NO don't you understand?" Silence filled the room. All eyes were on the girl who had burst into tears. People were stunned that the assistant was reaming this young girl out one minute, then talking to someone else politely the next, never skipping a beat. People were equally appalled by the fact that Crystal allowed it to happen. After the girl was publicly humiliated, her mother took her out of the room.

I learned two valuable lessons that evening.

Lesson 1: No matter how famous you are, money doesn't buy class.

Lesson 2: Even famous people hire idiots for assistants.

8. The Greatest Showman

Gabby

"I hope you know CPR because you just took my breath away."
"Your eyes are like the ocean; I could swim in them all day."
"If being sexy was a crime, you'd be guilty as charged."

If I didn't know better, I'd swear I was listening to someone reading the inside of greeting cards or watching a romantic comedy. In this case, it was neither. My client, Bella, had shared with me what Theo had told her the first time they met at college. They were both freshmen. He was tall, dark, and handsome. Very charismatic. Well-known around campus. Bella was the All-American girl: long blonde hair, blue eyes, and a body to die for. Bella was the envy of her girlfriends and the ultimate fantasy with all the guys. She was very athletic and intelligent. So was Theo. They made the perfect couple.

Bella could not stop talking about Theo whenever she was in the studio. She was smitten with him. I remember those days, but I also needed to impart some wisdom. "Speaking from experience, take your time, Bella. Don't jump into anything. Guys always put their best foot forward, initially."

"I know, but he is different from the other guys I dated.

Honest. I hear what you're saying. Theo isn't trying to jump in bed with me right away like the other guys. I'm not used to that."

When Bella was in the studio the following six months, it sounded like the honeymoon period was waning. She didn't have that excitement in her voice or the look of a schoolgirl crush about her. When I would ask how things were going with Theo, she would tell me they were fine, followed by something he had said or done that most would find offensive or inconsiderate, but Bella would laugh it off. Over the next several years, I suspected their relationship wasn't as rosy as Bella wanted us to believe. Sometimes, I think Bella trying to convince me was more for her benefit.

Theo became a police officer, and Bella couldn't be prouder. She showed me a picture of both of them at his graduation. Yes, he did look handsome, and they did make a good-looking couple.

I had heard that you only saw Bella with Theo or vice versa. On rare occasions, one would see Bella with her girlfriends—very rare occasions. Bella had mentioned how considerate Theo was, constantly checking on her and making sure she was okay when he was at work. He would also check in on her when she was at lunch with friends, inquiring if she had enough money with her or, in his usual charming fashion, would state, "I just wanted to stop in and say hello to the ladies."

Really Bella, in this day and age when texting is quicker, you find this endearing?

Bella continued to build up Theo's character to be this great guy. "He is so good with kids. He coaches youth soccer. The kids love him."

One day, when Bella was in the studio getting her hair done, I noticed what appeared to be bruising, covered up with makeup on her neck. I couldn't stay quiet. "Bella, is Theo hurting you?"

"No. Why?"

"Well, it looks like a bruise on your neck. Are you sure Theo is not hurting you?"

"This is kind of embarrassing. But sometimes, he gets a little rough when we're having sex." Bella tried to sound convincing, but my gut feeling wasn't buying it.

A couple of times, Theo showed up at the studio, in his uniform, of course. He was checking up on Bella, making sure she had an appointment. Being the smooth talker that he was, he came up with a convincing excuse for all to hear.

"Hey, Babe, I was in the neighborhood and wanted to see if you wanted to go to dinner tonight. Give you a break on cooking." If you weren't privy to what was happening, you would think Bella's boyfriend was lovely, suggesting eating out. I figured he must have beaten or verbally abused her the night before and thought being nice the next day would make up for it, and all would be forgiven, never saying he was sorry. That's usually the cycle of the abuser.

Gawd, the sight of him made me sick. I wish Bella would consider leaving him.

It was summertime, and Bella was scheduled for a color. She was wearing a bright orange, yellow, and red floral top with the shoulders cut out. It complimented her tan. I noticed scratches on her lower neck and several bruises on her upper arms as if someone grabbed her. She had strategically placed her top over the bruises, but it had shifted where I could see them in plain sight. Part of me felt she wore the top purposely to get my attention, knowing I would say something to her. I felt like she needed to talk but was too scared.

"Okay, Bella, enough is enough. Tell me now, what is

going on?"

"Gabby, I can't. He'll hurt me if I do."

"He's already hurting you, and you haven't said anything! You need to get away from him." I knew my comments fell on deaf ears. I put her under the dryer and turned around, only to see Officer Theo walking in and heading towards Bella. Her eyes got as large as saucers as he approached her. Grabbing her hair, he tried to pull her out from under the dryer.

"THEO, NO! STOP!" Bella screamed with such fear in her voice. It was a first for all of us to hear but was of no concern to Theo, who had become numb to the fear and pain he had instilled in her. With anger in his voice, he announced, "You're done here!" I immediately jumped in, grabbing and pulling him off her.

"You WILL NOT lay a hand on her in front of me!" He backed down and left, leaving Bella in tears. Now, we were all talking to Bella about leaving him. She wouldn't listen. A couple more times, Theo came into the studio. Bella immediately gasped with fear when she saw him. I stopped him before he could get close to her. His 6-foot frame never intimidated me, nor the uniform he was wearing. "Lay a hand on her. I'm ready." He would get mad and walk away, knowing I meant what I said, and witnesses were present.

Bella became pregnant by Theo, but she also found out that he was married, and he had gotten two other women pregnant simultaneously. She finally broke up with him, had her child, and moved out of Lockston.

Theo never got his anger under control. Luckily for Bella, she escaped his wrath for good. Out of Theo's two other pregnant girlfriends left in Lockston, one had an abortion. The other one ended up dead. Theo murdered her.

The only uniform Theo is sporting these days is a prison

uniform for life.

***

If you are experiencing domestic violence, reach out to the National Domestic Violence Hotline: 1-800-799-SAFE (7233) or Website: https://www.thehotline.org or Text "START" to 88788

9. Thanks to You

Celeste

By now, it is a well-known fact stylists are the "go-to" professionals no matter the issue. We are counselors, therapists, psychologists, mediators, mothers, and friends to a ·diverse clientele. We are not licensed in those professions that require it, but our clients don't care. They are looking for an unbiased sounding board to vent.

Grace was the exception. In her 70s, with beautiful short white hair, the roles seemed reversed. She had a standing appointment every 4-5 weeks. She would ask me about my daughter or a situation I had shared with her at the last appointment, then impart pearls of wisdom. The last time she was in, I had mentioned a disagreement my husband and I had over something stupid. Typical in any marriage.

"You know, Celeste, it's important to remember it's not about winning an argument that counts, but hearing what the other person is saying, validating their feelings, and respecting their point of view, even if you disagree. Agree to disagree." That has stuck with me and will stay with me until my last breath. Not only does Grace have thoughts to ponder, but she also has great recipes that she has shared with me. I reaped the benefit of tasting cookies when she made them with a recipe attached.

The last time she was in, I noticed a bump on her forehead while shampooing her hair. "Do you know you have a bump?"

"I noticed it. But I haven't paid much attention to it."

"Grace, that wasn't there four weeks ago. It's not a blind pimple. It's a solid bump. Does it hurt?"

"No."

"When did you notice it?"

"I don't know. Maybe it was a couple of weeks ago when I washed my face."

"Has it grown in size?"

"I don't think so." I was concerned and did not have a good feeling about this. Now the tables had turned, and I was playing doctor.

"Grace, I don't want to tell you what to do. But it would be best if you got that checked out. If nothing else, for peace of mind." Grace ended up going to a dermatologist.

The next time Grace was in, she updated me regarding that bump. "Thanks to you, I followed up with the doctor. I wouldn't have done anything if you hadn't noticed and pushed the issue."

The result: The bump was cancerous.

10. THE HOOK-UP CLUB

Arianna

Whore, slut, hoe, homewrecker! Pick a name that best describes the woman your husband of twenty-eight years became interested in, and you have my client, Sabrina's story.

Sabrina was an attractive woman who had been told by many that she resembled Mariska Hargitay, who played Olivia on *Law & Order SUV*. Though Sabrina's physical features were eye-catching, they were not enough to keep her husband at bay. Sabrina was the type of person who was easy to talk to, funny, a people person, and sensitive to the needs of others. She thought it was forever when she and Steve vowed before God and witnesses. By today's standards, twenty-eight years of marriage is considered forever.

In Sabrina's family, personal issues were kept within the family unit. So, she thought. During her last appointment, she told me what was happening with Steve and was determined to get to the bottom. Knowing for months something was up, Sabrina had asked him if there was someone else, and like all good cheating husbands, he convincingly denied it. Sabrina wanted so badly to believe Steve on one hand yet found herself second-guessing him when she thought about how distant he had become over the past year. She no longer had to second-guess after receiving a phone call one afternoon.

"Is Sabrina there?"

"This is she."

"Sabrina, you don't know me, but my name is Austin, and my wife is Meredith. I wanted to..."

"I'm sorry, but I don't know anyone named Meredith. Are you sure you have the right number?"

"Yes, allow me to explain. My wife has been sleeping with your husband for the past year." Sabrina could not believe what she was hearing. Not knowing the truth seemed more acceptable than hearing it at that moment. To think that just one phone call changed her life forever, exploding her world into a million pieces. What she had suspected for months was confirmed in a matter of seconds.

When Sabrina came into the salon two weeks later, I noticed she was eager to talk. I asked her if she had found out anything. She responded, "Oh yeah, Arianna. HER husband called me two weeks ago! Believe it or not, her sister works here, but I didn't ask for a name. I was too overwhelmed with the conversation. I do, however, know the whore's name!" I could not believe this guy had called her out of the blue, and now the cat was out of the bag.

"Don't keep me in suspense. What's this hoe's name?" As I leaned forward, Sabrina whispered, or at least thought she had whispered, "Meredith McBride."

One station away, a voice repeated the name loud enough that everyone in the salon could hear it.

"MEREDITH MCBRIDE!" So much for discretely disclosing the mistress. Marni was the hairstylist filling in for Celeste, who was visiting family in Malta for a month. Marni was known for being energetic, opinionated, and very much into everyone's business. I just wanted to crawl under the nearest counter or cape when she yelled Meredith's name. I felt so embarrassed for Sabrina and so disgusted with Marni. Just when I thought Marni had done enough damage, she took it to the next level, pulling out all the stops.

"I know Meredith McBride. She's part of the Hook Up Club. There are six siblings in that family, and they formed this club. They all actively seek out married spouses, have affairs with them, break up the marriages, marry the person they were involved with, and then eventually repeat the cycle. Meredith was a Vandergrift, then a Kaufmann, and now she's a McBride." Marni did not take one breath as she spewed out all the details about this other woman, which caused my client so much heartache.

"I heard she had left her husband and lived in the apartments across the street. She's seeing this new guy who is tall, nicely built, wears suits all the time, has salt and pepper hair and a goatee, and drives a Grand Prix with custom wheels. He's been married for a long time and has two kids who are both in school. One is almost out of high school. Not sure who this new guy is, but I'll find out."

Sabrina could not take it anymore. "Oh, I can help you with that. You're talking about MY husband!" You could have heard a pin drop. Blow dryers were silenced while talking ceased. The sound of running water in the shampoo bowls was nonexistent. The woman in the next station was adjusting her cap on her head only to freeze while her mouth dropped open. After a pregnant pause, Marni continued with her mouth on fast forward.

"Whoa! YOUR husband? How did you find out about it? What did he say? How long have they been together?"

I had had enough. "Sabrina, let's get out of here. I cannot believe that just happened." Sabrina followed me to the shampoo bowl, giving her the much-needed distance from Marni. Fuming at Marni and how unprofessional she was, I refused to let her know my true feelings at the time, especially in front of a salon full of clients. I waited until the end of the day to tell her what I thought. Sabrina left the salon that day shocked, hurt, and angry.

Thank you, Marni!

Since Steve had destroyed the trust in their relationship and continued to lie to Sabrina about ever knowing Meredith, Sabrina was not willing to rebuild any relationship with him or ever trust him again. Six months later, Steve finally moved out of their home, and within two years, their divorce was final. He lost his family, kept his job, married the whore-I mean Meredith, and became an alcoholic (alcohol was never part of his marriage to Sabrina).

For the first time, Sabrina lived independently, made her own decisions, and even returned to school to learn a new career.

She now has a thriving business at the local spa in Lockston.

11. It's Snot Funny

Matthew

The unspoken rule as a hairstylist is that you show up to work no matter how sick you're feeling. Self-care is essential, but so is money to pay the bills. I don't have allergies, but I have had sinus issues ever since I could remember. Today was awful for me. My nose was running, and I had a lot of drainage. I had to keep apologizing to my clients.

My last appointment walked into the salon. I struggled to get through the day and wanted to get out of there. Amber was getting a cut and dry, which was her usual. Thank God because I didn't know how much longer I could last.

I always felt bad for Amber. There seemed to be something "off" about her, but I just couldn't put my finger on it. She was in her 40s, had blonde hair, and was average height and size, but she looked like the Quaker Oats man. She never married and lived with her mother. Her brother wanted nothing to do with either of them.

As time went on, Amber was looking more stressed. Being a caregiver is a demanding job. Anyone who has ever done it knows what I'm talking about.

Sadly, Amber's mother passed away. Eventually, Amber was showing up high or drugged or both. I got the impression she was enjoying her mother's leftovers, as in medication. I'm not sure exactly what Amber was taking, but I'm certain muscle relaxers were the order of the day. She would usually sleep while I was doing her hair.

There wasn't much conversation as I washed Amber's hair that day. No doubt the meds were kicking in. On the other hand, I wished I had meds to stop my nose from running once and for all. As I leaned over Amber, continuing to wash her hair, I could feel my nose building up pressure, which wasn't good. I had no tissues available, and the next thing I knew, a big glob of snot had dripped out of my nose and onto Amber's forehead.

"What was that?" *Her medication must have worn off for her to be that alert.*

"Oh, it's just conditioner," I said calmly, blending it into her hair. I could not believe what had just happened. I finished washing her hair and added the actual conditioner. I about peed myself, trying not to laugh, but at the same time embarrassed, hoping no one saw it.

Once she returned to the chair, I started cutting her hair. Amber slowly slumped forward, falling asleep. I pulled her up by the back of her hair and continued cutting it. She never woke up. Thinking about what had happened at the shampoo bowl, I struggled to keep from laughing. I am always so professional, and my actions did not reflect it on this day. Holding back the laughter, I could feel my abdominal muscles tightening to the point I passed gas silently. I could only hope the smell wouldn't wake her up. I immediately turned on the blow dryer as if I were blowing hair off of her. She never budged, none the wiser, while I carefully breathed a sigh of relief. I woke Amber up to let her know it was time to leave. She paid me and slowly walked out of the salon, leaving me to wonder whatever became of her.

12. Did You Drop Something?

Celeste

I had just finished with my last client for the morning and was taking a quick lunch break before my next appointment. Mabel was a large woman, close to 300 pounds, easily. I often wondered how much weight my chair could handle, given there was nothing dainty about her, especially when she plopped herself in my chair. This particular day was going to be etched in my mind forever. I had no idea how and why until Mabel sat in my chair.

As she sat down, the aroma of a Burger King wafted through the air. I'm not a fan of Burger King, which didn't help. As I placed the cape on her, she was wearing mayonnaise, onions, and lettuce on her top. Literally. Thank God her hair was short, and the appointment would not take long, but more than the memory of Mabel wearing the Whopper would be the memory of her antics.

While cutting her hair, Mabel passed gas so loud that it startled me. Of course, I was standing behind her when it happened. She could have waited until I stood off to one side to cut her hair before she let it rip. My shock soon turned into a reserved laugh. I had to step away because I couldn't contain myself. I acted like I needed to grab something. Anything, only to return to Mabel justifying her "performance."

"Whoopsie! Sorry, I just had a Whopper." She did not have to convince me. I just rolled with it, quickly changing the subject and asking if she had any plans for the rest of the day. Small talk continued between us until it was time for Mabel to go under the dryer. I was looking forward to getting some relief from the aroma. As Mabel stood up, balancing with her cane, she gave her right leg a couple of shakes, and a ball of poop fell out onto the floor. She walked over to sit under the dryer as if nothing happened. I could not believe my eyes. It was gross. I wanted to say, "Did you drop something?" Instead, I was talking myself out of throwing up. There was no way I was cleaning that up, yet it needed to be.

"Oh, Matthew. I need you to do something for me."

"What is it?"

"I need you to pick up some poop on the floor."

"What? Are you serious? Some kid crapped on our floor?"

"Dead serious, and no, it wasn't a kid. It was an adult!" I figured, as manager, he would want to ensure 'it' was disposed of properly. He did. I disinfected the floor before Mabel returned to the chair. Part of me felt embarrassed for Mabel, but the other part couldn't stop wondering how you could not feel something moving down your leg. I was surprised that none of the other clients noticed what had happened. You couldn't help but notice the smell of Whopper exuding from Mabel when she walked past everyone.

I stopped trying to rationalize her behavior, chalking it up to the fact that this was one for the books.

13. Gotta Wash that Man Right Outta My Hair

Isabella

Week after week, we see women in their forties or older who are single due to divorce come into the studio. Their stories range from themselves going outside of the relationship to their exes having extramarital affairs. Few came in with their spouses of 30 years or more, a gentle reminder that marriage was not a total bust. But nothing could have prepared us for Charles and his wife.

Charles was tall and slender in shape with thinning grey hair, not an unusual trait for a man of sixty-five. Combine that with his quiet demeanor, and you have a man who appears unassuming and harmless. Since our studio was always busy, I noticed Charles when he sat down, usually on Wednesday evenings, around 6:15 p.m. His wife, Virginia, was a regular at our studio, but I knew her by name only, thanks to Charles. On several occasions, our manager asked Charles if he wanted any coffee or bottled water while he waited. Charles would always give the same response.

"No thank-you. I'm just waiting for my wife, Virginia."

I noticed that sometimes he would get up to stretch his legs and walk around the studio, making a point to stop near the shampoo bowls. I never thought much of it. I just figured he was curious and liked to watch how the stylists shampooed hair.

The visits with his wife, sometimes bi-weekly, were not unusual. I never saw him leave with Virginia. Then again, I had yet to see Charles arrive with her. I was always too busy and never gave it another thought. One day, I did notice him spending more time than usual at the studio. He was spending a good bit of time by the shampoo bowls. It had been well over an hour, and Charles was making his "rounds" in the shop, continuing to frequent the shampoo area. Looking at the stylists who were at the bowls, it suddenly hit me.

Check the appointment book to see which one is working on Virginia.

I checked Matthew's, Lexi's, Gabby's, Arianna's, and Celeste's schedules, but no Virginia was there. *Just take a deep breath, Isabella. Don't panic. You must be overlooking her name.*

I started looking for Virginia's name in our spa area, but to no avail. I checked the manicure and pedicure areas, and nothing came close to that name.

At this point, I was willing to accept any area Virginia was in. Unfortunately, no Virginia was found on the books that day. How could we have missed her all this time? By now, I'm watching Charles as he stands off to the side where the women are getting their hair shampooed. Keeping his hands in his pockets, he stood by quietly, intently watching with a smile of contentment on his face. Virginia's husband's harmless and unassuming appearance was now making me uncomfortable. Sensing someone was watching him, Charles glanced in my direction. I quickly looked down, pretending to write in the appointment book. Once back in the waiting area, as he sat down, he grabbed a magazine. Inhibited by his presence, I continued to peer down at the book. My mind was inundated with self-talk.

Oh my gosh. What should I do? This guy is giving me the creeps.

I needed to tell Matthew, but how could I do that without Charles noticing? That is if his name is Charles!

I decided to write down what I wanted to say, giving it to Matthew when he came in to check his messages. I had no sooner finished the note when Matthew approached the front desk.

"Any messages?" I handed him the note and went about my business as if nothing was wrong.

Matthew, "Charles," shows up every Wednesday with his wife, Virginia. He doesn't have a wife by that name! There is NO Virginia in the salon during that time! He spends a lot of time near the shampoo bowls. He has been doing this for weeks. What should we do? -Isabella

The next thing I knew, Matthew grabbed a pen and paper, walked over to Charles, and asked him to step outside with him. Minutes later, Matthew walked back into the salon alone. By now, staff were anxiously waiting to hear what had happened in the parking lot. Matthew returned with a look of disgust.

"I've never seen a man's expression change so quickly. I told him I knew what he was up to and that he needed to leave. I suggested he get a movie instead of coming around here. As I wrote down his license number, I told him that if he EVER set foot on this property again, I would call the police. That's when he gave me the evilest look I've ever seen. I knew I had hit a nerve but didn't care. He got in his car and drove away."

Charles never returned, but we heard he was making his presence known at other salons in the surrounding area.

Charles had a fetish with women getting their hair shampooed.

14. But Wait, There's More!

Matthew

In cosmetology school, we were taught (or warned) about specific clients we would encounter. The old saying followed, "Everyone has their cross to bear." There, my cross was on the books, first thing today, Felicity. Oh, how I dreaded it when I saw her name. I knew it would be a three-hour process, all for a cut.

Felicity came to me by referral of two other clients I had, and I was certainly not going to turn down making money. If only I had known then what I know now, I would have said I wasn't taking new clients at the time. Felicity lived in Alpine Estates, one of the most affluent neighborhoods in Lockston. First impression: tall, attractive brunette in her 40s, with hair mid-neck and teased. She was well-dressed, sporting designer shoes and a handbag, which coincided with her sense of entitlement. I could strongly sense trouble as she sat in my chair.

"I'm a picky person." It didn't take long to see that Felicity was a very, very picky person. Our first encounter started with her telling me how she wanted her hair cut and styled. Okay, we got that out of the way. No problem. Next, as she positioned her bag on her lap and opened it up, she pulled out her laundry list of demands.

"This is what I want you to use. I have my brush, teasing comb, gel, shampoo, hairspray, and blow dryer." My first thought was, *RUN MATTHEW, RUN!*

I brought Felicity over to the shampoo bowl and started using her shampoo. Unfortunately, that turned into an ordeal. I needed to wash her hair correctly. She told me where to scratch her scalp, ensuring it was a thorough shampoo. Gawd, could this get any worse?

I started cutting her hair, and she told me to stop. I wasn't cutting it right. To help me do my job better, she pulled out a ruler from her bag.

"What's that for?"

"To measure my hair and make sure it's even." Are you kidding me? I was insulted by her lack of trust in me to do my job. An hour and a half later, I finished cutting and measuring her hair, ensuring Felicity it was even. As she gave me her stamp of approval, I kept thinking it was almost over. There weren't enough words in the English language to self-talk my way through this appointment. All I could think of were cuss words at the moment. I had to change my mindset, or this would not end well. *Hang in there, Matthew. You can do this. Remember, she's paying you to do what she wants.*

But wait, there's more!

I started to blow dry her hair, second-guessing my abilities to do so for the first time in my professional career, waiting for Felicity to chime in. She did not disappoint. Rolling the hair around the brush was fine, but the brush needed to be held for 15 seconds when drying each section. Finally, her hair was dried and curled. I let the curls cool before brushing them out. Of course, it was not to her liking. By now, I expected only criticism from Felicity.

"May I see the brush, please? I brush out the curls like this; this is how you should tease it." Her appearance was a toss-up between her hair being put in a socket and looking like chicken hair, standing straight up on the top and in the back. At that point, I didn't care. It was over. She tipped me well and left.

I struggled the next couple of years with Felicity coming in. At least I knew what to expect, but my patience with her was waning. My dilemma: She was good friends with two of my other clients. I wondered how it would affect them if I no longer cut Felicity's hair. They were well aware of Felicity's obsessive, compulsive behavior. They both were surprised I had lasted this long. That's all I needed to hear. From that point on, every time Felicity called, I told her I had no openings. The last time she called, she inquired about my formula. She found someone else to carry the cross and wanted that stylist to color her hair exactly how I did hers.

"I don't think it's fair that you asked me for this. If whoever you are going to is a professional, that person should be able to figure it out." She didn't like my response, but I didn't care. Since then, I've heard she has tested the patience of several stylists in town.

I felt their pain, but that was one cross I no longer had to bear.

15. Keep Your Friends Close and Your Bridesmaid Closer

Celeste

We've all had that childhood friend we played jacks with, jump roped with, played Barbies with, or even pretended to get married. Maria and Brittany were those childhood friends. They had been friends since kindergarten. They were junior high and high school cheerleaders, successful in track, made homecoming court together, and had the same circle of friends. A friendship that would last forever.

Until...

***

Let me take you back to when Maria and Mario were dating three years ago. As close as Maria and Brittany were growing up, it appeared that Brittany and Mario were closer. The latter became a bone of contention between Mario and Maria, to the point that Mario did not give up his "friendship" with Brittany. That left Maria with only one choice: break up with Mario.

One year later, Maria and Mario were backed together and engaged. Does time heal all wounds? It must, because the woman who had come between them a year earlier was now one of Maria's bridesmaids. Maria told me she didn't want a rift between her and Mario, so she included Brittany. Brittany acted like they were good friends, who were closer now than when they were in high school. I could tell there was still something bothering Maria. I chalked it up to the typical girl drama of, "I don't like that color for a dress," or, "Why do we have to wear our hair a certain way?" Maria would have welcomed those issues, but it was more involved than that. Or should I say Brittany was more involved, which led to the drama?

Maria had shared her plans for the bachelorette party and was looking forward to it. They were making it a weekend event with massages, drinking, of course, dancing, and topping it off with a Sunday brunch. All the bridesmaids agreed with the schedule.

The week before the bachelorette party, Brittany informed Maria she was scheduled to work and couldn't find anyone to trade with her. Maria couldn't believe it. Brittany had known about this party for weeks. Everyone had checked their schedules, making sure it was a go. Maria felt like Brittany was pulling away from her but wasn't sure why, refusing to accept what might turn into her worst nightmare.

Brittany was a pro when it came to putting on façades. She had planned the next two weeks to make it up to Maria by shopping and going to lunch. During lunch, while shedding crocodile tears, Brittany provided a lame confession. "I wanted so badly to be there for you. I felt horrible. I could have lost my job if I had called off. I am so, so sorry." *Whatever, Brittany.*

Mario knew how upset Maria was over Brittany missing the bachelorette party. Inquiring if they had worked it out, Maria verbalized they had, but internally, she felt she couldn't trust Brittany.

The following weekend was the bachelor party in Myrtle

Beach, SC. Brittany was off that weekend and flew down to join Mario and his buddies, staying with the guys.

When Maria found out, she thought it was a joke. Not wanting to bother Mario while he was with his friends, she kept calling Brittany's phone. No answer.

She finally broke down and called Mario's phone. No answer. Anger, shock, and hurt were only the beginning feelings of betrayal Maria had towards Mario and Brittany. She had felt for some time that Brittany was too close to Mario, again, and him with her. When she confronted Mario once he was back from his weekend with the guys (and Brittany), he played it off like she was overreacting. "You know Brittany and I have always been close, but as friends," reassuring Maria that Brittany meant nothing to him. Maria was now in a no-win situation. If she confronted Brittany, Brittany would run to Mario, and Mario would get upset with Maria. It was too close to the wedding to call it off.

By the way, Maria never told me that Brittany had gone to Myrtle Beach. It was my son, who was one of the groomsmen. He was appalled that Mario welcomed Brittany with open arms when she showed up.

Just when you thought it couldn't get any worse, it was the night before the wedding, at rehearsal. As the whore, I mean Brittany, was walking down the aisle, Mario turned to my son, saying, "I'd like to run away with her and get married! I want her to stand on our side tomorrow."

"That's enough! We need to take this seriously," the pastor poured his wrath onto Mario. If my son hadn't invested in the tuxedo, he would have bowed out of this hot mess.

The wedding day had arrived and so had the bridal party at the salon. Maria acted happy, but I could tell something was bothering her. By now, word had spread about Brittany's antics. While I was doing Maria's hair, Brittany was sitting at the next station, having her hair done by Arianna. The entire time, Brittany talked about how close she and Mario were, that he was her best friend, and everything they had done together. Forget the fact that this was to be Maria's day. You would have thought Brittany was the one getting married. Maria never said anything, not wanting to cause a scene. Brittany also shared that her dress wasn't altered correctly and kept falling off her shoulders.

"I think it looks cuter off the shoulders." Of course you do, Brittany.

Little Sophia was the flower girl by default because the original flower girl got sick. Since it was short notice, Sophia wore the flower girl's dress, which was too tight on her, but no one seemed to care. One of the groomsmen, Sophia's uncle, came into the salon to talk with her. Sophia was excited to see him until he opened his mouth, "If you act up at all, I'm going to beat your ass!" In case no one heard him the first time, he repeated the phrase several times.

After listening to Brittany, I felt terrible for Maria, who would have burst into tears had her makeup not been done. Between listening to Sophia's uncle talk to her the way he did and wondering if I would have enough time to run home, change, and make it to the wedding, my head was beginning to throb.

The church sanctuary was beautifully decorated with lavender and white roses. The bridesmaids' dresses were a perfect match. The ceremony started with each of the bridesmaids entering the sanctuary and walking down the aisle. As the whore, I mean Brittany, entered, Mario walked up the aisle to meet her and escorted her the rest of the way, arm in arm, as he walked her over to the bride's side of the altar, chuckling. Everyone was appalled at what they had just witnessed. It was one of Mario's boldest yet tackiest moves, unbeknownst to Maria. I was sickened when I saw this.

It was now 8:30 p.m. at the reception. Maria and Mario had yet to cut the cake, the bouquet had not been tossed, or the first dance—complete, all because the groom was MIA. He had been drinking and smoking, but with whom? Was Brittany with him earlier? One could only assume. By then it was time for me to leave. I had seen enough. I left the reception without telling Maria or Mario goodbye. I was so disgusted with the whole event.

Now, one is left to wonder: Are these two still married? Is Brittany still friends with both of them or just Mario? Did Mario finally confess he wanted to run away with Brittany and marry her instead? These are questions only the future holds.

Last I heard, Maria's future wasn't looking so bright. Mario informed her he didn't want children. You'd think he would have had that conversation before they got married.

Then again, he probably did, but with Brittany.

16. Let's Be Honest, or it WILL Hurt

Lexi

I noticed Bailey's name on the schedule for today. She had heard about me through a mutual friend and was looking for someone new. I was getting a reputation among the 20+ year-olds for my highlights, lowlights, and extensions. At 61 years of age, that was a nice compliment. Many times, they would share stories that they would never tell their mother. My response was, "Suggestion? Listen to your salon mom..."

It was the first time I had Bailey as a client. She was in her 20s, with long, blonde hair. She was going to have her roots done but also wanted a trim. I discussed the color options with her. I also went over my standard questions when doing a consult before a chemical service.

"I want to ask you some questions before we get started. I do this with all my clients but especially my first-time customers."

"Okay," Bailey was hesitant while appearing a little nervous.

"Are you on meds?

"No."

Any medical illnesses, injuries, or conditions that would prevent you from getting your hair colored?"

"Nope, I'm good."

"Any surgeries?"

"No."

"Okay, good. Let's get started." Confirming how much she wanted to be trimmed, I inquired about the conditioner she used, given that her hair seemed a little dry. Bailey was soft-spoken but continued to appear a little nervous. I just chalked it up to being a first-time customer. Making conversation to put her mind at ease came to an abrupt halt as I was coloring her roots.

"MY HEAD IS ON FIRE! OMG, IT'S BURNING!"

I immediately got her to the shampoo bowl and turned on the cold water, only to have Bailey yelling, "RUN COLD WATER! TURN ON THE COLD WATER!" Having the cold water running to no avail, Bailey was at a crisis level and needed medical attention.

"Call 911!" Cami called, and what seemed like an eternity before the EMTs arrived, had only been about five minutes. Upon their arrival, I understood why Bailey was initially nervous. One of the EMTs recognized her immediately.

"Ma'am, do you have lupus?" knowing Bailey's mother did.

"Yes," as she cried out in pain.

"Then you already know you're not to color your hair."

What! She lied to me, putting me at risk for her selfish reasons. Thank goodness I had asked her the medical questions beforehand. I could see her trying to pin this on me. When I first saw her, I never thought she was the type to lie, especially about her health. The EMT strongly encouraged Bailey to be seen in the ER due to her scalp burns. Bailey said she was able to drive herself. I felt horrible and sorry for her, knowing that pain had to be excruciating.

Yet, Bailey could have avoided the pain if she had been honest with me initially.

I heard through the grapevine that Bailey's mother was upset with her after telling her not to go through with the appointment and that Bailey lied about not having lupus. Knowing the risks involved did not stop Bailey from playing hair coloring roulette all these months. Bailey never returned to the salon.

I often wondered if she learned the importance of telling the truth.

17. You Need Dethroned, Princess

Matthew

I can't say that money buys happiness, but it can make a young 22-year-old woman feel special for one week, especially if her parents are wealthy. The Lockston Ball was in its fifth year and had become one of Colorado's largest and most expensive pageants. To qualify, you must be a female between the ages of 21 and 23, a college graduate, ready to enter society, and currently serving her community. The preliminaries involved the queen and her court being selected several months before the Ball. This allowed the necessary time to make the exorbitant and lavish gowns.

The gowns alone were worth the price of admission. Containing Swarovski Crystals incorporated into the material and a detachable 20-foot train, only the upper class of Lockston could afford to enter their daughters. The gowns cost $50,000 and up. The crowns all the young ladies received weighed about five pounds and cost between $4000 and $7000.

Speaking of money, I would make $8,000 that week. It was the one time of year I looked forward to yet loathed, knowing the personalities I would be dealing with until it was over. Most of the young ladies were my clients' daughters. One in particular, Katrina (Kat for short), stood out among the rest. Being of average height and weight, she had just graduated from Stanford with a degree in finance. When I met with her earlier in the week to do a practice session with her hair and crown, her demeanor had overshadowed her already unattractive features.

Honey, if you were my daughter, you would not have that attitude living under my roof.

Her sense of entitlement went above and beyond. She was very spoiled, nasty, and disrespectful. Her ugly personality and appearance detracted from her designer clothes and accessories. I'm trying to be kind here, but there's no easy way around her appearance. Kat had strawberry blonde hair and a nose that looked like a beak, more or less like the witch in *The Wizard of Oz*. Ironically, she was witchy.

It was the day of the Ball, early morning, when Kat walked into the salon with her grande white chocolate mocha from Starbucks, warmly greeting me.

"Do you have a problem with me drinking this while you do my hair?" *No, but I do have a problem with your attitude.* Since her mother was paying me, I just had to roll with it.

"No, you're fine." She was my first of three "princesses" for the day. Each one was going to take about three hours to do. The crown had to be placed securely on the head with clips that closed and snapped back into the pipe cleaners that were already attached to the crown. The pipe cleaners were then strategically woven into the hair. The girls all had a Chignon hairstyle, fitting for a princess. I had my makeup artist, Whitney, with me on this day. Having never met Kat before, I waited for Whitney's observations as I was in the back getting everything ready. She didn't hold back.

"Wow! I must pull out the spackle and hope for the best."

"Yeah, I know what you mean. I'm thinking about pulling all the hair forward." Not only would it take an act of God to make Kat look presentable, but also like a princess. I turned to Whitney, "Let's get this over with." The only thing Kat had going for her was that her hair was in excellent condition. She used nothing but the best products.

"How long is this going to take? My schedule is tight today. I have a nail appointment at 1:00 p.m."

"You'll be out in time. Don't worry." The one-sided conversation focused on Kat's thoughts about the other girls and how her dress was the most expensive. Just when I thought she couldn't get uglier with her personality, she had taken it to the next level of bashing the other girls in between sucking down her Starbucks. All of a sudden, Kat stopped talking. Maybe she realized she was being too hard on these girls and having second thoughts.

"OMG, I don't feel so good."

"You'll be fine. It's probably just nerves. It'll pass." Kat was looking a little green, I have to admit. Having her fill of Kat's attitude, Whitney looked at me and winked.

"Don't some tacos sound good about now? What about some jellied donuts?"

The next thing I knew, Kat was projectile vomiting everywhere. She started to cry, stepping away to use the restroom as Whitney and I were left to clean up her mess.

"Gawd Whitney, way to go."

Not skipping a beat, Whitney smirked, "She deserved it." Kat returned to her "throne," now cleaned and sanitized. Her demeanor had softened. I'm sure it was out of sheer embarrassment. When it was all said and done, Team Matthew pulled through for Kat. Did she look like your typical princess? No, but she looked better leaving than when she had arrived. It was amazing what a little bit of makeup and a crown could do.

18. Man, I Feel Like a Woman

Celeste

Diana Ross, Cher, Tina Turner, and Dolly Parton. What do these celebrities have in common besides successful careers? They all wore wigs during their performances back in the day. In the 1960s, wigs were very popular. Ranging in styles from bouffant and beehive to afros and flicked-up bobs. Any celebrity donning one of these hairdos became instant money in the bank for wig designers.

Today was one of those days when my thoughts kept returning to the good old days when life seemed less complicated. Rather than texting someone on your phone, you could talk to them.

As I was applying the finishing touches to the hair extensions on my client, my mind drifted back to the days when clients requested a beehive or a bouffant. Starting my career in the early 1980s in Grand Island, Nebraska, I didn't have one part of my job that I favored more than the other. Whatever requests were in front of me usually made the customers look better when they left than when they arrived.

One client came to mind that I'll never forget. As she walked in, looking disheveled, in a gaudy house dress and large tennis shoes, I couldn't help but notice her light brown hair, which was clearly a wig. I knew what was coming next.

Greeting her, I asked what I could do for her today. "I just need my wig combed out."

"Sure, have a seat, and I'll be with you in a few minutes."

Although I had only been a hairdresser in town for three years, I was surprised I hadn't seen her before. As she sat down, she requested that her wig be kept on (as opposed to me putting it on a stand to comb it out). Either way worked for me; the result was the same. The wig was styled in a bouffant with bangs. It hadn't been combed out for some time, making it difficult to comb through without moving the wig. I asked the stylist next to me, Peggy, who was also the owner, to help by holding the wig in place. The look on Peggy's face when she positioned her hands on the edge of the cap, caught me off guard. I wasn't sure if she had seen lice or something else. I could tell whatever it was; it was disturbing.

Once we were done, I noticed Peggy deep in conversation with this intriguing client. As I approached the desk, Peggy announced, "She has a typewriter we can buy from her." Given the costs, Peggy was in the market for one for the salon but was holding off on spending the money. Yet, the price was right, so we got her address and scheduled a time for me to do the pickup. I thought Peggy got the client's name when she talked to her, which she had not. Well, as hairstylists, one thing is for sure: we may not remember your name (the first time around), but we certainly would remember your hair!

After the client left, I was curious to find out what had caused Peggy's strange look.

"Whiskers!"

"What?"

"I swear I felt whiskers. I tried to get a closer look without being obvious, but I couldn't see anything. I could only feel them."

"Did you see anything move?"

"No, I kept watching for movement, but nothing happened."

"Well, that being said, I don't know if I'm comfortable going to her home to pick up the typewriter. Since you talked to her more than I did, would you like to ride with me tomorrow?"

Peggy reluctantly agreed to the road trip.

The address was Vieregg Township, about ten miles from the shop. It was a rural area with homes separated by fields and hills. The dirt path guided us to the house. Thank goodness Peggy was with me. Anything could happen out here, and no one would ever know.

Approaching the porch, I knocked on the front door and was greeted by a male. This male wore a nurse's hat, makeup, uniform (a dress), white nylons, and white tennis shoes. Oh, and wearing the wig I had combed out the day before. She had cleaned up but looked like a dumpy woman.

It was her; it was him; it was both. He was a nurse, and this was the patient's home. Remaining on the porch, he brought out the typewriter. I paid with cash, and we left. Now, the whiskers made sense. Of course, back then, cross-dressing in Nebraska was not as acceptable as it is by today's standards in our country.

After getting over the shock that he was a cross-dresser, we realized we never got his name!

19. My Son Can Do No Wrong

Arianna

When I'm with a client, I usually focus on that person, blocking out those around me. If I'm not playing therapist, then I'm the sounding board, making suggestions when solicited. On this particular day, I was hard-pressed not to eavesdrop on the conversation in the station beside mine. She was a regular of Celeste's. Savannah was known for being very loud and obnoxious. We all knew when she came in, we could expect a one-sided conversation that the entire salon could hear. We've heard about the neighbor having an affair with the other neighbor. The teacher picked up for driving under the influence, the catfight between her sister and sister-in-law, and her only son, Jacob, getting married.

Jacob was 24 years old when he married Beverly, working as an auto mechanic. I knew of Beverly through a mutual friend but never admitted to Savannah out of concern that she might feel compelled to share every detail she loathed about Beverly. It didn't matter. Savannah did not disappoint. Everyone knew about Beverly, thanks to Savannah's disdain for her.

I could only imagine what Savannah was like as a mother-in-law. Being a good judge of character, I had a good idea. I felt terrible for Beverly, and I didn't really know her. It was almost as if Savannah was obsessed with ruining Jacob and Beverly's marriage from the get-go, hoping ultimately it would end in divorce. Beverly could not do anything right. Jacob was always complaining to his mother about Beverly, which didn't help.

Hearing Savannah talk about Jacob, I realized he was the perfect son in her eyes. He was so loving towards his mother. He was always helping around the house when she needed him. Jacob's father had passed away in a car accident several years earlier. At 17, Jacob took on the role of the man of the house. That said, I think Savannah resented Beverly from the beginning because she took Jacob away from her. It didn't matter who it was; Savannah was determined not to like Jacob's choice for a wife.

Beverly was of average height and weight, with shoulder-length brunette hair and bangs. In the looks department, she was more on the plain Jane side. She worked as a teacher's aide at one of the elementary schools. I had heard through the grapevine that Jacob had been controlling and abusive towards her throughout the years. Given his mother's personality, it would not have surprised me.

For sixteen years, Beverly endured the abuse from Jacob and Savannah, finally divorcing Jacob. Savannah could not have been happier. I thought we were finally done hearing about it until a significant turn of events several months later caused Savannah to broadcast an update on Jacob while in the studio.

"Well, since Jacob was convicted of murder [for killing Beverly], all he wears is orange. I knew it was going to happen. They had a rocky relationship for 16 years. I never liked that b**ch. She got what was coming to her."

Wow! Savannah had so much hatred for Beverly that she couldn't let it go, even after her son took Beverly's life.

20. THE GREAT PHYSICIAN

Gabby

Most people are great as parents. Others, you have to wonder why God allowed them to reproduce. Then there are the ones God hand-picked to be parents of children with special needs.

Mia was on her second marriage. She had her first three children with her former husband, whom she affectionately called the "wasband," and had a son with her current husband, Nick. Mia was very active in her church. She was also involved with her kids' school activities. There was always enthusiasm in her voice when she talked about the kids, updating me on each one of them. I always looked forward to her appointments.

She and Nick had decided they didn't want any more kids. Between the four kids, with the youngest one being four years of age, they were plenty busy. Knowing they were not having any more children and not wanting to live on birth control for the next ten years, Mia scheduled an appointment for a hysterectomy. She was not one to look forward to doctor's visits, but she couldn't wait to get this surgery done and over with.

Her story had such a profound impact on me that I felt I needed to share the day she was in to have her hair done, and she told me about her pre-op appointment from the week before.

"I had everything planned out with my mother and Nick's mother when it came to helping with the kids the week of surgery. Once home from the hospital Nick was taking off a few days from work to ensure I could get around. I'm a fast healer, so I told him two days should be plenty. I had meals made up and frozen to make it easier on all of us. The house was thoroughly clean, and the laundry caught up.

"Mia, you are too organized. I need you to come to my house after surgery when you feel up to it." We both laughed. She thought I was joking.

"My gynecologist performed the usual testing at my pre-op appointment, including bloodwork and a urine sample. I waited in the patient room when she entered and asked how I felt. I told her I felt great and looked forward to the surgery."

"You're not going to have surgery," as she watched for my response, knowing it would shock me.

"What? Why not?"

"You're pregnant!"

"WHAT! I can't be. I've been on three different kinds of birth control for four years; I only have one ovary that works, and I haven't been pregnant. Are you sure?"

"Positive, no pun intended. I'm canceling the surgery."

"Gabby, to say I am depressed is an understatement. I am devasted. Expecting another child was not what Nick and I had planned. I'm embarrassed to say anything to anyone. Aside from Nick, you're the only other one who knows. I'm 40 years old. I'm not ready to raise another child. We already have four kids between us. I don't know what people will think. There are days I don't want to get out of bed. Now, we have to think about turning one room into a nursery. Before my doctor's appointment, we talked about having a garage sale. Thank goodness we hadn't had that garage sale yet. All that baby stuff I had put away, including the crib, would have been part of the sale. Now I have to drag it all out."

It had only been one month since Mia had shared the news with me, but I noticed she was preoccupied with her thoughts during this appointment. I didn't want to pry.

"How have you been feeling?"

"I've had some morning sickness, which has been a real treat."

"Have you told the kids?"

"No, we haven't said anything yet. I wanted to wait until I passed the three-month mark. We'll tell our parents after the first trimester, but I'm unsure when we'll tell the kids. I think I'm still in shock over this. I kept waking up thinking this was all a dream. Gabby, I can't believe I must go through another pregnancy."

"Mia, the one thing I know is that there's a reason for everything. You might not understand it now, but you will. It'll all work out."

Over the next six months, I was concerned about Mia. I wasn't seeing the happy-go-lucky person I saw before her pregnancy. There wasn't enthusiasm in her voice when she talked about the kids. She appeared more tired with every passing month. The depression had a hold on her, and it wasn't letting go. I didn't see her until after the baby was born, and she updated me.

"Two weeks before my due date of November 9, I had gone for my prenatal checkup. I told the doctor I wasn't feeling right. Staff who usually do the ultrasound were gone for the day, so the doctor did it himself. Between the ultrasound and blood pressure results, the doctor was concerned, admitting me that day to the hospital. While in the hospital, I crashed. They rushed me to surgery. I ended up with a C-section.

"October 26, 2004, our precious Nickolas Jr. entered the world at seven pounds six ounces, 17 inches long. As Nickolas emerged, the cord was wrapped so tightly around his neck that the doctor jumped on the table, straddling my body as he worked feverishly, struggling to get Nickolas out and unwrap the cord. It was a race against time. He managed to get the cord off of Nickolas's neck. The result: Nickolas had Down syndrome. When I came to and was told the news by my husband, my world shattered. I became numb with the information. I wanted to see Nickolas, hoping his diagnosis wasn't obvious. It was. I thought I was depressed before, but I had no idea how much more profound depression could be until that day. I was mourning the loss of a healthy baby but didn't realize it at the time. I was sure I had done something wrong during the pregnancy, but what? I had four healthy kids. What could have gone wrong?

"Just when I thought it couldn't get worse, we were told Nickolas had a congenital heart defect: a hole in his heart. All I kept praying was, 'God, why did you let this happen? I can't deal with this. What did I do to deserve this? My baby is too little to have these problems.' God never answered me. I didn't want to see anyone, and I didn't want anyone to see my baby. Was I embarrassed? Maybe? Was I devastated? Definitely."

"Oh, Mia, I can't even begin to imagine how horrific the whole ordeal was regarding the delivery. It had to be scary for everyone involved."

"It was. We ended up taking Nickolas to a pediatric cardiologist. Well, we thought he was a cardiologist. He ended up being a pediatrician with some knowledge of cardiology. So we ended up at the Children's Hospital in Denver. The cardiologist, Dr. Parda, came highly recommended. During our first consult with her, I was very nervous. Given the size of the hole, we knew it would be a long recovery (6-8 weeks). Dr. Parda put our minds at ease as best she could, reassuring us she would take excellent care of Nickolas. This wasn't her first rodeo, and her reputation preceded her. We had heard she was the best in her field. That brought some comfort. Of course, we wanted the best for our son. The surgery was a life-or-death procedure.

"We reached out to our church and started a prayer chain. Those members had friends outside of the church reaching out to them. We had prayer warriors from Colorado to Pennsylvania and everywhere in between. Nickolas was going to need all the help he could get. Heck, Nick and I would need all the prayers we could get. Nick, my mom, and I sat down and devised a schedule of how much time we would need to take off work."

"You know Mia, prayer never hurts. It brings comfort even in the darkest times, especially when others care enough to pray for you, and they don't even know you."

"I know. We were terrified. Nickolas was so tiny, and all I kept thinking was that this was such a major surgery that was very hard on adults. How was my Nickolas going to be strong enough to endure it?

"This was the problem. Not only did Nickolas have a large hole in his heart, but he also had mixed red and blue blood. You don't have blue blood. When the blood returns to the heart through the veins, it has less oxygen (deoxygenated). It is still red but appears darker due to the light traveling through the skin, making it appear blue. The arteries carry the oxygenated blood from the heart to other parts of the body. Several tests confirmed the red and blue blood were mixed.

"Our last appointment with Dr. Parda was before Nickolas's surgery. She ran more tests and did a final echo.

During the echo, I noticed everyone getting these weird looks. It was giving me a creepy feeling. Dr. Parda started calling other doctors in to look at the echo. I could see the look on Nick's face, but it hadn't dawned on me what was happening.

"Looking at me, Dr. Parda said, 'Do you see the red?'"

"Yeah."

"Do you see the blue?"

"Yeah."

"They're not mixing. Do you see that?"

"Yeah." At this point, staff have tears welling up in their eyes. I was so programmed for the surgery that what I saw was not registering.

"I'm telling you, Gabby, I was acting so stupid in front of everyone. I asked Dr. Parda what we were going to do next. She said, 'Nothing.' Then, as we were saying goodbye to the staff, they were crying, and I was still acting stupid, asking Dr. Parda when we should make the next appointment. She smiled and said, 'Honey, this is no next appointment.'"

"Sorry, Mia, but now my eyes are welling up with tears. So you're saying Nickolas is healed."

"Well, it wasn't until our drive home that I said to Nick, 'Gee, I guess I don't have to miss work, and you don't have to call off.'" That's when it hit me. I rolled the window down and stuck my head out while crying and yelling, "OH MY GOD!"

"Gabby, there was a handprint on Nickolas's heart on the echo. It was directly over the hole that was in his heart. Now I understood why everyone was crying. It was God's handprint. He IS the great physician."

Now, I couldn't hold back the tears. I shared the box of

tissues with Mia, and we both had a good cry. Mia called her in-laws and had them get in touch with others to meet in the church parking lot that day. They had a big prayer fest, thanking and praising God for healing Nickolas' heart. Ever since that day, Mia's faith has become stronger than ever. It wasn't long after this happened that Mia's attitude changed, and the depression disappeared. She now proudly boasts about Nickolas Jr.'s milestones and her other children's accomplishments.

21. BROTHERLY LOVE

Isabella

As a child growing up with two sisters, I often yearned for a brother. Despite the close bond with my sisters, I couldn't help but imagine the joy of having a big brother. My love for sports and athleticism, a stark contrast to my sisters, only intensified this longing. Unfortunately, that dream never came to fruition.

Despite my tomboyish nature in my younger days, I found my true calling as a stylist. If I had to do it all over again, I'd still pick the same profession. I so enjoy meeting people and hearing about their lives. Each client is a new chapter waiting to be explored, and I find immense joy in being a part of their journey.

On this particular day, I had a new client, Chayton. Chayton was Native American. Noting his name was different, he mentioned it was nature-inspired, meaning Falcon. Interesting. Mine was mom-inspired, meaning devoted to God.

Chayton did look Indian. He was six feet tall, with dark brown hair, that surpassed his shoulders by six inches. His beard was about a couple of inches in length. His appearance, with his strong build and long hair, might have deterred some from approaching him. However, I was taught not to judge growing up, which also transferred to this profession. His calm and gentle demeanor despite his imposing appearance was a testament to this.

Chayton was a construction worker by day and, in his spare time, did woodworking with his brother. They have successfully sold their wares out of Chayton's garage for the past ten years. Without asking, he pulled out a business card and handed it to me.

"Check out the website if you need bookshelves, furniture, etc."

"Sure. I'll post your business card in our break room. Thanks. So what would you like done today?"

"I want all my hair cut off!"

"All of it?"

"Yes. My brother and I have a ritual of growing our hair out for a year. Then, after a year, we get it cut off, usually above our shoulders. This time, I want it all cut off. We've been doing this for several years. He's my only brother. I have five sisters. I've offered to cut their hair, but they were against it." As Chayton shared this, I couldn't help but feel a mix of curiosity and respect for their unique tradition. It was a testament to their bond as siblings.

It was an unusual request but not far-fetched. Chayton's hair was in good condition. I was curious about what they did with their hair once cut off, but I did not have the nerve to ask. They probably donated it to Locks of Love or a similar organization. As I removed his hair, I carefully placed it in a bag. Looking at himself in the mirror, Chayton gave his approval as I handed him the bag of hair. It was then that he volunteered what he would do with it.

"I'm going to put this on my brother's grave," as his eyes welled up with tears.

My heart sank. "Oh, I am so sorry." I didn't know what else to say. So many questions were running through my mind that I had no business asking. But what stood out above the questions at that moment? The profound love and loss that Chayton was experiencing and the depth of his connection with his brother, were palpable in the room.

That is true, brotherly love!

22. In the Name of the Father, Son, and Holy Spirit

Matthew

I'm not religious, but I have several clients who are. They've never pushed their religion on me, which I always appreciated.

Lillian was 72 years old, very outspoken, but funny. She would always impart thoughts to ponder that left one thinking the rest of the day about them.

Having short salt and pepper hair that was blended evenly, Lillian was the envy of many of her peers. She was the youngest of five sisters; the oldest living one was 92. Lillian contributed her sister's longevity to living right and giving God all the glory.

Winters in Colorado can be brutal. That said, the cold can physically wreak havoc on one's body. Mine was no exception. I had knee problems for some time, and the cold wasn't helping. Standing for extended periods only worsened it, forcing me to decide soon what to do about it.

My next appointment had just shown up as I finished Lillian. I scheduled Lillian for four weeks out as she paid me. I directed my other client to the chair and talked to her about what we were doing today. The next thing I knew, Lillian stood beside me while my client was talking. Interrupting her, Lillian chimed in, "Matthew, I heard your knee is bothering you. Do you mind if I pray for it?" As mentioned earlier, I'm not religious, but at this point, I could use all the help I could get. "Sure."

Lillian knelt next to me, holding onto my knee, praying while I tried to do my client's hair. I thought a quick prayer would suffice. Five minutes later, I heard, "...in the name of the Father, Son, and Holy Spirit, Amen." Okay, now I have three more, plus Lillian looking after me. Cool!

I thanked her, and she left. I was uncomfortable about the whole ordeal, especially since it lasted so long and I was in the middle of something. I appreciated Lillian's thoughtfulness and the fact that she always seemed to look out for me. My knee ended up improving on its own. At future appointments, Lillian would periodically ask how my knee was doing. I told her I was healed!

Gotta love that woman!

23. You're Lucky She Doesn't Understand English

Lexi

I've always enjoyed learning about different cultures and am fascinated by their customs, which are so different from those in America. I especially like trying recipes for various foods from other countries. Lord knows I can use all the help I can get in the kitchen. When it comes to hair, I can hold my own.

Sometimes, it can be challenging when a client speaks broken English, and you're trying to decipher what she wants done. It becomes very challenging when the client does not have a great command of the English language. Such was the case with Ezra. Her husband, Daniel, who accompanied her into the salon, would translate for her.

Ezra had long dark hair and was an attractive woman who wanted highlights. It was apparent she had dyed her hair, making it difficult to meet her requests...or should I say her demands?

Daniel was well-spoken, attractive, and about five feet seven inches tall. I explained to him the color could not take because of the dye currently on Ezra's hair. It would come out in different colors. As he was translating, Ezra kept giving me dirty looks. Disappointment would have looked better on her. I'm still determining what Daniel translated because Ezra was not giving up.

"She wants to know if you can still do it. She said it would be fine." *No, it won't be fine. What part of "it's not going to work because your hair is dyed" don't you understand?*

"The only way I can show you is by testing a sample of her hair. I'll cut about 1/8´´ off, apply the color, and we'll wait and see what happens." Smiling at me and nodding her head, "Yes," I could tell Ezra thought she would get her way.

The look on Ezra's face when the true colors appeared was more of a shock. The orange, black, and yellow samples of her hair were not what she had expected. This would typically be a deterrent for anyone contemplating moving forward with the request unless you are Ezra.

"She wants to know why you still can't do it."

Are you kidding me? I had just shown her and Daniel. He may have pointed out the obvious, but his focus seemed to be on his wife getting what she wanted-or was it him?

Looking at me, Daniel quietly countered, "You do something for her; I'll do something for you."

"No, thank you. We don't do that in America!"

I applied toner to Ezra's hair and returned it to her natural color. They paid me and left, never to return, with Ezra none the wiser of her husband's indiscretions.

24. Shame on Her, She Knows Better

Celeste

I always appreciated the cosmetology classes, conferences attended, and books I read regarding hair. Of course, any hairstylist will tell you there's nothing like on-the-job training. Even that can't prepare you for all that you'll encounter. Hence, Dorothy comes to mind.

Dorothy was about 72 years old, had white hair, and dressed frumpily. During the first several appointments, she was friendly and respectful of my skills. After that, the real Dorothy came out. She never gave me a chance when she sat down to ask, "What are we doing today?" Dorothy would automatically tell me what she wanted and how she wanted it done. She watched my every move, which I wasn't used to, but it didn't make me nervous. I knew my stuff and was confident I would do an acceptable job. She would have never returned today if she didn't like how I did her hair the first time.

She was very negative about life. I could never talk to her about anything positive without her turning it into a negative. We referred to her as the Senior Debbie Downer. She mentioned that she lived in the senior community apartments.

"I heard those are nice. Do you like it there?"

"No! I like my place, but I don't like the people. They're too old. I don't have a car. I need to get places, like here today. Nobody would give me a ride. I finally found someone. No one is nice." Dorothy didn't have any family in the area to help out.

After getting to know the real Dorothy, I understood why no one wanted anything to do with her. I wondered if she had always been this bitter or if it was later in life. Changing the subject to something I hoped was more pleasant, I asked what she did for a living before she retired.

"Oh, I was a hairdresser for a little over 20 years. My license is in escrow [on hold]. I just reached a point where I wasn't enjoying it anymore, so I knew it was time to quit." I did not see that coming. She had to wonder what her customers thought of her.

As I finished with Dorothy, she seemed pleased with the results. I scheduled her next appointment as she paid me.

No tip, as usual.

25. And the Oscar Goes to...

Gabby

We were always taught not to judge. You never know what a client is going through. But once in a while, one client shows up that makes you wonder: Is something wrong with him, or is it an act? Those were my thoughts every time Clyde and his mother came in. Clyde was 28 years old, skinny, with stringy blonde hair. His mother always spoke for him while he looked down at the floor. I wasn't sure what was happening with him, but his mother seemed to control him. Clyde lived with her. It had seemed Clyde should have moved out years ago. Was his mother what they called a helicopter parent? It would appear.

As Clyde sat in the chair, his mother sat down and started reading a magazine. Putting the cape on Clyde, I asked him, "Is this what you want? Your mother said this is what you want."

"Yes," he replied softly, as if afraid to speak. That was the extent of our conversation. The next thing I knew, Clyde was sliding out of the chair. His mother saw him and yelled, "OMG, he's passed out. Lay him on the ground."

"Do we need to call 911?"

"No, he's done this before." As Clyde lay on the ground,

among the hair clippings, his mother yelled, "I need a cold towel." It was our busiest day that week, with clients occupying every chair available. One of the male clients waiting his turn got up and announced, "I don't need this crap. I'm outta here."

Lexi handed Clyde's mother a cold towel, only to have her reply, "This isn't cold enough." She grabbed the towel, went to the shampoo bowl, and ran the cold water over it. Not taking the time to wring out the towel, she ran back to Clyde, splashing clients as she passed them. Putting the towel on the back of his neck, she talked to him as he came to.

"It's okay, honey. You're going to be fine. Remember, we're going to get you a kitty. You're okay." Once Clyde regained consciousness, we helped him back into the chair. I finished cutting his hair, which was to his mother's liking. She paid me, and they left.

"Gabby, are you okay?" Lexi noticed the perplexed look on my face.

"Yeah, I'm fine. But that whole situation was weird. Didn't you think so?"

"I thought it was weird that his mommy is always with him at his age."

Later that day, I stopped at Dollar General to pick up a few items. When I went to check out, I couldn't believe my eyes. It was Clyde working the register.

"Hey, are you okay?"

"Ya, I'm fine. No big deal."

Are you kidding me? Everything he put me through today, and he is working this register, talking to customers with his mother nowhere to be found? What the heck was going on with him? I wondered if it was more of attention-seeking behavior. Clyde never showed up at the studio without his mother glued to his side. Yet, he could independently hold down a job without her presence which made no sense. That whole situation was questionable.

Yes, Clyde, you do deserve an Oscar!

26. Like Father Like Son

Isabella

The majority of my clients are incredible. Some stand out more than others for one reason or another. Such is the case with Luke and his three boys. You can always tell the great parents, and Luke was one of them. He was very doting to his boys, Jeffrey, who was 13 years old; Jonathan, who was 10; and Jacob, who was five. They were well-behaved and well-spoken.

Luke always enjoyed planning family vacations, and this summer was no exception. They had just returned from Disney World, and the boys were eager to talk about it. Each one outtalking the other with excitement about all the things they had experienced, including the Star Wars exhibit.

It was Jacob's turn to get a haircut. His reddish blonde hair complemented his freckles. He was very animated when he talked, with his hand gestures and eyes getting more prominent with every story he told. Personality plus! It was a joy to cut his hair. It was a reminder of the simple things in life that bring such joy to children.

Much to my surprise, I saw Jacob and his father walking into the salon the next day. That is never a good sign. My first thought, "What did I do wrong?" After looking at Jacob, it was apparent what had happened. I was not the culprit. Jacob was. I couldn't wait to hear this story as his father shook his head, still in disbelief. I acted like I hadn't noticed.

"Hi. What brings you guys back?" Trying not to laugh, Luke proceeded to tell me.

"You will never believe this one. Last night, Jacob said he was going upstairs to take a shower. The next thing I knew, he came walking down the stairs with a towel wrapped around his head. Thanks to Elmer's glue, pieces of his hair had been cut and glued to Jacob's chest. Before I could ask what he had done, he proudly boasted, 'Look, Dad, I look like you!'" Now, I felt it was appropriate to laugh.

"Awe, Jacob, you wanted to look like a grownup, like Daddy." Nodding his head up and down, "Yes," this animated five-year-old was not so animated today, as he dropped his head, looking away. "It's okay, buddy. We'll get you fixed up."

Yes, Luke, imitation is the best form of flattery, but this went a little too far. Jacob did not do a good job on his hair, so I had to shave his head completely. Fortunately, Jacob was okay with the decision, as we all made a big fuss over how cool he looked.

27. You'll Pay for This

Lexi

Early in my career, I lived in Doylestown, PA. I owned a little salon. Being the sole owner, I needed protection when I worked. I'm not big on owning a gun, so a dog was the next best thing. A Rottweiler Lab mix named Goliath. Before he could be with me at the salon, I had to get him licensed and put him in obedience school. He was the best protection I could have ever imagined. He was a staple around the salon. Goliath was always gentle with the clients. He doesn't like his paws touched for some unknown reason, and my clients were aware of that. Goliath never bit one of them. However, when he was outside one day, a drunk walked past. I warned him not to touch Goliath's paws. Of course, that is precisely what he did, and Goliath bit him. For a split second, the drunk sobered up, "Boy, you weren't kidding!" Fortunately, stitches were not required.

Seeing a fresh face walk into the salon—or a paying customer is always nice. Evan was in his early 70s, with grey hair, a mustache, scruffy-looking, a large nose, and big cheeks. He was a truck driver. I didn't care what he did for a living as long as I got paid. His social skills were lacking, so I smiled and greeted him with a "Hello." In return, I got a response in a gruff voice.

"I can't find anyone to do my hair!" *It's a comb-over; how difficult could this be?*

"Have a seat and tell me what you would like."

"I just want a trim off the top and tapered around the ears." That seemed to be an easy request. So, I did exactly what he asked. He appeared to be satisfied with the cut. He paid me and left. He was the last appointment of the day, and I was eager to get home and relax. It was wintertime, and I had to scrape the snow off my car windows. It would have been nice if the company that cleared our parking lot would have paid it forward and cleaned off my car. Since that didn't happen, I started cleaning off the snow when Evan suddenly appeared yelling at me.

"You SOB. This is the worst haircut I ever had. You're going to fix it!" Not to be imitated by his approach, I stood my ground.

"I'm not fixing it, but I'll return your money."

"I want it fixed! I can't go around town looking like this." I could not believe I was having this conversation that needed to end.

"Man, you got an old man comb over. Nobody will stop you on the street to say you have nice hair." Well, my response didn't help the situation. He continued to cuss me up one end and down the other. He got in his car and peeled out of the parking lot, cussing and screaming with the window down. Honestly, he could have kept the window rolled up. I would have heard him loud and clear. Given his demeanor, now I understood why he couldn't find anyone to do his hair.

The following week, the state inspector stopped by. I was baffled as to why he would be here, given that I had just passed an inspection about six months ago.

"Are you the owner?" Hesitantly, I admitted to it. I did not have a good feeling about this.

"I'm here due to a complaint about you being drunk while cutting your clients' hair, and your dog was violent towards clients, and he was filthy."

Trying to maintain my composure, I knew Evan was behind this. "Sir, I have *never* cut hair drunk, and as you can see, my dog is not filthy or violent."

"I'm sorry, ma'am, but you are expected in court next week and can tell it to the judge at that time," as he handed me the papers.

I couldn't believe what had just happened. I was so thankful no one was in the shop at the time. I had to drive to Philadelphia and plead my case in a court of law. I felt like a criminal. Guilty until proven innocent. I knew I hadn't done anything wrong but was a nervous wreck. I had notarized statements from 20 clients verifying my integrity and Goliath's certificate from the dog obedience school. I also had a picture of Goliath that happened to be taken ironically on the day Evan was in the salon.

After presenting my evidence I believe my testimony was sincere and honest. I felt this judge understood me. After the judge considered everything, he ruled in my favor, thank God! He cautioned me to choose my words more carefully when talking to my clients in the future. I agreed I should have never commented about Evan's comb-over in the heat of the moment and reassured the judge it would not happen again.

It never did. Evan never returned.

28. Do You Smell That?

Mathew

Beverly was 62 years old, petite, with blonde hair. She had been coming to me for several years. She was a waitress at one of the nicer restaurants in Lockston. Her quiet demeanor made it challenging at times to carry a conversation. I didn't take it personally. Truthfully, I welcomed the change of pace from playing therapist on most days. Beverly was excited about her appointment on this particular day because she was getting highlights. A product called Sunglitz, a revolutionary hair highlighting product that had recently hit the market and became popular, was the reason for her excitement. It was a different way to highlight hair. Having used it on other clients with remarkable results, I was confident Beverly would be pleased. We had discussed the color she wanted, along with trimming her ends.

While I was coloring her hair, Beverly's excitement turned into lengthy conversations as she shared some stories about her recent customers. As I finished her up, I put the cap on her head and had her sit under the dryer. The salon was filled with the familiar scent of hair products and the low hum of dryers. I was about five feet away when I smelled something. It was a faint, acrid odor that was out of place in the salon's usual atmosphere.

"What's that smell?" I walked back over to Beverly and lifted the dryer hood, only to see the top of her hair smoking like a chimney! I couldn't believe my eyes. I had never had anything even remotely close to this happen before. My heart raced, and I could feel the blood draining from my face. I started fanning the smoke with my hands. Lydia, our shampoo girl, was watching the entire time, her eyes wide with shock and concern. I motioned with my lips, "Shhh," trying to keep the situation under control.

Sensing something might be wrong, Beverly asked, "Is everything okay?"

"It's fine. Let's finish up your hair." As Beverly approached the shampoo bowl, I continued fanning the smoke off of her from behind, trying to maintain a calm façade. I looked at Lydia and said, "Rinse, now!" Thankfully, Beverly's hair turned out to her satisfaction and my immense relief. I called the company to report the incident. They had never heard of such a thing. The incident never repeated itself, but the mystery of why Beverly's hair was smoking that day remained unresolved.

29. When OJ Isn't Enough

Arianna

I'm not one for working out as much as I should. My schedule doesn't permit it. In a way, I'm thankful. I hate working out but watch my food intake without stressing over it. I am always in awe over those who can eat anything and never gain a pound. I can look at a cream stick donut and automatically gain two pounds. I had just finished a client who was a fitness instructor. While cleaning up my station, thoughts of needing to take my health seriously ran through my mind. I decided I needed to walk three times a week.

Celeste's station was next to mine, and of course, it's hard not to listen in when she has a client and vice versa. One of her newer clients, Yasu, was scheduled towards the end of the day on this particular day. He was of Japanese American descent and in his 50s, with dark hair, a slender build, and very healthy-looking for his age. He was always polite and well-spoken. He worked in the lab at Lockston Memorial Hospital. Celeste has forever been intrigued by different cultures and their customs. She had asked Yasu previously what his name meant.

"It means peace or quiet." No doubt, that was the vibe he always gave off. Very fitting.

I noticed there wasn't much conversation taking place

between the two of them on this appointment. Usually, Yasu would ask Celeste how her day was going and how the family was doing, and she would reciprocate. Today, he told her what he wanted done, leading Celeste to ask how his day went, trying to get some conversation going.

"It was fine." Yasu became quiet as if to say he wasn't in the mood to talk. Okay, we all have those days. Celeste finished cutting his hair and asked if everything looked okay.

Yasu was looking in the mirror but not responding. Celeste and I noticed he was sweating. Celeste told me to call 911.

"Maybe he's a diabetic and just needs some orange juice."

"CALL 911 NOW!" So I called, and the EMS showed up within minutes. Yasu gave them his name and wallet, which contained his information. As the ambulance pulled away, my heart was pounding so fast I thought I would have a heart attack. Celeste and I were both concerned, hoping, and praying Yasu would be fine.

We hadn't heard anything for several days and thought the worst. Yaus's son showed up to pay for Yasu's haircut. Talk about a family with integrity. He also took the time to thank us.

"My dad had a major heart attack. You guys saved his life!"

My heart sank. I was certain Yasu just needed some OJ. Celeste was the one who saved him and should get all the credit. A month later, Yasu walked into the salon. He was a welcome sight for sore eyes. We hugged him, telling him how good it was to see him. He thanked us for looking after him. When we asked if he remembered what happened that day, he did not. He did not even remember getting his haircut. My chances of Yasu not hearing my stupidity of wanting to give him OJ instead of calling 911 had increased.

That day, I learned a valuable lesson: Always err on the side of caution! You can give OJ later.

30. I Could Not Agree With You More

Celeste

I've always enjoyed little kids. When they come into the salon, we usually have suckers for them to occupy their time. Although nowadays, they have iPads that seem to do the trick when it comes to distracting them. Sometimes, kids may be a challenge, as you can imagine, yet there are times the parents can be. Sometimes, the parents are more nervous than the kids, which certainly doesn't help matters.

I had one of the most beautiful babies, under a year old, who had long, curly, dark hair and a lot of it. Little T, as his mother affectionately referred to him, was as pleasant and as happy as you could want in a baby. His mother told me she just wanted him to have a trim. Easy request. It was not a problem. Sitting Little T on her lap to get his haircut, she did not waste time talking on her phone. I placed a cape around him, lifted a piece of hair on his head with my fingers, and trimmed it. The curl fell to the floor. Little T's mother stopped talking on the phone, looking at me in disbelief as she combined a tapestry of cuss words while questioning my ability to cut hair.

"What the hell? What did you do?" She looked at me as if I had just scalped Little T.

"I'm trimming his hair like you said." I know a trim was

all she wanted for Little T. How could I have screwed it up on the first cut? I hadn't. I had no idea what was taking place at the time.

"You need to go back to school."

"Okay, I will go back to school." There was no way I was arguing with this one.

"You need to learn how to cut hair!"

"I agree."

"You don't know what you're doing."

"You're right; I don't." She kept getting upset because I was agreeing with her. I refused to get into an argument. For someone who wasn't pleased with me from the very beginning, she allowed me to finish cutting Little T's hair. I had to wonder if the theatrics were her way of getting out of paying for the "trim." As she walked out, she announced, "Not one of you SOBs stood up when I walked in," referring to the other two stylists waiting for their next appointment.

I felt terrible for Little T if this was how his mother usually acted. They left, and our phone did not stop ringing for the rest of the day. Little T's mother called numerous times, demanding to talk to the owner. Matthew finally took the call only to hear her order him, "I want that b**ch fired! You should see how this b**ch cut Little T's hair. She needs to go back to school!"

Of course, that didn't happen, and Matthew reassured me that I did the right thing by staying calm. I told him it did not matter how I would have reacted; she was determined to make a scene. That was evident by her not hanging up her phone as she continued talking to that person—or, I should say, as that person on the receiving end continued to listen in on the drama.

Little T's mother never returned. Fine with me, but I missed seeing Little T.

31. I'm With You Till the End

Isabella

Cosmetology school offers hands-on experience with clients in cuts, perms, and coloring. That is how I met Clarise. She was one of the first clients I got to practice on, or I should say, she was one of the first to trust me with her hair. We had an instant connection, and throughout the 24 years I did hair in Florida, she was uncomfortable going elsewhere, though she tried. She would tell me, "I tried someone else, but it didn't work. They need to know haircare and style. They either knew one or the other, but not both." We formed a special bond throughout the years. She was tall and medium-built, with brown hair that came to her shoulders. She was a classy lady who was always up-to-date on the latest fashions and hairstyles. The latter made my job easier. She was very conscientious about her appearance, always professional and beautiful, inside, and out. She was a minister, and no doubt, she had the demeanor to bring a sense of calm to any situation.

When Clarise was on the books, I knew it would be a good day. Given how long she had been coming to me, we went through everything together. Meeting our husbands, getting married, having children. We would encourage each other, especially when it was one of those days that every mother goes through when you want to throw your hands up in the air and say, "I quit."

I remember the day she shared with me her news that had rocked her world and turned mine upside down. Clarise had breast cancer. I never thought in a million years everything we had gone through that cancer would be on the list. She was calm about it when she told me—putting her trust in the Lord to get her through this. I was determined to be with her throughout this journey. She would need chemo, which meant eventually she would lose her hair.

"That's alright. I'll still be coming to you when my hair falls out. I'll wear a wig, and you can style it." Talk about a positive attitude. I don't know if I could have been that upbeat or matter-of-fact regarding my hair or health. It was apparent that Clarise trusted God throughout this ordeal, and I needed to as well.

Clarise had been receiving chemotherapy for about two weeks when she came in for her appointment. She appeared tired but was still in good spirits. Knowing the routine of what she wanted done on the last couple of visits, we headed over to the shampoo bowl, and I started shampooing her hair. As I was washing her hair, it was falling out. My heart broke for her. I told her what was happening.

"I knew it was going to happen. If it is, I'm glad it's with you." We had a moment of embracing each other, hugging, and crying. What she said next caused me almost to sob uncontrollably while trying to be the strong one.

"I told you I'm with you till the end. I mean it." She was killing me at this point. I could not put into words the love we had for each other. After we discussed what few options Clarise had left, she told me to shave her head.

"I already have a wig. It's okay." We both shed more tears as she was now completely bald. From then on, she would come in every two weeks for a wig style. I would wash and massage her scalp, taking the extra time to pamper her the best I could. She was a class act through the following months. Her hair was growing back, and she looked great.

Ten years later, I was still cutting Clarise's hair. She had been in remission and still is today. Thank you, Lord!

32. There are Some Things More Important

Gabby

Evelyn was a regular of mine and one of the sweetest ladies. She was in her 80s, with short salt-and-pepper hair. Married for 60 years, Evelyn often shared stories about her husband that did not always put him in the best light. She also happily shared stories about her grandchildren. I always looked forward to Evelyn's appointments, knowing she would not be at a loss for words. As much as she talked about family, Evelyn always asked about mine, which I appreciated.

Evelyn was always on time. Today was no different. Known around town for her driving, or rather her lead foot, I often wondered if she ever got a speeding ticket. "Believe it or not, I have only received two in all my years, but my husband doesn't know about them." I couldn't let the moment pass, continuing our conversation at the shampoo bowl.

"Evelyn, were you a driver in the Indy 500 in your past life?"

"Oh no, honey. I wished it was this life, but I never went so far as to get sponsors."

As I finished washing her hair, I heard someone ask for Evelyn. Looking up, I watched as the police officer walked towards Evelyn, who was calmly looking at him as she sat up in the chair.

"Ma'am, are you the owner of that white Oldsmobile?"

"Yes."

"Ma'am, you can't leave the scene of an accident. You left your car *in* the store!" Evelyn had run her car through the front of the drugstore, two stores down from the salon. Not skipping a beat, she replied, "Well, I had to get to my hair appointment. I couldn't be late. "

Talk about loyalty. With a towel wrapped around her head, Evelyn went outside with the officer to talk. He allowed her to come back in and finish getting her hair done.

"Looks like I have to call my husband to come and get me. He'll be cussing up a storm when I tell him what happened. Just hope he gets it out of his system before he gets here."

When the car went through the front of the store, it knocked over the wall of glass bottles inside. The pharmacist thought someone was firing gunshots. No, it was just our sweet Evelyn stopping by.

The incident had a profound effect on Evelyn, leading her to reconsider her driving habits. It was the last time Evelyn ever drove.

33. Can You Keep a Secret Till I Die?

Lexi

Martha was a bank manager at Lockston Federal Savings and Loan. She was petite, five feet, three inches, with natural blonde hair and blue eyes. Her husband had died, leaving her to raise her young son, Chad. Several years later, she was lucky to find love again, marrying a great guy, Grady, who took in her son as if he were his own.

Martha would come to the shop twice a week to have her hair done. Throughout the years, she never missed an appointment. When the main road was closed and detours set up, it added 30 minutes to her drive. She didn't care. The weather could be bad; she would take her time driving and still arrive on time. That was how dedicated she was to me, and I never forgot it.

I had to laugh when I thought about putting hairspray on Martha. She would remind me, "Do heavy on the sides, medium on the top, and light on the back." I had three different kinds of hairspray. If I grabbed the wrong one, she would snub her nose up at me. I made sure I memorized the hairspray ritual, preventing future nose snubs.

Martha was very close to Chad. It was hard for her to accept when he was old enough to move out and be on his own. He eventually bought a lovely home that Martha and

Grady would frequently visit. Knowing how picky she was about her hair, Chad would go that extra mile, having her park in the garage so her hair wouldn't get messed up on those days of inclement weather. As endearing as this sounded, it only lasted for about a year. Eventually, the car was left outside. Martha never complained, just thankful to spend time with Chad.

Well, let me rephrase that. Martha never complained about parking the car outside the garage; however, she did complain about Chad wanting a motorcycle.

"At his age, he doesn't need one. My husband sees nothing wrong with Chad owning a Harley. The way drivers are these days, you can't be too safe. The last thing I want is for him to be killed on one." I understood where she was coming from, having a son of my own who wanted one.

Knowing how badly Chad wanted a Harley weighed heavily on Martha's mind. She didn't want this to come between them, yet she also wanted her son protected from careless drivers. They had recently experienced the loss of a friend who was killed on a motorcycle by a drunk driver, which was still fresh on Martha's mind and, I'm sure, Chad's. Martha told me she didn't have a good feeling about Chad wanting a Harley, but she also recognized that he was not only a grown adult but also a very responsible one. When Martha wasn't worried about Chad, she was concerned about her mother's health, whose lungs were deteriorating. According to Martha, her own lungs were getting just as bad.

Martha could not keep her appointment for the first time in thirty years due to declining health on the Wednesday before Mother's Day. Knowing how faithful she had been to me throughout the years, I didn't hesitate to go to her house. I would do it as long as need be.

When I walked in, Martha was wearing oxygen. I thought her lungs had taken a turn for the worse, but I found out she had been wearing oxygen for years, just not when she came to the salon. She was appreciative of me coming to her home. Given her loyalty, I told her I would continue doing so as long as she needed me.

On that Saturday, Grady called me to say Martha had passed at the age of 68. I couldn't believe it. I just saw her three days earlier. I was so upset. To this day, she has been the most loyal client I ever had. Grady told me one of her last requests was that I fix her hair for the funeral. It was a pleasure to honor one of her two requests. When styling hair for the deceased, you usually only have to concern yourself with the top of the hair and maybe a little on the sides. In Martha's case, I only had to focus on the top. I only used one can of hairspray. *You can't snub your nose at me now, Martha.*

The day of the funeral was very emotional for me, as one can imagine. Pulling myself together so I didn't sound like a blubbering idiot, I gave my sympathies to Chad and Grady. They couldn't thank me enough for being such a special friend to Martha. Now, I needed to share Martha's second request.

"I need to tell you both something. Martha had another request. She asked me to keep this secret until she died. When I told them, they both stood there in shock, speechless. She knew Chad had purchased a Harley and had been hiding it in the garage all these years. She wanted to preserve the relationship with Chad and was willing to at all costs...even risking her hair getting messed up.

34. Good Thing I Shaved My Legs

Arianna

I've always had a soft spot for kids with disabilities. I have a cousin who has Down syndrome. Maybe that's why. I would always volunteer at the Special Olympics in Lockston every spring. It was so rewarding for all involved. I also learned a lot about communicating with those who were deaf, blind, nonverbal, etc. Little did I know those formative years would benefit me later on as a hairstylist. Back in the day of cosmetology school, they didn't teach us how to provide services to someone with a disability. It was on-the-job training.

Most people would have been uncomfortable with someone like Tommy. He was 42 years old, in a wheelchair, blind, mentally retarded, and wore a helmet. His caregivers were wonderful with him. So patient. Two things I always keep in mind when talking with a person who is blind: 1) Don't talk louder; they're blind, not deaf, and 2) Tell the person before you touch him, so he is not startled.

I greeted Tommy as he was wheeled up to my station. I told him I was glad to see him and asked his caregiver to remove his helmet.

"Tommy, I'm going to comb your hair." He nodded "yes" while leaning forward. He always leaned forward when I cut his hair.

It was summertime, and I had decided to wear my short denim skirt. When I say short, I mean it was right above my knee. Knowing what was about to happen next, I was thankful I remembered to shave my legs that morning. Tommy always liked feeling my knee the entire time I cut his hair. It helped him stay calm.

His caregivers were not comfortable with his actions. "Tommy, stop that. That's not nice."

"Leave him alone. He's not hurting anything. He's fine." It bothered his caregivers more than it bothered me. My mantra when helping people with disabilities has always been: Whatever it takes. Switching to the other side to cut his hair, Tommy would touch my other knee.

Emphasizing to his caregivers that Tommy was fine, I reassured them, "In all the times I have cut his hair, he has never moved his hands up or down my leg. He is focused on my knee for whatever reason. If this is what brings him comfort, so be it. It helps me do my job."

They understood. I also understood their point of view. But at the end of the day, I needed Tommy's cooperation and was willing to put up with his odd behavior.

Whatever it takes!

35. The Principal Will See You Now

Gabby

The selection committee had narrowed their decision to two candidates for the Harding Middle School principal's position. It was between a colleague and me. I was pulling out all the stops on this one, including the PowerPoint presentation I prepared, hoping it would prove I was the one for the job. Now, I just had to look the part.

I was excited about the new outfit I had bought. It was a two-piece navy blue double-breasted pantsuit. It was comfortable, and I felt good in it. Accompanied by a single strand of pearls and pearl earrings, I had dressed to impress. Eyeing me up and down, my husband disgustingly gave his unsolicited opinion.

"I don't know what possessed you, Amy, to buy that outfit. You look so thin you remind me of a starving African teacher."

My eyes welled up with tears as I stood there hurt, angry, and devastated, listening to Todd proudly laugh about his "one-liner." He could barely get the rest of it out from laughing so hard. I could hardly wait to hear the punch line.

"Do yourself and me a favor, and don't pick out any more clothes yourself. Get your friend Monique to help you. Now there's someone who knows how to dress."

And that's how the most important day of my professional career started.

You would think after ten years of marriage, I would be used to Todd's insensitive and discouraging remarks toward me. He never hesitated to embarrass or degrade me, privately or publicly. The more witnesses, the better he felt. Other husbands would have been proud of their wives' achievements. Mine was the exception. Any accomplishments I had ever received resulted in me crying afterward. I had silently hoped this would be the one time Todd was proud of me. That never happened.

After a grueling two-hour interview and five more hours of waiting by the phone at home, the committee had finally made its decision.

I cautiously yet anxiously called Todd, "Honey, I got the job!"

"Well, Amy, that's great. Maybe now you can start contributing to this family financially instead of me doing all the work. Do you think you're big stuff now that you're a principal? Remember, you're just a wife when you walk through those doors. I'm still the one in charge here." I could hear the guys in the background laughing. I should have known better than to call Todd at work and tell him the news. Waiting until he came home was an option. I just thought and hoped (again) this would be the one time he would be happy for me.

And that's how the most important day in my professional career ended.

***

If I had to name two things that I loved about my job as a hairstylist, it would be 1) helping people look good and 2) hearing about the professions they have chosen. Anything else disclosed is a bonus, sometimes. That being said, Amy came to mind.

She was a tall, attractive woman in her late thirties. Her shoulder length reddish brown hair and piercing green eyes added that "WOW" factor when she entered a room. She always came across as confident and professional. I admired her so much for pursuing her dream job as a principal. She was the only female candidate out of six applicants for the position, which was impressive.

I remembered when she got the job. She was so excited, and I was excited for her. But her excitement was tainted with Todd's negative comments playing repeatedly in her head. I felt so bad. I knew how hard she had worked over the past two years to get her principal's license while caring for her family of two girls, ages six and eight. For her husband to be such a jerk about it even surprised me. I thought this would be the one time he was supportive and proud.

Amy had been coming to me for several years. We instantly connected from the first time I cut her hair. I never pried into my clients' business, but I was all ears if they wanted to share information.

Knowing how important this principal's license was to Amy, I always asked how things were progressing during the two years she prepared for it. She always gave me the same response.

"I can't wait until these classes are over so I can get a principal's job. That's where my true passion lies." She mentioned in passing she had hoped she was selected so Todd wouldn't have to work so much overtime, allowing them to have family dinners at a decent hour. I was taken aback by her comment, knowing that's when he was verbally abusive. I knew dinnertime had to be taking a toll on the kids. It certainly was on Amy.

I kept asking myself why any woman would want to stay with a man who was degrading to her on a daily basis. I've heard that women in abusive relationships will remain out of fear. It's equivalent to the Stockholm syndrome. I would think there would come a time when one would say enough is enough. Pack the kids up and get out while you're able. It's easier said than done when you're not in a toxic relationship.

Several months after Amy started her new position, I noticed a change in her. I couldn't quite say what it was, but something was different. She told me she worked out three days a week and walked daily. She also mentioned that she had been thinking about getting highlights and wanted to do it on her next appointment. Someone had told her she would look good with them, and I agreed.

Amy's request caught me by surprise. I knew she was always watching her money, spending only what was necessary on her hair. I started to notice that she cared more about her appearance. Her style of dress even changed. One might chalk it up to her new leadership position, but I could tell there was more behind it. Once she got the highlights, I sensed this wasn't just for her benefit. It was as if she was trying to impress someone, and it wasn't her husband.

Watching Amy come in month after month, I could tell she was struggling with wanting to tell me something but was holding back. I never pressed the issue. I figured she would tell me in due time. About five months passed before she finally opened up.

"I have to tell you something." Here comes the moment of truth. I knew there was someone else.

"You know how you want to tell the world when you're in love? I am, and it feels so good."

"Really?"

"Yes. Oh, Gabby, he treats me so well. He respects me, and he doesn't yell at me. Best of all, he makes me feel good about being me. He is the opposite of Todd."

"So, where did you meet him?" It wasn't hard to figure this out, but I wanted to hear it from her first.

"He's a teacher in the same building as me. We've been seeing each other for about a year. I can't believe I'm talking to you about him. It feels so good to finally tell someone about him."

"It must have been hard to hold it in all this time, Amy. How did you do it?"

"I have no idea. I knew I couldn't say anything to anyone, but I've always felt I could trust you. We are so in love."

"Your life is so busy; how do you find the time to see each other?"

"Well, it started with us going to lunch. Then, eventually, we were able to go to conferences together out of town. We meet about once a month for a weekend out of town. We tell our spouses we have to go to a conference."

"He's married?"

"Oh yeah, I left that part out. Sean has been married for twelve years and has two kids. His wife is verbally abusive towards him. What a coincidence. I have a picture of him. You wanna see it?"

"Sure, if you don't mind."

Sean was biracial, had a great smile, was built, and was very good-looking. I could understand why she would be attracted to him. The last time Amy was in, there was talk that both were leaving their spouses.

They were waiting for the right time.

36. My Lips are Sealed

Isabella

Hairstylists are more than just professionals who cut hair. We are not only counselors and therapists, but we are also our clients' biggest confidantes. I've always wondered why couples cheat on each other instead of just getting a divorce if they aren't going to try to fix their marriage. It's also interesting how creative one becomes when cheating on one's spouse. Such was the case with Louise and Doug.

Louise was a plain Jane type of woman. Slender build with shoulder-length hair. If only she had applied a little make-up, that could have gotten the ball rolling in the looks department. Speaking of appearances, Doug was at the bottom of that list. There was nothing masculine about him, which explains the squirrely look and very slender build. They say opposites attract. These two were the exception. They both had been coming to me for ten years. Having a rapport established with them, it was no surprise when they both opened up about the other. That is when my talents for juggling their stories and keeping them private came into play.

Louise had confided in me that she suspected Doug was cheating on her. Doug suspected Louise was seeing someone, although she never said anything to me. I'm looking at both of them and wondering how that was possible. Neither one had the looks or personality. There's someone for everyone out there, and eventually, there was someone for Louise.

"Isabella, I am seeing someone who makes me happy. I've been seeing him for the past year."

"Oh! Does Doug know?"

"Nope. He is clueless." Wow, I did not see that coming. Then again, they had many issues when I think back to their relationship. Louise showed me a picture of her new flame. He was a big, muscular dude—the total opposite of Doug. I guess opposites do attract. I wanted to say, "That's funny that you thought he was seeing someone when you are the one," but better judgment prevailed. On Doug's next visit, he strongly suspected Louise was seeing someone.

"Did she say anything about anyone?"

"No."

"You sure?"

"I'm sure." The last thing I wanted was to be pulled into this hot mess. It got to the point that I dreaded when they both had hair appointments, even though they were on different days. Doug was becoming obsessed with finding out what Louise was up to, to the point that several months later, he started waiting for me out back once a week whenever I was going to my car. It didn't matter what time of day it was. On the day Louise had an appointment, Doug would be waiting out back to accuse me of not telling him what was happening. He had gone through Louise's phone, checking text messages and phone calls. I had yet to text her anything. That did not stop Doug from his interrogation.

"What did she say? Did she talk about him?"

"No."

"I know you know what's happening and aren't telling me. I know Louise told you about him. I have a right to know, and you are withholding information!"

"Doug, you have to stop doing this. You can't keep

coming here and asking me about her. I have nothing to tell you."

When I told Doug he couldn't keep coming here and questioning me, I should have clarified that it also meant he should not follow me home to continue his interrogation. Now, I am terrified. I've watched this mild-mannered man turn into some psycho. I finally told Louise what was going on, and she confirmed my diagnosis of him.

"I'm worried about you, Isabella. He has a secret box at home with all my text messages, your name, phone number, and home address, and what time he's been to the salon to talk to you." Now I tell my husband about it because I'm so scared. He wanted me to go to the police, and I told him I wasn't going to because Doug just wanted to know what was happening. He hadn't threatened me verbally, so I couldn't justify filing a report.

Eventually, we needed to contact the police. Doug had shown up at my home at 11:00 one evening. It was the same day Louise had her appointment, but he had missed me. My husband answered the door. Doug said he needed to talk to me. As soon as I saw who it was, I said, "That's him. That's Doug!" My husband immediately went into protective mode. "Get the hell off my porch!"

Doug became more aggressive, demanding to talk to me. The fact that my husband was six feet, four inches tall, towering over Doug meant nothing to Doug. Both ended up in our front yard, with Doug throwing the first punch. Now, the police were involved. Instead of a date night, my husband accompanied me to a day date in court, as I appeared on behalf of Louise and Doug.

While on the witness stand, I was asked when this all started and if I ever requested Doug to stop, to which I responded I had asked him several times. I still had the text messages I sent him saying he needed to stop. He didn't care.

I also told the court he had been by my home twice before coming onto the property. Of course, Doug's rebuttal was, "That never happened."

What benefit would it have been for me to make this stuff up? My goal was not to end up in court, but to get Doug to stop stalking me. When he was on the stand, he said it was illegal to hide this information and that I was hiding secrets. Then it turned into Louise and me sleeping together. He had written scenarios of Louise and me having this affair and stored them in a tackle box.

Doug acted normal before all this went down. He lost his mind and ended up in a psych ward for a while. Louise ended up marrying her man, who cherished her, and they are still married today. I have no idea what ever happened to Doug.

All I knew was that I could no longer have either of them as clients. I felt terrible for Louise, but I didn't care. My well-being was more important.

37. Hair to Die For

Gabby

My first job as a hairstylist was in the small town of New Paltz, NY. Fresh out of cosmetology school, I worked in a salon with three stations. It was a popular salon, given its size. Since I was the new kid on the block, I was told that Frances would be one of my regular clients. I needed the money and was not in a position to pick and choose my clientele. I heard she was elderly but friendly.

How bad could it be? I like elderly women, especially the nice ones.

Meeting Frances for the first time, I understood why they gave her to me. She was in her early 90s, with a petite frame and short white hair. Her husband would drop her off. Bathing was not a priority for either one of them. That was tough for me, given I'm a neat freak. But I pushed through it every week. You could tell Frances wasn't healthy. I felt horrible for her when her husband passed away. Now, she relied on her family to drop her off and pick her up. One time, she came in with fleas on her legs. It was horrible. They weren't in her hair, just on her legs, which I never understood. The owner called the family to come and get her. Frances just took it all in stride.

Watching the six o'clock news one night, I heard an elderly woman was missing. I looked up, and it was Frances. She had taken the car without telling anyone and was driving around. They couldn't find her. Here she was in the next county. When she came in the next week, I told her I saw her on the news.

"Oh, people made such a big to-do about nothing! I just wanted to go for a drive!"

She always got a shampoo set involving shampoo, rollers, the dryer, and a comb-out. Once I finished rolling her hair, I had her sit under the dryer. Something about the warm heat on your face makes you want to doze off. Most of my clients, who were elderly, would fall asleep, leaning forward. I was careful to gently raise the hood so I would not startle them when their time under the dryer was up.

As I lifted the dryer hood off of Frances, she fell forward, faceplanting on the floor. "Frances! OMG, I killed her!" No, I didn't kill her, but I thought I did. She wasn't moving. The EMTs arrived, but it was too late. Frances was dead. My boss removed the rollers from Frances's hair before they took her. Well, at least her hair was dried before she left, if there was a positive to gleam from this day. I was so upset that it took everything in me to get through the rest of the day.

I attended the funeral, crying and apologizing to the family. "I'm so sorry. I thought I killed her." Her death had such an impact on me that the family sent flowers to my home.

To this day, I think of Frances every time I need to check on my elderly ladies. I no longer gently lift the dryer hood. I knock first on the hood, ensuring they are just sleeping.

38. Make Me Look Good for My Mug Shot

Lexi

It had already been a hectic day, scheduled at the walk-in station. I was anticipating a break in the action when Joy Larson walked in. I knew she was going to ask for me. I should accept it as a compliment; however, this was one of those occasions I would have readily passed on having my ego stroked.

Joy was in her sixties. Her dark brown hair unsuccessfully shrouded the grey roots. She wasn't the most pleasant of clients. I didn't feel like her name matched her personality. She was respectful, but the tone in her voice offset the pleasantries. As she walked with a limp over to my station, she was wincing along the way.

"Joy, arc you okay?"

"No! I'm in pain. I had a knee replacement, and that SOB of a doctor won't return my calls. He wants to wean me off my meds, and I'm in too much pain to do that right now. Of course, he doesn't know how much pain I'm in because he won't call me back!"

"I'm sorry to hear you're in so much pain."

"Yeah, me too."

To keep the conversation from escalating, I quickly

changed the subject. "So, what are we doing today?"

"Make my hair look beautiful because I will be in jail by the end of the day." Chuckling to myself, I pushed for clarification.

"Joy, what are you talking about?"

"I'm going to that orthopedic surgeon's office to kill him! I want my hair to look good when they take my mug shot."

I could not believe what I was hearing. Joy was joking. Right? I'm sure of it. Then again, she was upset. Maybe she was serious? The tone in her voice came off that way. The only thought running through my head was: How do I handle this? "Oh, you don't mean it, Joy."

If looks could kill-she eliminated all doubt. Now, what do I do? Do I have someone secretly call the police while Joy is still here? Do I try to talk her out of it, risking her becoming angry with me? I could barely keep my palms from sweating. I was certain Joy could hear my heart pounding out of my chest.

She had earlier volunteered the orthopedic specialist name, Dr. Blanc. His office, Mountain Top Orthopedics, was only two blocks from the studio. If Joy held to her word, time was of the essence. No sooner did she walk out the door than I was looking up the phone number for Mountain Top Orthopedics.

"Good afternoon, Mountain Top Orthopedics. How can I help you?"

"Hi, is Dr. Blanc available?"

"I'm sorry, he's with a patient. Would you like to leave a message?"

"This is urgent. My name is Lexi. I work at My Preference Hair Studio, two blocks from your office. I just cut Joy Larson's hair. She is a patient of Dr. Blanc's. He did her knee surgery. She just left here and said she was coming there to kill him. She's very upset with him."

"What? Oh my gosh. I'll notify security and the police. Thank you so much!"

I no sooner hung up when sirens sped past the salon a few minutes later. I found out later that security was waiting for Joy as she approached the building, gun in hand, behind her back. Security asked Joy if she had an appointment, and she told them, "No, I'm just stopping in to see Dr. Blanc." Dr. Blanc was secured in his office while Joy was interrogated. They arrested Joy for carrying a gun without a permit and confessing to wanting to kill Dr. Blanc.

For Joy, the chances of Dr. Blanc ever returning her calls had just dropped to zero.

39. WE WERE OUTDONE

Arianna

I was raised not to judge people by their appearances. But sometimes, you can't help but notice individuals because of their appearance. Anita was one of those people. Her 5-foot 9-inch slender frame outlined her seventh-month pregnant body. It was Anita's second pregnancy, and she glowed. Her beautiful, long black hair framed her face. She could be featured on the front cover of Essence Magazine; she was that stunning. Gorgeous was the word that came to mind when you mentioned Anita's name. Anita was one of Celeste's regulars. Everyone around town seemed to know Anita due to her height and beauty.

While doing my client Leonette's hair, I overheard Anita talking about how excited she was to have a boy this time since she already had a girl.

"I'm so blessed. I get one of each. I already have the name picked out. Davonte." His sister's name was Davita.

Anita eventually switched the conversation to the purses that had been stolen from women around town. "I can't believe someone would be that brazen, or is it desperate? Whoever is doing this needs to get a job." We all agreed. We couldn't believe that no one had witnessed this person stealing purses. Whoever it was they had perfected their craft, and became very talented.

Anita left the shop looking just as beautiful as when she

entered. I had finished Leonette's hair and was getting ready to schedule her next appointment when I heard panic in her voice.

"My purse is gone! Where's my purse? I had it right here on the stand. Someone stole my purse!"

"Are you sure you didn't leave it in the car?"

"I am sure I brought it in with me. When I sat it down, I thought I probably shouldn't leave it there, but I have in the past, and it was never an issue. I'll go double check my car, but I know it's not in there," and it wasn't.

I felt horrible for Leonette. As women, we know our purses contain our entire lives. Now she had the daunting task of canceling credit cards, shutting off her cell phone, getting a new driver's license, etc., but her focus shifted to not having the money to pay me. Typical Leonette, always putting others first. She had to call her husband to come and pick her up. "When Keith gets here, I'll pay you."

"Leonette, it's fine. You have enough on your plate right now. You can pay me on the next visit. I am so sorry this happened."

It wasn't until a couple of days later when I was cleaning up the kitchen while watching the local news, that I saw Anita's picture featured on TV. Not hearing the storyline leading up to her picture, I thought something horrible had happened to her. I was wrong. It was because of her that something terrible had happened to numerous women. Across the bottom of her picture, it read: Pregnant woman caught stealing purses.

What? Are you kidding me? Anita was responsible for stealing Leonette's purse. As it turned out, Anita stole several purses from seven different salons. She made it a one-and-done visit with the other salons except ours. She meticulously plotted out which salons to hit, selecting the most vulnerable clients. Yes, we were outdone! What a shame that someone so beautiful and pregnant would go to jail. Was it worth losing both of your kids, Anita?

I seriously doubt it.

40. Down on the Farm

Celeste

I've always respected those who do farming for a living. It is a demanding profession that requires dedication seven days a week. Depending on what part of the country a farmer lives in, it can be a year-round job. Julia was one of my lifelong customers who lived on a farm, selling meat from her cattle. At 43 years of age, she had a thicker build, which was probably a combination of genetics, birthing five children, and working on a farm. Her pixie undercut with brown hair and blonde highlights looked good on her.

Having healthy relationships has not always been Julia's strong suit. Her last marriage ended with a guy who was physically abusive toward her. At one point, he had pinned her against the wall. She tried to grab a knife to stab him. He told her to go ahead and do it. Instead, she called the cops, having him arrested.

She always felt like she had to have a man in her life, meeting Chris about eight months after her divorce was final. Julia was a Christian, and Chris was a Catholic. They dated for six months, marrying shortly after. Chris was a financial advisor. Julia had gone back to school to be a health coach. She kept busy with the kids and the farm while learning more about becoming an herbalist. She had talked of earning a degree in that field someday. A people pleaser who burned the candle at both ends, she was always late for her appointments because she didn't know how to say "No." One time, Julia showed up for an appointment with a baby lamb in the front seat of her car with her kids. The Dam had twins and abandoned the one ewe, requiring the family to bottle-feed her.

Unfortunately for Julia, the only difference between this relationship and the last one is that Chris was not physically abusive, only verbally abusive. Julia endured Chris's narcissistic behavior for years. He constantly reminded her he did not want to live on a farm and never had that desire. Knowing how important it was to Julia, Chris didn't care. Month after month, as she came in for her appointments, she looked more defeated than the previous month. He would tell her she was not attractive and needed to lose weight. Their sex life was horrible. Julia recalled the one time that devasted her.

"While we're making love, he could not even make eye contact with me, only saying, 'Are you done yet?' That was hard to hear, and it was harder to feel sexy after hearing that."

Julia's kids didn't like Chris. She had two daughters from the previous marriage. The eldest one was married. The other daughter was 16 years old and had an attitude that caused many problems, adding to the stress in the marriage. This daughter worked two jobs to stay out of the house but also suffered from depression. She wanted to move out because Chris bullied her all the time.

Chris was becoming more challenging to live with and to love. Divorce was not an option, though it did cross Julia's mind several times. Julia wanted them to go to counseling but knew Chris would refuse if she suggested it. She had to make it look like it was his idea. She also knew he would not go for it unless it was affiliated with the Catholic Church.

Of course, in Chris's typical fashion, when Julia said she needed to talk to someone, his immediate response was,

"Well, I think you should. You need the help." Asking if he would be willing to accompany her, adding she knew the Catholic Church worked closely with a Catholic agency in town that provided spiritual direction regarding marriages, his response was, "If it's going to straighten you out, sure." Julia felt there was hope, given that Chris would do this. She also knew it was vital that it was a male counselor since Chris didn't respect women, especially herself.

For the first time, Julia believed their marriage would take a turn for the better. The counselor would see how Chris was and constructively call him on it. After several sessions, the counselor pulled Julia aside to tell her nothing else could be done due to Chris's narcissistic ways and his never-admitting wrongdoings.

Once again, Julia felt defeated. In Chris's mind, he had won. When Julia told Chris there wasn't anything the counselor could do for them, Chris responded, "I could have told you that. I didn't care for him that much, to begin with."

Tears slowly streamed down Julia's face as she felt crushed, shouldering a sense of helplessness. She told me she wanted a divorce. She couldn't take Chris anymore, but she was concerned about being able to keep the farm, and what if he wanted to take the kids out of spite just to hurt her? A lot of decisions needed to be made. The best advice I could give her was to pray about it. "You need just to say, Lord, slap me with a 2x4 and help me make a decision!"

Julia laughed but knew I was serious about the praying part. I'm not sure what the future holds for Julia, but she knows who holds the future. If nothing else, this will bring her closer to God.

41. Pretty in Pink

Isabella

When you're a hairstylist, it's not unusual for a family to request you to do their hair. I could provide discounts, though certain individuals secretly hoped for a freebie every time. I try to avoid doing family for two reasons: 1) They may not like what you did, and now it's caused a rift in the relationship, and 2) I can't pay bills with handouts and discounts. I learned that from my mother-in-law, a hairstylist for many years.

Of all the things they taught me in cosmetology school, the one thing they left out was how to work on dead people in a funeral home. If you've never done that before, it is an experience you will never forget. It is a very raw, unreal experience. Early in my career, a family asked me to do this person. I was hesitant, but it meant a lot to them. Now, the pressure was on. I was feeling the stress over being in a room with a dead body and making sure I didn't disappoint the family. Allow me to paint a picture for you of how this went down.

First, I was in a room with empty caskets, thank God. Music played in the room next to mine while the embalmer worked on a body. I put in my earbuds and started playing my music to distract myself. I was so thankful I remembered to bring my earbuds.

Taking a deep breath as I looked at this lifeless body that was pale as a ghost and cold, I started applying makeup. I applied the foundation, blush, and mascara. The lip gloss was in her favorite color, pink. I kept thinking she would wake up and say, "Boo!" She was ornery like that. Next, I fixed her hair. I only had to focus on the top and sides. She had short hair that was between a grey and sandy blonde. She liked her hair spikey and messy, with the bangs down. Very particular. Finishing up, I had hoped I did my mother-in-law justice. She had passed away from Stage 4 cancer. One of her last requests: "I want you, Isabella, to do my hair and makeup when I die. You will be the only one who can make me look like me." I had an excellent relationship with her. We never argued in the two and a half years I had the pleasure of getting to know her. How I wished my mother-in-law would have lived longer.

Everyone knew how much she loved pink, so the family gave her a pink casket. The one daughter worked in the paint department of Sherwin Williams. The son worked in the stain department. Between the two of them, they provided their mother with a beautifully stained pink casket. The funeral director said they had never had a pink casket.

Everyone who came to calling hours complimented on the casket: "How cool she got a pink casket." "Never saw one like that before." "It's so beautiful."

My mother-in-law was well-known in the community. The 239 guests who paid their respects confirmed this. She did look beautiful. She would have been pleased. Do I want to extend my services to the funeral homes? Not a chance. But it was an honor and privilege to make up my mother-in-law and have that private time with her.

42. HE IS NOTHING LIKE HIS BROTHER

Gabby

Family dynamics have always fascinated me. It's amazing to see a family where the kids all resemble each other, yet another family consisting of children that look nothing alike. Throw in a mixture of personalities that leaves you wondering what they will be like when they grow up. Watching these children grow up, sometimes we can be spot on with our predictions, while other times we miss the mark.

I have to wonder about the brothers Aaron and Andrew and what they were like growing up. Aaron was the older brother, with a nice appearance, in his early sixties, very social, genuine, and funny. It was always a pleasure to see him in our salon. On the other hand, Andrew was in his late 50s, with grey hair that barely covered the top of his head, average in the looks department, short in stature, and always sporting a golf t-shirt and shorts or khaki pants during inclement weather. Rumor had it that Andrew had a roving eye for women, acting like a lady's man. I'm still trying to figure out why. His reputation did not make women comfortable. He was a regular client of mine. He was flirty, always complimenting me about my hair, clothes, and shoes. I had heard he was a pervert. It wouldn't surprise me. I was always on my guard with him. He wasn't married, which was understandable. He had a daughter my age.

I've always followed my gut instincts. Chalk it up to a woman's intuition, but he undresses me with his eyes. I would check my appointment book the night before to see what kind of day I would encounter with clients. When I saw Andrew's name in the book, I knew I needed to dress conservatively that day.

On this particular day, Andrew was my last client. As usual, he was all smiles, greeting me. I was my typical cordial self. Part of me didn't want to converse with him, knowing it would give him a reason to maintain eye contact. The other part of me thought I needed to come up with something, anything, no matter how mundane, to talk about, killing the silence that was about to fill the air. Either way, I was in a no-win situation.

As I finished trimming what little hair he had on top, I moved to his right side and started cutting his hair when he said the unthinkable.

"I so badly want to shove my face in your boobs!" It took about a nano-second for me to respond.

"Don't you EVER say that again to me! Don't EVER do that!"

"Oh, sorry. I didn't mean to upset you."

"Don't ever say that again!" I was so mad at him that it took everything in me not to ruin cutting the rest of his hair. I found myself cutting faster than I ever knew was possible to get him out of the salon. Upon finishing, he paid me, including a $20 tip. Thanking him for the tip, I never asked if he wanted to schedule his next appointment. I didn't care if I ever saw him again. His parting words: "Let's keep this between us." *Fat chance, Andrew.*

The other girls in the salon refused to schedule him after I told them what happened. Matthew made it clear that if Andrew returned, he would be the only one cutting Andrew's hair. I'm so thankful Matthew had my back.

I never said anything to Aaron. I did not want to embarrass him. I'm sure he knows the way his brother is, but I have no idea to what extent. To my knowledge, Aaron never found out; if he did, he never mentioned it.

43. Reach for the Stars

Lexi

There are so many facets to becoming a hairstylist. Knowing different textures of hair from all cultures and how to work with them can be challenging. When I think back to being in cosmetology school, I remember one particular client, Jamar. He was an identical twin. While his brother, Javon, was going to one of our stylists who was black, Jamar came to me. Immediately protesting, his mother spoke up, "Oh, absolutely not! I don't want someone white to cut my son's hair." My manager intervened, saying, "Lexi is one of our best. She'll do a great job." Now, the pressure was on for sure.

I introduced myself to Jamar, who was outgoing and eager to greet me.

"Hi, I'm Jamar."

"Well, Jamar, it's nice to meet you. I'm Lexi. Let's get you set up over here." Jamar's personality was bigger than him. He was six years old and had a super thick afro. I heard he was learning to ride a bike and loved playing football and basketball.

"I'm the best one in my class. They always give me the ball to score." He was chatting away about school and his friends. If I had any questions or comments, I would have to wait till he took a breath or stopped talking. Suddenly, he stopped. I thought something was wrong when all of a sudden, he let out the biggest fart.

"Did you just fart?"

Laughing, Jamar proudly admitted it. "Yeah. My dad told me if you have to fart, just let one rip!" By now, we both were laughing. Regaining control and focusing on Jamar's hair, Jamar announced he wanted a star on the side of his head. This is an easy request to fulfill if you are an artistic stylist. If not, your day is about to get ugly.

"We need to check with your mom first. As long as she says it's okay, I'll do it." Jamar's mother agreed to it, which excited him. "You'll need to hold very still. If you move, the star will no longer look like a star."

"Okay, I can hold still." Jamar did an excellent job, contributing to my star's perfect appearance. His response was priceless when I inquired why he had chosen a star.

"So I could shine!"

You already shine, Jamar. But now even brighter.

44. In the Right Place at the Right Time

Matthew

Nanette has been a regular client of mine for years. I've always enjoyed my older clientele. Everyone appreciates the special attention they receive from their stylist, but something about my clients in their 70s and 80s makes me want to go out of my way to ensure they feel extra special.

Nanette was 74, with silver and grey hair blended beautifully throughout, with a touch of grey around the temples. She was a classy woman who never spoke ill of anyone. It was so refreshing when she came in, knowing we could have a pleasant conversation, unlike some of my clients, who were all about the town gossip. As juicy as that could get, I made a point of steering clear of voicing my thoughts.

Nanette was getting a perm on this day. She mentioned she was going to lunch with friends, so she didn't have to fix dinner. It was just her at home. Her husband passed away three years earlier.

I had Nanette at the shampoo bowl and was rinsing her hair. I opened the cupboard door above Nanette to grab a towel, only to have the door fall off the hinge, hitting her in the mouth.

"OMG! I'm so sorry. Are you okay?"

"I'm fine. Don't make a scene, honey. It's okay."

Nanette was not feeling any pain because she was numb. I wrapped the towel around her eyes as it draped over her face so I could finish rinsing her hair. I always do a thorough rinse, especially when a perm solution is involved. Lifting the towel off of Nanette's face, I noticed blood oozing out of her mouth. Now I'm in panic mode but trying to stay calm. I asked Nanette to hold the towel against her mouth while I got some ice. I ran to the kitchen to grab some ice out of the freezer, to no avail. Go figure. I saw a glass of lemonade that had ice in it. I emptied the glass, rinsed off the ice, and ran back to Nanette so she could apply the ice-filled cloth to her mouth. The bleeding slowed down.

"Honey, don't make a scene. Really, I'm fine."

It just so happened that Dr. Yuricic, the local dentist, was getting his hair cut at the same time this debacle took place. He came over and checked Nanette's injury. "My office is five minutes away. Just stop by when you are done here."

What were the chances a dentist would be in the studio when a mouth injury occurred? What were the chances you came to get your hair done and a door fell off the hinges and hit you in the face? I felt horrible for Nanette. Not wanting to draw any more attention to herself, Nanette self-diagnosed what she couldn't see. "I'm fine. The bleeding has slowed down. It'll stop soon."

Dr. Yuricic did not let up. "I need to fix your injury. Applying pressure isn't going to be enough." I could tell by the tone of his voice that this was serious.

Nanette kept applying pressure to her mouth with the cloth while in the studio. I packed Nanette's mouth with toilet paper to ensure continued pressure as she drove to the dentist's office.

"Honey, honestly, you don't need to make a fuss. I'm

fine."

Nanette received three stitches that day. Her labial frenulum, which is the thin tissue connecting her upper lip to her upper gums, had been sliced.

From this day forth, the cupboard door remains open when I have clients, never risking this day to be a repeat.

45. Oh No You Didn't

Arianna

The teenage years are a fascinating and complex period. Adolescents are neither adults nor children, navigating a unique space. They experience significant physical changes, expanding or contracting social circles, unpredictable attitudes and mood swings that rival the heights of Mount Everest. Understanding the complexity is key to fostering patience and empathy in dealing with teenage behavior.

When you're 15, you're chomping at the bit to have a job and learn how to drive, check out the opposite sex, and fantasize about your next boyfriend or girlfriend, unless you're Clark. His focus was on hunting. Always dressed in black or camo outfits, he had spikey blonde hair and was tall with a thin build. He didn't play sports, although, in regular clothes, I would have pegged him for a basketball player. I wasn't into hunting. I hate the thought of innocent animals killed but am willing to act interested, breaking the awkward silence that would otherwise fill the air.

I recall reading about the prefrontal lobe, which does not fully developed until around 25. This part of the brain controls decision-making, self-control, and problem-solving. On this day, Clark proved science to be spot on. After cutting his hair, I stepped away momentarily, telling him I'd be right back. I was gone for a total of two minutes. When I returned, Clark decided to use his problem-solving skills to cut his shoestrings with the scissors I had left on the counter.

"What are you doing? Do you have any idea how much those cost? I paid 475 for them!"

"Oh, I'll give you $5." Clark was eager to make it right.

"Five dollars! No, I'm talking four hundred seventy-five dollars."

"For those scissors? They're so little. I can't believe you paid that much for them." It took everything in me to contain the thoughts I wanted to verbalize.

"I can't believe you used them to cut your shoestrings! Why was it so important to do that right now?"

"I'd been meaning to cut them and kept forgetting. So when I saw the scissors there, I figured I'd do it while I had the chance. My bad." Given the size of the scissors, I could tell Clark couldn't grasp why I was so upset. I had to keep reminding myself he didn't know better.

Note to self: Never leave my scissors where clients can access them. Especially a teenager!

46. You Take My Breath Away

Celeste

Glenda was a 75-year-old woman with COPD. Getting out to socialize was a thing of the past for her. She had become so weak and depended on oxygen. As a result, her home was where social gatherings took place. It was also where I would be cutting her hair.

Arriving that day, I was hard-pressed to find a parking spot. So many cars lined the driveway in front of Glenda's house.

I hope nothing happened to her, and no one told me. Walking up to the front door, I could hear laughter and music playing, which was a good sign. No one heard me knocking, so I helped myself and entered the house. There sat Glenda, greeting me with a smile. The music had stopped at her request, and she directed everyone to leave. Thank God, I didn't want that big of an audience watching me do her hair. Plus, I get selfish with my clients, wanting to have that time with them and only them.

Before we got started, Glenda had a request. "Can we go in the bedroom? I want to smoke a cigarette before we get started." I was in no hurry and wanted her to be as relaxed as possible, so I complied. Entering the room, the smell of cigarettes hit me like a ton of bricks. It wasn't as strong in the living room, probably because the windows were open. Beside her bed was a large coffee can almost overflowing with cigarette butts. I wanted to throw up. But I knew I'd never get paid, so I resorted to keeping my mouth slightly open, breathing through my mouth, preventing the odor from consuming my nasal cavity. Glenda turned off the oxygen machine, sat on the bed, and lit one up. As I sat with her, I couldn't help but wonder why someone would be so selfish and jeopardize her health, especially when she was on oxygen.

Once she finished, we entered the kitchen, and I started to perm her white hair. Glenda was easy to talk with, and we talked about everything and anything. At one point, I noticed she was struggling to breathe. She kept trying to take deep breaths, resulting in short, quick ones instead. "Oh, Glenda, maybe you shouldn't have had that cigarette." For me, it was a no-brainer. If you can't breathe, smoking makes it worse. I was getting concerned. Her breathing was becoming labored. No one was around if I needed help. I'm trying to stay calm but at a loss as to the next step to help her.

She slowly leaned forward. *That's it. She is going to die in front of me, and no one is around.*

"You're standing on my chord, for God's sake! Get off my chord!" I was thankful Glenda had figured out the next step. I was clueless that I was the reason she couldn't breathe. I felt horrible, apologizing profusely. On this day, I learned a valuable lesson: Before passing judgment, I must make sure I'm not cutting off someone's oxygen.

47. Take Your Queen Home

Matthew

Every hairstylist has mixed emotions during this time of year: Prom season. Being inundated with appointment requests can lead to a potential spike in income, accompanied by attitudes, a sense of entitlement, tears, and mood swings. If appropriate, I would have told the girls or their mothers to make sure it's not that time of the month. That's when I charge extra.

Ella had dropped by to schedule an appointment for her sister, whom I had never met. "Matthew, my sister Elizabeth is going to the prom and needs her hair done. She is *very* particular about her hair and only wears it a certain way when it's a special occasion. I told her you are very popular with the high school girls regarding prom night and making them look good."

"Thank you for the compliment, but I need you to make it clear to her that I have one rule. If she gets crazy on me, I'll quit, and she'll have to leave. I don't have time for drama." I was already dreading doing Elizabeth, hearing how particular she would be about her hair.

The day arrived, and Ella strolled in with her sister. Not to sound mean, but there was nothing attractive about Elizabeth. I assumed she was going to the prom with her girlfriends. I couldn't picture her going with a guy. She was overweight, had long nails, false eyelashes, an attitude that sucked, and a sense of entitlement that set the tone for the rest of the appointment. The only natural thing about her that was positive was her long, beautiful brunette hair. After discussing how she wanted her hair, I felt this would be doable and painless. I then felt a tinge of guilt for my ill thoughts of Elizabeth.

I had finished the sides and back and started doing the top when Elizabeth burst into tears. "It's too big! I don't like it."

"Okay, I got you." I took it out and flattened it some more. She started crying again.

"I don't like it. It doesn't look right." Through the tears, she told me what she didn't like. That's fine. I corrected it, only to have her burst into tears again. No matter what I did, she didn't like it. A constant flow of tears accompanied her displeasure. By now, the girl was working my last nerve. I was almost done with her hair when Elizabeth looked at Ella and started crying again.

"I don't like it!"

That's it! One and a half hours later, my patience had left the building, and I let her know it. "I have shown you 80% of my work, and you allowed it, only to have you sit there and cry because you can't make up your mind." I swung Elizabeth around in the chair so fast that she grabbed the arms of the chair. I looked at Ella and ordered her, "Take your queen home! I'm done!" I didn't care that Elizabeth's hair wasn't completely styled as she wanted it. Ella paid me $20, and I never saw Queen Elizabeth again.

Thank God.

48. One Hair Makes All the Difference

Isabella

I have a cousin who has autism. She is six years old, bright, very articulate, and takes everything you say literally. I enjoy spending time with her. Her innocence and childlike ways make it easy to accept her comments that have no filter. Having her in my life made it easier for me to understand and work successfully with children on the spectrum, especially Tyler, when cutting his hair.

Tyler was a chunky four-year-old with thick, straight poker hair. He was used to getting a haircut at home, but it was always a struggle for him to sit still. It would be his first haircut in a salon, which explained the mother with a camera in tow, grandmother, uncle, and cousins, who showed up. His mother was concerned about me using clippers, noting, "His father has to hold his head in place so I can use them. Tyler screams the entire time."

Remembering how my cousin's mother would always explain each step of an event ahead of time to her, keeping it simple so there were no surprises, I knew I needed to do the same. First, I started by raising the chair up and down (without him), then having him get in the chair, raising it, putting the cape on, and ending with him holding the clippers. Knowing clippers are the most challenging to use on any child, especially someone with autism, I showed them to Tyler first, letting him hold them. Then I held them, turning them on so he would be familiar with the sound. I let him feel the vibration of the clippers, saying, "It tickles your hand." He giggled.

As I was getting ready to cut his hair, he started to yell in the cutest four-year-old voice, "I don't wanna haircut."

"Tyler, I have to cut your hair. It's getting too long."

"NOOOOO! I don't wanna haircut. I want it ALL cut!" Wow, it all made sense now. Talk about taking a word literally.

"Tyler, I'm going to cut ALL your hair just like you said, okay? I'm not cutting just one hair."

"Okay, you cut all of it." I knew by now that he trusted me. The rest of the time went smoothly, including when I used the clippers. Ever since that day, Tyler and I have become good buddies. He is always excited to see me, as I am him.

49. Trick or Heat

Gabby

Fall is one of my favorite times of the year. Throw Halloween into the mix, and it's the perfect way to wrap up the end of October, in my opinion. I look forward to seeing the kids in the neighborhood get excited when they come to my door. I'm known around our development for passing out popcorn balls. My mother used to make them with melted marshmallows, butter, vanilla extract, and, of course, popcorn. She would tint the melted marshmallows orange before pouring the mixture over the popcorn. It was a hit then and still is to this day.

Today, Jada was on the books. She came from money; her father was a doctor. She was 17, average height, skinny, with naturally curly hair to her mid-back. Her eyebrows were as thick as Oscar the Grouch's. I was in the back when she and her friends arrived, so I had my assistant wash her hair, rinse with conditioner, and put her under the dryer, keeping me from running behind. Little did I know, a health issue was about to unfold. Jada told my assistant about all the Halloween costumes she was considering, having been at the Halloween shop before her appointment. No matter what she selected, she would do it justice, given her artistic abilities, especially with makeup.

Once Jada's hair was dried, my assistant had Jada return to the shampoo bowl to trim Jada's eyebrows using my scissors. Suddenly, my assistant saw something small drop into the bowl. Several specks dropped at the same time. Again, it happened repeatedly. Yes, Jada had lice. The heat from the dryer acted as an incubator, hatching the eggs. Jada had tried on several hats at the Halloween shop before coming in, and maybe that was the culprit. It was too coincidental. I took Jada aside, ensuring her privacy and dignity, to discuss the situation. I then made a discreet call to her mother. "Your daughter got sick, and you need to get her." Her mother was appreciative of the call and kept the matter between them.

After Jada left, I had to throw away the cape and towels. I also disinfected and sanitized my scissors and the shampoo bowl. I felt terrible for Jada. I knew she was embarrassed, and it was out of her control. It's situations like these that remind us of the importance of handling health issues with sensitivity and discretion, especially when it comes to young people like Jada.

50. If You Were My Child

Lexi

I remember when I was little, I always listened to my parents. Having raised to respond, "Yes, ma'am," "No sir," "Please," and "Thank you." Anything less was not acceptable in our home. I don't have children, but my parents were good enough role models that if I ever decided to have children, I'd know what to do, for the most part. Today's teens appear to have a sense of entitlement. It astonishes me when I see them talking to their parents the way they do and get away with it.

More impressive is when they are younger than a teenager and have better manners. I thoroughly enjoy having those children for clients. And then there's Carly. She was eight years old with natural blonde hair, blue eyes, and the look of an angel. The 'ole saying, "Looks are deceiving," fit Carly to a tee. I could tell there wasn't a warm, loving connection between her and her mother. It was almost as if Carly resented her mother. I had no idea how much resentment was there until the day they were both in the studio. It was unclear what Carly's mother said to her, but how Carly felt was apparent.

"No!" The disdain in Carly's voice was interrupted by Carly hitting her mother on the shoulders. Carly's mother did nothing. She was undoubtedly embarrassed by her daughter's actions. The perm rods I had in my hands landed on the floor. I immediately walked over to Carly as we locked eyes. As I mentioned, I don't have kids, but the parent in me came out without hesitation.

"You better apologize to your mom right now!"

"No! She's mean to me."

"I don't know what happens in your house, but you will not act like this when you're here. You are to respect her." She still wouldn't apologize.

"Let me tell you something. You see that camera up there. I can have the police here, and they will deal with you if you don't apologize to your mother." There was no response. She couldn't care less. It was as if Carly had become immune to any discipline or threats. It was apparent Carly called the shots. It had me wondering how bad Carly had it at home.

If you were my child, you would be apologizing. Then again, you would be acting differently.

Carly was brilliant and knew how to play the game. Given the mother's lack of response, Carly took advantage of it. As a diversion from Carly's undesirable behavior, Carly quickly changed the subject.

"My dad is old."

"How old is your dad?"

"He's older than you. He's 49."

"I'm 62. Where's my wallet? Give this kid a dollar." Her mother immediately chimed in.

"She's not getting a dollar. Not the way she's been acting." Finally, Carly's mom acted like a parent instead of a human punching bag.

Unfortunately, Carly's behavior did not improve

throughout the year. If this was any indication of what she'll be like as a teenager, I hope she decides to go elsewhere. Her actions were not only disruptive but also disrespectful, making it clear that she needed a strong hand to guide her.

Rest assured Carly, I will only have so many Come to Jesus meetings with you, especially when you're a teenager. If your disrespectful attitude continues, you can take it elsewhere.

51. No Thanks, I'm Not Hungry

Matthew

Have you ever had that one person who stands out when you think of everyone you know? Usually, someone with a great personality and a sense of humor who knows no stranger and is friendly to everyone—just a joy to be around. But there is also that one person who is the opposite. You know the one I'm talking about. Someone loud and boisterous, is always on her phone, and of course, it's on speaker, and she has to be the center of attention. Yes, she is a regular client of mine.

Allow me to introduce Lyanne. Lyanne had poker-straight, dark blonde hair with highlights. Hair maintenance was essential to her, evident by her well-groomed appearance. Her hair was very healthy even though she washed it daily.

When I'm with my clients, I focus on them. My reputation for pampering them and giving them my undivided attention precedes me. I have to admit, it's challenging with Lyanne. It's as if it's a competition with her. Without sounding egotistical, being the studio's manager and lead stylist, I know many people who come through those doors. I could stop to acknowledge everyone, but my focus is on my client. Of course, if they greet me, I will say, "Hello." Lyanne, on the other hand, takes it upon herself to start talking with everybody and their brother. It didn't matter if they sat in the station next to her or in the waiting area. She is a retired teacher, so she feels it's a rite of passage to interview everyone.

"What's your name? Did I have your child in school? How old is he now? What is he doing?"

OMG, Lyanne. Stop talking!

Just when you thought you'd seen and heard it all, Lyanne's phone would ring. Of course, it was on speaker, and now we were all fortunate enough to listen to her conversation with her family doctor regarding her husband's test results. The results indicated that his issues all stemmed from his diarrhea. Did everyone in the studio need to know that information, Lyanne?

"Lyanne, shouldn't you have your phone off speaker in public when your doctor calls? I don't think your husband would have appreciated everyone hearing his results."

"Oh, it's fine. If it were more serious, I wouldn't have had it on speaker." I doubt that, but it sounded good for everyone who couldn't help but hear.

By the way, did I mention that Lyanne was always late for her appointments? She always walked in with a Tim Hortons bag and a McDonald's coffee. Would she ever call to tell me she was late? No. Would she ever offer to bring me something from Tim Hortons? No. Would she bring me a coffee? No. Thanks anyway, Lyanne. I'm not hungry. I don't expect my clients to feed me. Still, a simple gesture occasionally goes a long way, especially if you're consistently late because you're doing Meals on Wheels for yourself.

This last time, Lyanne arrived 10 minutes early. I was not in the studio but was arriving any minute. She told Cami she would be back shortly. Lyanne arrived 20 minutes late. "I'm sorry. I had to drop a meal off to my sister. She's been sick."

It was the first time she apologized for being late, which was a shock. I knew Lyanne made meals for her sister. The fact that her sister was ill, and she was caring for her allowed me to grant her forgiveness and see a different side of Lyanne.

The side that wasn't all about her.

52. Hands Down

Arianna

I'm always self-conscious about my body odor, ensuring I don't have that underarm sweat. That's the last thing a client needs to see or smell when you're washing their hair. I make sure I never wear perfume out of respect for my clients who may have an allergic reaction. I have a sensitive nose, so when my clients come in, I can tell who smokes, who doesn't, and who bathes and who doesn't. When you get clients from certain cultures who purposely don't bathe, I'll be honest; it is challenging to get through the appointment. The only saving grace is that they tip well.

Then you have those clients that mask the smell of cigarettes and weed with an abundance of perfume. Meet Chelsea. She's 62, skinny as a rail with fine, see-through, short, feathered hair. Her calico hair consisted of blonde and grey hair with highlights and lowlights. I can't remember a time she came in that she didn't reek of weed and cigarettes. Anytime I saw her name on the books, I knew the Lysol can needed to be accessible as soon as she left. Chelsea was friendly, talkative, and always on time, which made up for the odor. But not really.

On this particular day, she seemed preoccupied. She was quieter, making it hard to carry a conversation. That's okay. Sometimes, the client wants and needs silence, especially if they're having a bad day. Quiet time works for me, as well. So often, my clients look to me to solve the problems they have created that could have been prevented.

While cutting Chelsea's hair, she raised her hand. It was in my way, so I gently put it down. She raised it again, not saying anything. As I lowered her hand again, I said, "You must keep your hand down. It's in my way when I'm cutting your hair." She never acknowledged what I said. Instead, she tried lifting her hand a third time when I noticed her eyes rolling back in her head.

I grabbed my phone and immediately called 911. The first responders arrived in three minutes. I don't recall Chelsea telling me she had diabetes. She looked like she was going into a diabetic shock. Informing the EMTs what had happened, I mentioned Chelsea never mentioned anything about having diabetes. The EMTs assessed her and started an IV.

"It's not diabetes related. She's having a stroke." I couldn't believe what I was hearing. My heart sank. Poor Chelsea was trying to tell me every time she raised her hand that something wasn't right. I was so focused on cutting her hair that I ignored what she wasn't saying. I felt guilty, yet I knew it was out of my control.

That experience changed my outlook on my clients. I thought I was perceptive before. Now, I watched for any sign of distress when cutting my clients' hair, regardless of age.

The good news is that Chelsea was able to get the medical attention she needed within the time frame of having a stroke.

The better news: Chelsea made a full recovery.

53. I Was His Only Hope

Celeste

I've always enjoyed cutting kids' hair. They have great personalities and are so intelligent. It's like having a miniature adult in the chair. Of course, toddlers are a different story. If they aren't comfortable the first time they get a haircut, the parents, me included, don't have a fighting chance of them cooperating in the future. Part of getting a child comfortable with me is ensuring I don't overwhelm him with my voice. I also make sure I am on his eye level when we first meet, so I don't tower over him. Adults easily inhibit children. Building that trust factor is critical, especially when using the clippers. But on this day, the trust went beyond a child trusting me with the clippers.

It was my first time meeting my next client. As I watched him walk in with his father, his head down, I thought somebody either didn't want a haircut or was in trouble. It was neither.

"Hi, I'm Celeste. What can I do for you today?"

"My boy needs a haircut."

"Sure. Hi. What's your name?"

"His name is Donny." Donny never made eye contact, looking at the floor the entire time. Sensing he didn't want to be here, I tried to lighten the mood.

"Hey, Donny, come over and sit, and you can tell me

about your soccer team." He was wearing a Stallions soccer shirt that looked like it was part of a uniform. I was hoping that would break the ice.

"He's not playing sports this year. That's from last year," his father interjecting quickly. Donny sat in the chair, continuing to look down, glancing briefly in the mirror at me. There was no life in his eyes. Something wasn't right, but I couldn't quite put my finger on it. I asked his father what we were doing with Donny today, and he told me he wanted his hair cut shorter because summer was coming. Anytime I asked Donny a question, his father would answer for him while hovering over Donny. When children are above five, the parent does not have to be beside them when they get a haircut.

"You can sit over there, and we'll be done shortly." Donny's father reluctantly went over to sit down, but it was short-lived. While I cut Donny's hair, his father was pacing the floor, watching us like a hawk. I understood why. Getting a closer look, I noticed bruises on Donny when he sat in my chair. We are trained to watch out for child abuse and how to handle it. I was already using a soft voice when talking to Donny and continued to do so, now more than ever. Slowly turning my back to Donny's father while cutting Donny's

hair, I quietly said to Donny, "You are safe here. Are you safe at home?"

"No."

"Does anyone hurt you or beat you?"

"They hurt me really bad. I get bruises and open sores. My dad does it."

"If your dad asks, you didn't say anything." Out of my peripheral vision, I saw his father walking back to us to see what we were discussing. Acting like I didn't notice, I kept talking to Donny so as not to raise any suspicions.

"So, Donny, what's your favorite video game?" Donny never had a chance to answer because his father interrupted any thoughts Donny may have had of his own.

"How's it going over here? You're looking pretty good, Bud."

"We're almost done. Your dad's right. You do look good." When we were finished, I told Donny it was nice meeting him. His father paid me but did not include a tip. I wrote down the license number of their car and called Child Protective Services.

I often wonder what became of Donny, never seeing him in the studio again.

54. Could You Be Anymore Insensitive?

Isabella

I enjoy my job and my clients. No two days are ever alike, and no two clients are ever alike. That's what makes each day interesting. I'm never bored in this profession. I get tired from being on my feet all day, but I'd still be a hairstylist if I had to do it again.

I relish watching the kids grow up right before my eyes. One minute, I'm letting them pick from the treasure box for a treat after a haircut. The next minute, I'm fixing their hair to go to prom. As a hairstylist, you sometimes feel like part of their family. That certainly was the case with Diana.

Diana had been coming to me for the past 12 years. She was a down-to-earth girl who had the sweetest personality. She was married to a great guy whose personality rivaled hers. It was no surprise that Diana was successful as an elementary teacher. She was great with kids, especially her own. Delilah, her four-year-old, would come in with her sometimes. I would cut Delilah's hair as well. She was so well-behaved and well-mannered for her age. It made up for the ones who let their children walk all over them.

It was summertime, and Delilah accompanied her mother to the salon. Diana was scheduled for a cut and blowout. In typical Diana fashion or mom fashion, she had packed the iPad for Delilah, along with some books to occupy Delilah's time. Delilah was sitting on her mother's lap, which I didn't mind as we discussed what Diana wanted done today. Knowing Diana wanted to keep Delilah close, I told Delilah, "We're going to wash Mommy's hair. You can watch."

Lying Diana back into the shampoo bowl, I started wetting her hair. Suddenly, she was convulsing, having a seizure. I put her on the floor, turning her on her side while yelling, "Call 911." Removing the cape so it would not constrict her neck, I placed my hands under her head to prevent it from butting against the floor.

"Mommy, Mommy," Delilah was crying out her name, trying to get close to her.

"Lexi, take Delilah." As Lexi picked up Delilah, she struggled to get out of Lexi's arms, holding her arms out towards Diana, who was still seizing. "NOOOO! Mommy, wake up. I want Mommy!" Lexi reassured Delilah that her mother would be okay and that special people were coming to help her.

No sooner did Lexi finish telling Delilah than the EMTs showed up. By now, Diana's seizure had stopped. The EMTs asked me what had happened. I told them, and they concluded when Diana laid back onto the bowl, a nerve was pinched in her neck, causing her to seize. I knew Diana had told me she had seizures in the past, but in the 12 years I've known her, this was the first time I witnessed her having one. The EMTs put her in the ambulance, and Delilah joined her. They gave Delilah a teddy bear to comfort her, which I thought was sweet.

As the ambulance pulled away, my thoughts and prayers for Diana were interrupted by Sara, a client sitting in Arianna's chair who was getting her hair cut. Sara was known for gossiping, having no filter, and being opinionated and today was no exception.

"I'm appalled that mother came into the salon and didn't have her seizures under control. Plus, she brought her daughter, subjecting her to it. How selfish can she be? That kid is going to be scarred for life."

I'm appalled at your lack of empathy for this mother.

Diana is very special to me, and I'll be darn if I'm going to let someone talk negatively about her. As calmly as possible, I walked over to Sara and shared my thoughts. "I'll have you know, Sara; Diana has been coming to me for 12 years, and this was the first time I ever saw her have a seizure. And if you must know, it wasn't her fault! She is an excellent mother, and I can assure you she would never put her daughter in harm's way for selfish reasons, such as getting her haircut. I apologize to you and everyone in the salon if Diana's seizure made you uncomfortable. I'm sure it made all of us uncomfortable. The good news is that we were able to get her the help she needed in a timely fashion. She and her daughter are safe; that is where our focus should be."

Sara left the salon that day, needing an attitude adjustment. As Arianna approached my station, I braced myself for her disapproval of talking to her client like I did. It was necessary to speak up for Diana and protect her integrity. Maybe I crossed the line. Sara was not my client, but Diana was.

"Thanks, Isabella. I was going to say something when Sara took a breath, but that's when you came over. I couldn't have said it better myself. She needed to be called out. In Sara's world, it's more important to voice her opinion than to consider someone else's feelings. Could she be any more insensitive?"

Probably, if given more time.

55. Feed His Ego, Starve Yours

Gabby

Somedays, I feel like I make an emotional difference with my clients when they come in with their problems. On other days, I know I have, especially with these teenagers. Having a good role model for a mother, I learned so much from her about life, and I am still learning. When need be, I impart those words of wisdom to my clients.

Stacey was referred to me by her best friend, a client of mine. Her natural color was a sandy blonde. With fine hair down to the middle of her back, it was fringy, angled on the sides. She started coming to me about two years ago when she was a junior in high school. I noticed she had gained significant weight since the last time I saw her. Stacey was very good at softball, receiving a college scholarship, but turned it down due to the love of her life. Or was it the loser of her life? I'm leaning toward the latter.

Brad and Stacey dated throughout high school. It was an on-again, off-again relationship for four years. I inquired if she and Brad were still together on this particular appointment.

"Yes." I could tell she was regretting her answer.

"Stacey, why are you still with him?"

"I don't know. I guess out of comfort." Out of comfort? This is a guy who has narcissism written all over him. From what Stacey had told me over the last two years since they graduated, he doesn't seem to respect women, especially Stacey. Brad told her, "You're heavy, and you will never find anyone who will treat you as good as I treat you."

He didn't get along with his parents, so he moved in with Stacey and her mother, who was divorced. Stacey's mother always supported Brad, leaving Stacey out in the cold. It only fueled Brad's ego. In her mother's eyes, Brad could do no wrong. Stacey was the problem. It's no wonder Stacey's self-esteem was in the crapper. She recently had gone through Brad's phone only to confirm what she had suspected. He was calling another girl. She wasn't sure how to approach him about it. Of course, once her mother heard what she had done, Stacey would have to listen to her mother taking Brad's side.

"You have no business going through his phone. You wouldn't like it if he went through yours."

While Stacey was at work the next day, her coworker, Kelsay, approached her. "Hey, Jeannie said your boyfriend has another girlfriend," It took everything in Stacey not to burst into tears. When she got home that night, she asked Brad about it. Of course, he played it off as if it was no big deal and not true.

A few days later, Brad announced he was staying at a friend's house. At this point, Stacey felt like Brad was pulling away. She found out through the grapevine he was going out with his "girlfriend," and it wasn't Stacey. Feeling crushed and defeated as she told me, I couldn't stay silent.

"Why are you still with him? Why don't you leave him?"

"I don't want to start over. I don't want to be alone."

"Honey, let me tell you something. This is the best time of

your life. He made your life miserable during your four years in high school. Here you are two years later, still not appreciated by this guy who disrespects you, treats you like you know what, and has the nerve to say, '...you'll never find anyone who treats you as good as I do.' Believe me, you don't want someone like him. Your 20s are the best years of your life. It is when you should be spreading your wings and figuring out what you want to do in your life instead of being tethered to a narcissist. You need to find out who you are and not what Brad is deciding for you! By staying with him, you give him permission to treat you like crap. You build up his ego only to have him tear yours down. That's not love. You are worth more and deserve better." I had to be the mom she never had at that moment.

It had been about eight weeks since Stacey's last appointment. My words of wisdom had fallen on deaf ears. She was still with Brad and no doubt Brad was still playing the field. Thanks to Brad laying the foundation on how to have an unhealthy relationship and her mother's lack of support, Stacey is setting herself up for one toxic relationship after another whenever Brad decides to leave her.

56. Can You Hear Me Now?

Lexi

I had twenty-one years in the hairstyling profession, yet nothing could have prepared me for what I had experienced on this day. It was crazy, hectic, non-stop with walk-ins, and I had six more hours 'til we closed. There must have been a full moon in the forecast. A few customers were in rare form, sharing their negative attitudes from recent conversations with a spouse, teenage daughter, or coworker. The common thread with them was, "Make me look and feel better than when I walked in here!" It could be challenging, knowing they would rather talk to Lexi, the counselor, than Lexi, the hairstylist. Trying to decipher what they wanted in between the "Ums," "I don't know," "I think I want highlights, no, just color the roots… wait, I'm not sure what I want today," I was about ready to pull my hair out. Knowing their frame of mind, they weren't in the position to be of sound judgment under such duress, so I took the initiative to make two suggestions.

"Cut, style, and blow dry?" Or "Just touch up the roots and a trim?" I felt like the parent. "You only have two choices. Pick one!"

When I saw Ed walk in later that afternoon, I welcomed him with open arms, in my mind. He was 83ish, about 5 feet

10 inches, a veteran, and a retired mill worker who had moved to Lockston with his wife to be closer to their children. He had a sense of humor that was different in a subtle way.

He was a regular at the studio and known around the shop as one of the nicest guys. His wife of 60 years and the love of his life had recently had a stroke, affecting her left side. Coming in for a haircut was Ed's way of getting some respite from what had become a very demanding, emotional, and physical job as a caregiver. I had just finished up a client and was ready to take Ed.

"Hi Ed, you ready?"

"Sure, Lexi. But I don't know how you can improve on perfection." Staff and clients sitting nearby chuckled.

"I'll do my best. Just sit here and make me look good today, instead."

"Sure, I can do that. I need a trim around the sides with a little more off the top." His soft white hair would make any actor in his eighties jealous, along with most men in their 60s. He took pride in his appearance. Always dressing nicely in casual pants and shirts to match, he was not your typical 83-year-old. His pants were at a respectable position on his hips rather than hiked up under his armpits. Rumor around town: he received a sizeable undisclosed settlement for an accident he had years earlier in the mill back in his hometown of Steubenville, Ohio. Maybe he did, but he never acted like he was rolling in the dough.

While cutting his hair, he opened up about his wife, noting all she had gone through with the stroke. Keeping a positive attitude, he reminded me, "You know, it could have been worse. She's able to speak slowly. She always tells me she loves me. I wish there were more that I could do for her." I could feel my eyes welling up with tears. Thinking about my husband of six years, who barely remembers to call when he's going to be late for dinner, let alone tell me he loves me, I got lost in my thoughts. Starting to feel sorry for myself and somewhat jealous, I refocused on Ed.

Finishing up his haircut, I just needed to trim around his ears and clean up his neck. Knowing the sound of clippers around the ears or on the neck can leave one a bit unnerved, I made light of it, jokingly using a standard line as a diversion.

"Gee, if we could remove these ears, it would make my job a lot easier."

Pulling the top of Ed's ear down to trim behind it, I had just finished "my line" when suddenly, the clippers nicked his ear, causing the entire ear to fly off, landing on the floor! Standing there in shock, speechless, with my mouth wide open, I looked dumbfounded as his ear lay there. He had a prosthetic ear that snapped on (and off) unbeknownst to me all these years. Trying to catch my breath, I blurted out, "Oh my gosh! I'm so sorry. Why didn't you tell me about your ear?"

Laughing by now, Ed responded, "I never tell anyone. Half the fun is watching the expression on everyone's face when it comes off." I didn't know whether to be grossed out, laugh, or throw up. Then Ed requested the ultimate, crossing the line as far as I was concerned.

"Well, are you going to pick it up?"

"I'm *not* picking that up!"

"You have to, I can't. I'm sitting in the chair with hair all over me. I need my ear back." Reaching down with my index finger and thumb, I picked up Ed's ear, quickly tossing it to him like a hot potato. It looked unbelievably real and felt exactly like skin. Shaking his ear back and forth before blowing the hair off it, he snapped it back on, never skipping a beat.

"An accident in the mill damaged my ear on the outside, leaving me with minimal hearing on that side. It's no big deal. Don't worry about it." No problem, Ed! Are you kidding me? Don't worry about it. It's easier said than done. From then on, every time I looked at a pair of clippers, it was a trigger for me for the longest time. I could not trim around a customer's ear for months without thinking of Ed.

The next time Ed came into the salon, Arianna cut his hair. I was so traumatized by what had happened. The image of his ear popping off the side of his face was still vivid in my mind, not to mention how the prosthetic ear felt when I picked it up. It was going to be a long time before I got over this. As long as I knew Ed, I couldn't believe he had never told me about his ear. I felt hurt by it, not to mention embarrassed.

My standard line became history that day, and I never used it again.

57. Desperate Times Calls for Desperate Measures

Arianna

I enjoy hearing about my clients' children. Having two boys, I can relate to the excitement of reaching milestones: the first tooth, the first steps, the first day of school, and those lovely teenage years when you are no longer called "Mom." Instead, the eye roll and snarling of the lip put you on notice you are no longer cool to be around. I especially enjoy it when my clients ask me about my boys and how they're doing. Such is not the case with Grayson.

Once Grayson assumed the position in my chair, every appointment was about his only child, Gregory. Every visit. He never asked about my boys.

"Gregory made the honor roll again—the third time this year." "Gregory made the golf team." No surprise here. Grayson was a golfer. "Gregory is in the math club. They're going to the State competition." Enough about Gregory, please.

Grayson was short for a guy and wore glasses. He was average-looking but on the nerdy side. He had alopecia, resulting in baldness in some areas. Grayson never talked about his wife. I recalled what she looked like from the picture he showed me on his phone once. It was all three of them at an awards ceremony for Gregory, of course. She was homely looking. According to Grayson, she worried about everything. Drove him up the wall. Grayson, on the other hand, gave Gregory anything he wanted. I was getting a better picture of why this was Grayson's second marriage.

On this particular visit, Grayson did the unexpected. He didn't talk about Gregory. He spoke of his wife and how they were falling out of love. "My wife told me she wants a divorce but still wants us to live together. I don't know if I want to do that, but I also don't want to go through the hassle of getting a divorce. Let me ask you something."

I couldn't wait for this one. What could I possibly help Grayson with, knowing he had never asked for my advice over the past four years that he had been coming to me?

"Do you know of anyone who wants to have sex? If I'm going to live with someone and not have sex, I need to find another outlet."

"Sorry, Grayson, I can't help you in that area. I got nothing." Are you kidding me? Of all the subjects to seek my advice, this was the best he could come up with. I don't know why he thought I would know someone.

Grayson ended up with a divorce. I have no idea how that affected his sex life, and I didn't care to find out.

58. When Your Man's Away

Matthew

Women are beautiful, and I especially enjoy making them feel beautiful. I have built up quite a clientele over the years and am very proud. Of course, boasting about doing celebrities' and politicians' hair doesn't hurt when new customers consider me. It also helps when you look like Kasey, who refers new clients to me.

Kasey was the mother of two daughters, who were both attending Colorado State in Fort Collins. One majored in Journalism and Media, while the other majored in Political Science. Kasey's husband was a regional manager for Accenture, which is based out of Denver. He traveled a lot, leaving Kasey to find different ways to occupy her time since she didn't have to work. Plus, her girls were away at school, which allowed for plenty of "me time," according to Kasey. She would always talk about day trips with her girlfriends and sometimes weekend getaways, especially when her husband was gone. She never seemed bored.

If you have ever seen Van Halen's "Hot for the Teacher" video, that was Kasey. The only difference was that Kasey had long, medium-brown hair with many highlights. When she entered a room, heads turned, male and female alike. That's not bad for someone in her 40s. She also knew I was probably the only male she could trust not to undress her with his eyes.

Kasey arrived on time, dressed to the hilt, wearing her Versace jeans and a purple zebra sheer silk shirt, leaving nothing to the imagination. Her Kate Spade black hobo bag complimented her black platform wedges. She looked like she had just stepped out of a magazine.

Today, Kasey was getting a touch-up with her blonde highlights. While foiling her hair, she told me her daughters were coming home for the weekend. She looked forward to it since they hadn't been home in several months. They would Facetime in between visits. She rarely spoke of her husband, which left me wondering if she was staying with him because of the money, the girls, or both.

Finishing up Kasey, I just needed to add the toner. When a client gets highlights or color, a toner is required. The hair is toned as the last step in the coloring process to remove any remaining unwelcome tones, leaving the hair looking neutral. I gasped as I leaned Kasey back onto the shampoo bowl to wash out the toner. I couldn't breathe for a split second. She had grabbed me between the legs.

"If we only had a couple of hours. My husband is out of town." It was the one time I had wished I wasn't gay.

"Sorry, I'm flattered, but I'm not interested. I don't think your husband would appreciate it."

"What he doesn't know won't hurt him." Could she be that desperate for sex, and how many other men has she acted this way towards them? She was so natural about it I had to wonder.

I finished her appointment as fast as possible while she stared at me with that "come hither look." I have never had a woman make me feel as uncomfortable as Kasey did on this day. Since that incident, I always make sure I am out of reach of a woman's hand when they are at the shampoo bowl.

I don't care how old they are.

59. ALL IN THE FAMILY

Celeste

I know it's our responsibility as stylists to show up for work regardless of how we feel. People's appearances depend on us. It's also our responsibility to respect our clients when we are under the weather. I only wish our clients would reciprocate.

It was that time of the year when cold and flu season was at its peak. Almost every one of my clients this day seemed to have one or the other. It was inevitable I was going to catch something. It was just a matter of time.

Melinda arrived without her son, Mikey, who also had an appointment for a cut. "I'm going to get my haircut first. My mom is bringing Mikey." Melinda always respected my time and the studio, knowing that a six-year-old would be bored out of his mind waiting his turn for a haircut, risking the chances of him not sitting still. I appreciated her consideration. Melinda was about 5´4´´ tall, chubby, with short, brunette hair. She was a stay-at-home mom but very involved with her son's school. She always volunteered to help with the class parties and was active in the PTO. My mother never did that. She was a nurse and didn't have the time.

Melinda was usually a happy-go-lucky type of person. Today, she was not feeling it. She had a horrible cold, which became apparent between coughing and sneezing while her nose was running. Secretly, I wished Melinda would have canceled. I would have been okay with that. I was finishing up with her hair, and like clockwork, Melinda's mother walked in with Mikey, who was also sniffing and sneezing. It was just a matter of time before Mikey had a nasty cold. Why she never canceled was beyond me. I am so anal-retentive about that stuff.

It was Mikey's turn. As he sat in my chair with the cape on, he apparently had picked up his cold from his mother. His nose was running, and his way of handling it was to sniff the snot back in or use the cape as a tissue with a quick swipe. Mikey was chubby with auburn and brown hair. He was very animated when he talked. I have to admit he was a cute kid.

"I'm thirsty." His mother asked if he wanted the rest of his orange juice left over from his breakfast at McDonald's. I usually don't want kids eating or drinking while I cut their hair, but in this case, I was willing to be flexible and let him have one drink. What could it hurt?

He eagerly grabbed the bottle and started gulping the OJ down. He no sooner gulped it down, and it came back up, projectile vomiting onto the cape, floor, and splashing on the counter. He started crying. Reassuring him it was okay, and we'd get him cleaned up, I carefully removed the cape, and his grandmother picked him up. Melinda didn't hesitate to grab towels and clean the floor, which I appreciated. Other clients would have left it for me to do. I did disinfect the area before Mikey sat back down.

Once Mikey calmed down, we finished his haircut without any more OJ or incidents. It was a miracle that I never caught his or his mother's cold!

60. Sorry, We're Booked

Isabella

I've been married for 17 years. My husband and I have always gotten along. We both have a sense of humor, which has come in handy throughout the years, especially when I just wanted to cry. We've always taken our vows before God seriously. I've never understood the couples that don't. In today's society, it's nothing for couples to spend thousands of dollars on a wedding. Within five to ten years, they are getting a divorce. This is where premarital counseling could have come in handy, saving them both heartache and money. Maybe if someone had suggested premarital counseling to my next client, the outcome would have been different.

Heather was a pretty woman, 5´8´´, and in her late 30s. She was a bigger-boned gal, but that did not deter her from her long bronde hair (brunette and blonde combined), contributing to a very sexy look. Her husband, Steven, was very good-looking. They had a daughter, and Heather had two boys from her previous marriage. They were a very nice-looking family. They were very family oriented. The family portraits Heather would share were beautiful. The fall and Christmas ones were my favorite. Their kids kept them busy with school and sports.

"Heather, you and Steven do so much with the kids. Do

you two ever have a date night? It would help if you had that. My husband and I have date nights a couple of times a month. We also pretend to have affairs *with* each other. If I call him, he'll say, 'Oh, I just finished talking to my girlfriend. Your timing was good.' My response is usually, "That ho! When is she going to give up?" Heather and I laughed, and then Heather shared what I didn't expect and would have been okay not knowing.

"Well, we have date nights with another couple, Jim and Tammy."

"Oh, that's nice."

"They are the only couple. We're swingers."

"Omg, I love watching swing dancing. I always wanted to learn it." Chuckling, and to my embarrassment, Heather corrected me.

"That's a different kind of dance. There is music and dancing if you go to a Swingers' Club, but it's not your typical nightclub. People are there to have sex with each other. We prefer to keep it between Jim and Tammy at their house."

Allow me to retract my last comment. I did not see that coming.

I was speechless. I had no idea how to continue this conversation and wished it had never started. I didn't have to; Heather answered all my questions and then some.

"We commit to them, and they to us. It's like having a verbal contract. Steven made it clear we were only having sex with Jim and Tammy. No one else is welcome into our group."

"Don't you get jealous that Steven is with another woman right in front of you?"

"No. I'm with another guy in front of him. It turns us both on. You and your husband should check it out sometime. You meet a lot of nice people."

"That's okay. I think I'll pass. Thanks anyway." Knowing marriage is a sacred institution, the concept of couples agreeing to have sex outside their marriage is very foreign to me, and enjoying watching your spouse do it with another person is unconscionable.

About a year after Heather had shared her lifestyle with me, she announced Steven wanted a divorce. I had heard through the grapevine that Heather broke their agreement, cheating on Steven. There was no way I was broaching that subject with her. God only knows where that conversation would have led.

Unfortunately, over the next year and a half, I noticed a significant change in Heather's personality. She became evil and nasty, starting with stealing my flat iron. She would book appointments but did not have the cash to pay. Even the credit card companies caught on to Heather. She would say she was running home to get another card and would be back, never returning. I would no longer put up with her new attitude and refused to do her hair. One time, she had extensions put in and ended up stiffing the other stylist who did them. It got so bad that Matthew put an end to this fiasco. "Enough of her antics! The next time Heather calls in to make an appointment, I don't care who answers the phone. You tell her we are booked. Eventually, she'll get the message."

Eventually, she did.

61. She's a Walking Nightmare

Gabby

It's amazing to me when I'm at a clothing store, and I watch kids running around, playing hide-n-seek in between the racks while their mothers focus on the latest items on sale instead of their kids. Or you're in the waiting room at the ER, already feeling like crap, and you have kids laughing and screaming with excitement as they chase each other, taking advantage of their parents being on their phones. Thank goodness the triage nurse or patient liaison steps up to be the parent, kindly telling the children they can't do that and asking the parent to keep their children close, so they don't run into any patients.

When an adult oversteps their boundaries, that is also a head-scratcher, accompanied by thoughts that can never be verbalized in public. That said, Elliana comes to mind. She was a regular of Lexi's. Lexi was off sick that day, but when Lexi called Elliana to say she'd have to reschedule, Elliana insisted that she needed her haircut today due to an event she was going to that evening. Lexi had texted me asking if I had any openings for a cut and blow dry. I told her I could squeeze Elliana in around 3:00, but she might have to wait a few minutes. Elliana arrived 15 minutes early, which made her stay longer, knowing the client I had in my chair and what was left to do. When she walked in, I remembered seeing her before when Lexi did her hair a few times, except last month. I also remember Lexi telling me Elliana could be demanding despite appearing reserved. That's okay. I can handle demanding. I'm not too fond of it, but I can handle it.

Elliana was of ethnic descent with black shoulder-length hair that was layered. She was about 67 years of age. She was somewhat attractive and nicely dressed, wearing several bracelets matching her dangling earrings. She could have left the heavy eyeliner at home.

After waiting for 25 minutes, it was Elliana's turn. We were never officially introduced. As I introduced myself, I asked her what we were doing today. I already knew from talking to Lexi, but I thought I better make sure. In her broken accent, Elliana responded, "You gonna just trim. No change style. I no wanna cut short. Okay?"

That seemed easy. We talked, well, Elliana talked most of the time, telling me her plans for the evening with her husband and another couple. Dinner sounded like the only thing on the agenda. Elliana made it sound like a significant event when she talked to Lexi. It was essential to get her hair done. Now, it was all making sense about Elliana's demanding side.

Elliana reached forward as I finished towel drying her hair, grabbing the blow dryer. *Oh, she's going to hand it to me. How thoughtful, unusual, but thoughtful.* Wrong. Instead, she turned the blow dryer on and started to dry her hair.

"What are you doing? I can't let you use that!"

"Why not? The other girl let me do it." The other girl? There is no way Lexi would allow this. Then it dawned on me. Marni had filled in for Lexi, who had surgery earlier last month. It seemed like chaos ensued every time Marni filled in for a stylist. For example, when she had filled in for

Celeste, she shared with the entire salon about Meredith McBride, the mistress, who was sleeping with some guy. The guy's wife was in the salon while Marni ran her mouth. Now Marni had done it again. She was allowing Elliana to use the blow dryer. I was peeved.

Are you kidding me, Marni? Why would you do that? You know better. Gawd, I hate it when she fills in for someone.

"Elliana, I could get in trouble for allowing you to use the blow dryer. It's against State Boards to permit a client to use *any* appliance."

"This no appliance. It's a blow dryer, no?"

"It is considered a hair appliance. I will finish blow-drying your hair." Much to her displeasure, she handed me the blow dryer.

I never got a tip from her that day. At this point, I was just glad this nightmare was over, and she wasn't on my permanent clientele list. I told Matthew what had happened, and he said I did the right thing.

Once in a while, I will help out at one of the smaller salons in Lockston. Several weeks later, Elliana walked into that salon. I did not want her to see me, so I stayed in the back. I overheard her asking to use the blow dryer when the time came. Fortunately, the stylist told her, "I can't let you do that. I'd get in trouble."

"Why not? I no tell anyone. I no understand. The other girls let me." I wanted to walk out there and say, "There are no other girls. Just one that allowed you to do it, and that should never have happened."

Fortunately, this stylist stuck to her guns, repeating what I had already told Elliana, who reluctantly allowed the stylist to do her job. By the way, that stylist did not get a tip either.

Lexi, you OWE me big time for this one!

62. The Juggler

Lexi

Reflecting on my diverse clientele over the years, I realized that no amount of cosmetology school could have prepared me for the unexpected: From an ear popping off when the clippers nicked it, to dealing with the likes of bridezilla, momzilla, and auntzilla, and even a client with a vendetta against her doctor. The list goes on, and I can now add Tunisia, the juggler, to this colorful cast.

As I was attending to Tim, a first-time customer, Tunisia sauntered in with one of her friends. I knew from previous visits with Gabby that the studio was about to be infused with her vibrant and lively presence. Tunisia was a character like no other, a whirlwind of energy and laughter, who knew everyone's name and never failed to bring a smile to our faces.

Tim was a businessman, very professional, and polite. When Tunisia entered the studio, I could see him in the mirror, trying not to laugh.

"Hey, y'all. I'm here. Let's get this party started!" Tunisia's arrival was like a burst of energy in the studio. If you were having a downer of a day, she unknowingly helped you forget about the problems you couldn't solve. Her bubbly, animated personality filled the studio with life, putting any conversations on hold. Little did I know this day would be filled with entertainment, leaving us all speechless.

Tunisia was African American, somewhat attractive, and in her early 50s, but more importantly, she was a survivor. Having cancer that required treatment a couple of years ago, she never let it get her down. "God ain't ready for me yet. I ain't go'in nowhere." I guess she was right. Three years later, she was stronger emotionally, physically, and verbally. On this visit, she bragged to the entire studio about her body.

"I'm on my fifth body," she declared, her voice filled with pride and resilience. "I had a kid body, high school body, 30-year-old body, cancer body, and now this body." Moving between my station and Gabby's, she stood close to Tim, her next act about to unfold. Cupping her hands under each breast, juggling them up and down as if they were large cantaloupes, she announced, "Now I have these babies and am proud of it. I'm a Christian and believer in Christ, and that's what helped me get through cancer. Thank you, Jesus!"

I couldn't believe what I had just witnessed. Tim kept in his professional persona, acting as if it didn't faze him, but I knew differently. Hoping she was done became a fleeting thought as she continued. "No matter how much you weigh, you should be comfortable in the skin the good Lord gave you. I'm ready for my class reunion." I'm unsure if she was saying it for her benefit or her friend sitting in the chair that easily weighed 300 lbs., or both. As Tunisia walked back over to sit down, she boasted, "My boyfriend be coming back around. He sorry he left."

Wow! There was nothing left for Tim and me to discuss. I couldn't remember where we left off. It didn't matter at this point. I knew whatever we had to say couldn't come close to what we had just witnessed. I finished up with Tim, apologizing for what had happened. "I must admit, Lexi, I never expected entertainment with this appointment." We both laughed, agreeing there was a first time for everything.

Tim paid me, tip included, thanked me again for a memorable time, and noted that he would stop in the next time he was in Lockston.

I hope it's not on the same day Tunisia is here.

Note: The client, who witnessed this event firsthand while on a business trip, told the author about it. It needed to be told, but from the stylist's perspective.

63. Breaking the Sound Barrier

Arianna

I know being the mother of two can be demanding. Having two boys close in age can be challenging. Boys are usually full of energy, rambunctious, and louder than girls. They can also be adorable, warming the hearts of those within earshot.

Cody was four years old, had blonde hair, and was average in size. It was the first time he was in our studio. He was accompanied by his parents, clinging to his mother as I greeted him. He appeared withdrawn, which was typical behavior for his age and understandable given the environment. It's usually a crap shoot with four-year-old's when it comes to getting their hair cut and cooperation. I'm pretty good with kids and can get them to warm up to me. Somehow, I didn't have a good feeling about this four-year-old.

"Hey, Cody. My name is Arianna. It's nice to meet you." Cody scoped out my chair, the other clients, the studio, the floor, and anything else to prevent making eye contact. "Let's have Mommy and Daddy bring you to my chair, and you can see what it does." I pumped it up, making it go higher but not too high. Then I hit the release pedal, and he watched the chair come back down. "How about you go for a ride? Mom, why don't you put him in the chair." Surprisingly,

Cody didn't make a fuss, which I was thankful for. *You got this, Arianna. It might not be so bad after all.* I figured if I repeated the phrase enough times in my head, it would come true. Inquiring how Cody's hair should be cut, his mother started the conversation with what every stylist dreads hearing.

"Well, it can be a challenge, but we work through it. We always cut his hair at home. Make it shorter on the top, clippers on the side."

I started on the top, cutting his hair while talking to Cody. His parents stood by him the entire time, which didn't bother me. I'm used to it with kids this age. Cody was still acting withdrawn. I could tell he didn't want to be here. Heck, I feel the same way on certain days. As I pulled out the clippers to do his sides, this quiet, withdrawn four-year-old let out piercing, blood-curdling screams followed by yelling.

"NOOOOO! STOP! LET ME GO! NOOOOO!" Of course, the other clients in the studio were just as surprised at the outburst as I was, followed by whispers to each other. Truth be known, the whispers between clients were no longer whispers. One client talked loud enough on purpose, I'm sure, for all to hear. "Does the kid have to scream like that?" I understood why she said it, and I also understood why Cody was scared. By now, Cody was sitting on his father's lap while his father held Cody's body tightly against his. The screaming became louder as his mother held Cody's head firmly in place while I used the clippers on both sides. I'm pretty sure he had broken the sound barrier. I was so stressed between the screaming and yelling, coupled with Cody trying to get out of the hold his father had on him, that I could not and would not attempt the clippers around his ears.

Looking at Cody's mother, I decided enough was enough. "I don't want to do this. I don't want to hurt him."

"No, you *have* to finish it." His mother was adamant. I couldn't get the clippers around his ears. There were straggly hairs, and I pointed out the obvious: It was not safe, given how upset Cody was. As Cody's screaming was lowered a decibel or two, his mother begged me, sounding like a five-year-old wanting to go outside.

"Please, please, you have to finish. It looks stupid." Repeating why I couldn't fell on deaf ears. Now, his mother went to Plan B. "Can I have the scissors?"

"I can't let you do that."

Looking at her husband in disgust, she grabbed Cody off of her husband's lap and announced, "C'mon, we're leaving!" As Cody's father got up, he looked at me with disappointment and embarrassment, saying, "We'll take care of it at home."

That was fine with me and the other clients. When the family left, I waited for the salon to break out in applause, but it never happened. Cody's parents paid me for my time but did not tip me. At this point, I was thankful I had been paid anything.

I never saw Cody again, often wondering who the poor stylist was in Lockston that would have her patience tested. I hope she had earplugs.

64. LORD HELP ME

Matthew

Do you ever browse the GoFundMe pages? Millions of people from around the world are going through challenging times. If you're unfamiliar with the organization, it is a crowdfunding site. People make financial donations to those needing medical assistance, memorials, emergencies, financial emergencies, etc., to name a few. If you're ever having a bad day, peruse those pages, and you'll realize your life isn't so bad. Sometimes, I would like to refer clients to that site when they start their "woe is me" attitude. We should remind ourselves daily how fortunate we are, appreciating the simple things in life. Some people always look for a handout instead of taking responsibility to better themselves.

Tamika was that person. She was in her 40s, always well-kept, and dressed nicely, but her appearance clashed with her personality. Tamika had a sense of entitlement that was getting on my last nerve. She came to me via a referral from a previous client who had moved out of town. I wish the client would have taken Tamika with her, knowing now what I didn't know then.

Her first appointment was a red flag, but I didn't realize it. She showed up on time, which was critical in my book. I am anal-retentive about adhering to a schedule. Tamika told me what she wanted done, which was a shampoo and a blowout. I had just finished blow-drying her hair when she asked how much I would charge to cut it.

"A full cut or trim?"

"I want a full cut but didn't bring in enough money. I'll make up the difference on the next visit." Now, I have to decide if I can trust this person I don't know to follow through with what she said or make an excuse as to why I can't do it today. She did keep her word, thank God. Yet, the next month Tamika showed up late. Not cool.

"Oh, I had to drop off my kids at my mother's." *How long have you known about this appointment? You couldn't plan better?*

"What are we doing today?" I wasn't in the mood for pleasantries. That ship sailed when Tamika walked in late.

"I want a trim. Keep it the same style." That's good; I didn't have time to do anything else because she was late. I finished her hair, and she pulled the same stunt with me.

"Oh, I switched purses and don't have enough money. Can I pay you next time?" What am I supposed to say? *"Sure, I love it when my clients stiff me. That's my favorite part of my job."*

"You can, but I also need you to make sure you have enough money in your purse to cover my services for that day. I can't keep allowing clients to pay me every other month. I have bills to pay." Tamika claimed she understood.

The following month, Tamika walked in late again. "Sorry, I had to stop at the store." *Seriously, you couldn't do that after your appointment.* Now, she has thrown the rest of my day off. I am not pleased with her again. This time, Tamika had enough money to pay me for the day's services and her previous appointment. Maybe the last conversation I had with her sunk in. Only time will tell.

The next month, Tamika showed up late. It was a double whammy for me. She was late and had an excuse for being unable to pay me. "I ran short this week; can I pay you on my next appointment?" *Oh my gosh! I'm going to start a GoFundMe account. I'm not sure if it will be for Tamika or myself.*

"Tamika, this has to stop. You can't keep coming in here late. It's not fair to me or my other clients. It throws everyone's day off. I also need you to have the money to pay me on the day of the appointment. I can no longer accept payment a month later. I've been more than understanding with you. Now, I need you to understand where I'm coming from."

"I do, Matthew. It's just being a single mom and all. I don't always have the money on me."

"Well, you need to budget better. If you don't have the money, we need to arrange your appointment so you can put $5.00 a week back."

"Let me think about it." Her "thinking about it" would lead to another weak excuse. Whenever I would look in my book to see who I had the next day and saw Tamika's name, I had no choice but to cry out to God. I'm not religious, but at this point, I needed all the help I could get in dealing with Tamika. "Lord, I can't take much more. You got to help me. She's upsetting my day and my clients. I can't afford to lose them. Please do something. Anything."

The last time Tamika was in, she had the money to pay me. When I asked her about scheduling her next appointment, she told me what I had longed to hear. She was moving and would not be back. I silently did a fist bump and a happy dance in my mind.

I guess God does answer prayers. Thank you, Lord!

65. It Just Got Cancelled

Celeste

Before we moved to Lockston, my husband and I lived most of our married life in Grand Island, Nebraska. He loved to hunt; I enjoyed doing hair and target shooting in my free time. That said, it was common for us to buy guns. Depending on the type of gun purchased, it either came from the gun shop or one of the residents in town. Once in a great while, when I bought a gun, I would have the seller drop the gun off at the salon at the end of the day, right before I left. It was always in a case, preventing eyebrows from being raised. If anyone asked, I would tell them it was a little something for the house. I wasn't lying; I just wasn't transparent.

It was early afternoon on this particular day when this guy walked in with a box and placed it on the desk. I didn't order a gun, but I thought maybe my husband did and forgot to tell me he was having it delivered to the salon. He was out of town that week for work, so it might have been for him.

I didn't have a good feeling when this guy walked in. He was African American, thin, 5´10´´, with a beard, shabbily dressed in worn jeans, a dull brown shirt, and very scary looking. As I cut my client's hair, this guy started walking around the salon. He kept looking up toward the ceiling. I caught myself looking up as well, thinking he saw something. There was nothing there that I knew of. He stopped at each of the stylists' stations between his glancing upward to ask questions about hair.

"I want to bring my daughter in for a haircut. She has wavy hair, and she wants the waves out. Can you do that? My granddaughter's hair is curly. How can you get the curls not to be so tight? My other granddaughter is biracial. Do you do that kind of hair?" Now, I am on alert. What was in the box, and why was he making the rounds? The next thing I knew, he was walking towards me. Great. I couldn't wait to hear his question.

"I want you to cut my hair and make it the last appointment."

"Sure, let me check the book. Is 5 p.m. okay?" It wasn't my last appointment, but I didn't tell him.

"Ya, thanks. Bye." He grabbed the box and walked out. I grabbed the phone and called the police. Come to find out, he had been drunk and had been at the car lot before stopping here. They had called the police as well.

The police arrived outside of the salon. They inquired about what he was doing, and he replied, "I have a hair appointment."

"Not anymore. It just got cancelled." The cops placed him in the squad car. The police believed he was scoping out the premises to see how he could access the salon ceiling, hoping that it connected to the drugstore next door where he could steal medication. I'm thankful I followed my gut instincts.

66. It's All in the Name

Isabella

Throughout our careers, specific clients are memorable for one reason or another. Those are usually the clients for whom we will provide well-deserved nicknames, such as Curly Cue Sue, Chicken Hair Hazel, Tight Perm Patty, and Loose Lips Lucille.

But no one came close to Harriet when it came to well-deserved nicknames. At the first salon I worked in, my clientele grew thanks to Harriet's son, who started coming to me first. Through word of mouth, his mother and neighbors were coming to me. Harriet and I hit it off immediately.

Harriet was very short. My first impression was that she was a little person. She used to be skinny but had put on weight due to health issues. Her breasts were huge. It was evident she required extra support. Harriet preferred the relaxed look instead, throwing her bras away back in the 70s. She had long black hair, like in the 80s, with short bangs that were puffy. A spiral perm was her signature style. She became a beautician and worked for a while, but I would do her hair weekly.

When I permed Harriet's hair, she always wanted the spiral curls to be as big as possible, with her hair just as tall. "Is this too close to God, or do you want it lowered?"

"Nope, that's good." It was nothing for us to be laughing the entire time. That could be why she always wanted her appointment scheduled when no one else was in the salon. She would giggle so hard that she would pee her pants. I told her once, "This is why they make Depends." She only laughed harder, which did not help the situation.

The time came to spray her hair. I could never use enough hairspray, according to Harriet. I would use almost a whole can of hairspray on her. When I thought her hair couldn't handle any more spray, Harriet would get in her car, and before starting it up, she would have a can of spray handy and spray her hair!

God help her if she or anyone within 10 feet lit a match. I chuckled as she drove away.

There goes Hairspray Harriet.

67. For Better or Worse

Gabby

I have a good relationship with my husband. He is so appreciative of everything I do for him. I know, without a doubt, that I can count on him to be there for me, no matter the situation. He has proven that over the past twenty-one years, religiously. That said, I am amazed when I see couples who have been married for a long time become so disrespectful towards each other or oblivious to the obvious.

George and Nan were married for thirty-one years. They always came into the salon together to get haircuts. I hadn't seen them for several months, thinking they must have been out of town. They loved to travel to the New England states in the fall. You could tell they got along, yet, like all couples, they would bicker about nothing. I would silently chuckle as they thought they were being quiet. Everyone knew them in the salon, so it was not unusual for us to take turns doing George's hair. Lexi usually had Nan. Today, I had George.

While George was talking to me about the price of gas going up and considering buying a new car, I glanced at Lexi. I noticed her struggling with brushing out Nan's hair. Lexi's hand was visibly shaking as she gripped tightly onto the brush while trying to brush through the hair. I couldn't believe what I was seeing. Nan's hair was so matted and knotted that it reminded me of a dog with big, matted hair. Nothing was going to get through it. I could see the embarrassment on Nan's face. Nan was not one to let her hair go, so seeing her in this condition shocked Lexi and me.

As I finished cutting George's hair, Nan announced that she and George had been in a car accident three months ago. She injured her arms and could not do anything with her hair for three months. Now, I was upset with George, and he sensed it. Three months of looking at his wife, whom he knew was meticulous about her hair, and he couldn't help her? I couldn't help it; my thoughts flew out of my mouth.

"Were your arms broken too?"

"No." George's demeanor now mirrored that of a scolded puppy. The fact that he could be so oblivious to Nan's hair for three whole months was unconscionable. It was a clear sign of neglect, a betrayal of the vows they had taken.

After Lexi made several attempts to work through the matted hair and a discussion of Nan's options, ultimately, the only solution was to shave off Nan's hair. The emotional weight of the decision was heavy. We held back our tears until George and Nan had left. Nan had already endured so much with the car accident, and now her appearance had been drastically altered, all because of George's neglect.

So much for the vows "...in sickness and in health."

68. When 20/20 Vision Isn't Perfect

Arianna

Nellie comes to mind when I think of clients that have stood out over the years. She never married, dated, or had kids. She always held down a job and lived in her parents' original home. Nellie was in her 50s and set in her ways. She was the epitome of an old maid.

She had short hair, and it was starting to thin on top. Month after month, I watched her hair get thinner and thinner to the point she only had about five to six hairs on the top of her head. She would try to blame her thinning hair on me. I would give plenty of suggestions, but she would never follow through. She finally quit getting perms. I still gave her recommendations throughout the years. Some were repeats, just rephrased, to no avail. There were solutions for her thinning hair, but once again, it was easier for Nellie to blame me than to take responsibility. She would implement one of my suggestions but not follow through, only to say, "It wasn't working, so I stopped using it."

When she didn't want to hear what I had to say, she took it upon herself to seek out the advice of the other stylists in the studio. "What kind of medicines have you heard help with thinning hair? Do you have any recommendations for products out there for thinning hair? I need something to help thicken my hair, and I'm not sure what to do. What do you suggest?" Once again, Nellie was given sound advice but never followed through.

When the time came for her to need cataract surgery on both eyes, she was looking forward to it. "They say you don't need glasses once you have that surgery. That's one less thing I have to lose around the house," as she chuckled. That was probably the first time I saw her laugh, making me giggle.

When you have cataract surgery, they emphasize the importance of having a driver. Nellie would not let anyone drive her. I even volunteered against my better judgment. She took a cab. The procedure was a success on both eyes. I was happy for her. Unfortunately, Nellie was not. This was apparent when she came in for her appointment after having the surgery. She was fit to be tied. She was fuming and there was no calming her down.

"Do you know that doctor fixed my eyes? Because of him, I can see every wrinkle, gray hair, and line on my face. I don't like it, and I made sure he knew it. I demanded that he return my eyesight to the way it was. He said he couldn't do that. I can't believe he did this to me."

I couldn't believe all the hatred she was spewing toward this doctor. Her reasoning dumbfounded me as I listened to her rant. I had no response. I felt confused and bad for this doctor, but I did not want to express my support for him.

He did his job, Nellie. What did you expect?

Nellie was always negative. All the years I did her hair, she had nothing positive to say. I would try to change the subject to something pleasant to cheer her up, and Nellie would still find something negative about it. Sometimes, she would yell at me and carry on when she wasn't complaining about life. Clients of mine and the other stylists made sure their appointments were not on the same day as Nellie's. Everyone was depressed when Nellie was present. If you remember the donkey in Winnie the Pooh, Eeyore, that was Nellie. Or should I say, Negative Nellie? It got that bad. Her family was reduced to a sister whom she refused to talk to and a nephew. I was the only one she had left. I always feared I would be the only one concerned if Nellie didn't show up for her appointment. There was a time I even called for a welfare check on her. I was emotionally exhausted in this toxic relationship, to the point my emotional tank had dried up. I put up with her for years, but I couldn't do it anymore. I finally told her I couldn't do her hair anymore. She begged me to continue with her. I stood my ground, feeling like a burden was finally lifted off of my shoulders.

I heard that Nellie passed away a couple of months later. It was sad to think that someone with that much hatred lived in a world filled with good people who could have helped her, and she died alone.

69. Heroes Wear Capes... Salon Capes

Lexi

Owning your salon has advantages and disadvantages. The one I had back in Doylestown, PA, before moving to Lockston held many good memories. I was blessed to have so many great clients. There were days that I questioned why I ever owned my salon, especially when it came to the repairs that hit at once. I always braced myself when one thing broke down, knowing it was only a matter of time before something else would need to be repaired.

Fortunately, I had learned the importance of putting money aside in an emergency fund. My father taught me early on about saving up for rainy days.

I designed my salon so that one feels peace and tranquility when entering. My clientele ranged in age from 20s up to 80s, but the bulk were between their 50s and 80s. I had quite a few who were wealthy. The tips were especially good and appreciated.

Today was a jam-packed day, and lunch had to wait until dinnertime. That's okay. I knew this would be one of the disadvantages of running your own salon. It's no big deal. I was used to it.

I had never had any issues with clients except when I first opened, and one client reported me because of my dog,

Goliath, who was licensed to be in the salon. I was thankful it ended in my favor. Oh, how I missed Goliath. I could have used him on this day.

My clientele was white. I had no African American women, but I would gladly welcomed them as customers. So, it threw me when this black guy walked into the salon and sat in the waiting area. If you remember the large car phones and how big and bulky they were, he held that in his hand, pretending to talk on it with the wires hanging out of the bottom. I instantly knew he was up to something.

"Can I help you?"

"No, I'm just waiting on somebody," he said, dropping his head back down and pretending to talk on the phone. As you can imagine, the women in my salon were terrified. As I slowly walked to the backroom, I picked up the phone and called 911. "I just had a guy walk into my salon. He's acting suspicious."

"Ma'am, don't hang up the phone. We just had a call and believe it's about the same individual. The cops are on their way. They're looking for him." As I was walking back out while I was talking to the 911 operator, she asked me what he was doing. I reported he was getting antsy, and she reassured me how close the police were to the salon. At that point, I asked him again, "Who did you say you were waiting for?"

"Never mind." He realized what was going on, and he bolted out the door. He had just gotten down the sidewalk when the police tackled him. He had beaten someone to a pulp with a brick and robbed him before walking into my salon.

On this day, I donned my salon hero cape.

70. You'll Go Blind

Celeste

The headlines on the news this morning: Gunman shoots clerk at the gas station, forgets to take the money. Sounds like this guy should be added to the list of Dumbest Criminals. That got me thinking back to Grand Island, NE, and this customer who walked into our salon to use the tanning beds.

We recently updated it with a couple of beds. As the owner, I had hired two girls to operate them. The beds were a huge hit, especially during the spring and summer. The bulk of the clients were women, although it wasn't unusual for a man to pop in from time to time to use the beds.

I've always been a clean freak. Our state inspections consistently passed with flying colors, and I wouldn't have it any other way. I stressed to the girls the importance of sanitizing the beds before the next appointment and that dirty towels were not lying around.

One of the regulars walked in to use the tanning bed on this particular day. This was his third time. The girls had mentioned this client made them uncomfortable. I understood why. He looked like a creep. He was of average build, tanned, with hair above his shoulders. He was wearing sweatpants, a tank top, and a shirt. His appearance was very nondescript. You wouldn't give him a second look if you passed him on the street. The last time he was in, the girls had told me they were sure he was using the tanning bed to pleasure himself. When I asked how they knew he was doing that, they mentioned the residue splashes on the inside of the tanning bed, and he always asked for extra towels. No other client asked for extra towels or left beds in that condition.

"We don't want to wait on him anymore. He's a creep, and we *know* what he does in those beds. It's scary knowing he doesn't care."

These girls were like my daughters, and I was not having anyone come into this salon and make them uncomfortable. I reassured them I would handle it. Mama Bear was in the house! Well, this creep showed up the next time.

"Yeah, I want 10 minutes."

"I'm sorry, we are booked."

"No, you're not. Your tanning beds are empty." Now, he was getting an attitude that did not sit well with me.

"I'm telling you we're booked up. Take your hint. You're not to come in here anymore." He went outside and sat in his car. He wouldn't leave. It was like he was trying to intimidate us. Nobody had walked in to use the beds while he sat in his car. Luckily, I have a photographic memory and stared at the car long enough to get a good description, including the license plate.

The creep came back in while I was in the back and approached the girls, trying to convince them to let him use the bed. I immediately stopped what I was doing and walked up to the desk. "I said we don't have a bed!" He opened his shirt, exposing the gun he had tucked in the front of his sweatpants.

"Okay. How 'bout now? You gonna let me use the bed now?"

"Listen, you MOTHER! If you're not going to use that on me, you need to get the hell out of my salon right now!" He looked at me and left. I called the police, giving them a detailed description of him and his car. They busted him at the shopping center. It turned out he was visiting several tanning beds in town but not to work on his tan. Pervert. I hope he goes blind.

The police interviewed me and asked if I was insane, and I told them, "No. First of all, I never felt threatened by that jerk. And second, who comes in and points to a gun aimed at his penis? I told him that unless he would use it, get out of here."

I wouldn't change anything if I had to do it all over. My staff's emotional well-being was more important than this jerk's sexual needs being met.

71. I Had That Gut Feeling

Isabella

Have you ever felt that something wasn't right, but you couldn't quite put your finger on it? That's exactly how I thought about the father who brought his three children in for haircuts every Sunday. I never saw the mother with them, leaving me to wonder if she was even in the picture. There were two girls and a boy. The girls were four and twelve years of age. The boy was seven. I never knew their names, but the routine was always the same. The youngest one always got a trim, the boy would get a haircut, and the oldest girl could not decide how she wanted her hair, always seeking her father's opinion.

"Do you think I should cut my hair? What if I get it cut this way? Maybe I should have the part on the side? What do you think?"

"I like it the way you have it. It would be best if you kept it like that. We'll have Isabella cut a little off," he said as he smiled affectionately at his daughter.

While cutting her hair, I mentioned that it was nice that her dad was off today and that they could all enjoy the day together. "Oh, that's not my father. He just goes to our church." WHAT? I couldn't believe it. Her brother, standing nearby, spoke up. "Yeah, he's like a mentor." A mentor?

Where are these kids' parents? They need parents, not a mentor! I finished cutting the girl's hair and watched as she walked over to her "mentor," seeking his approval. I watched the two of them interact while cutting the brother's hair.

The girl was wearing a mini skirt, which could have benefitted from another two inches of material. I don't know of any twelve-year-old with perfect sitting posture; this one was no exception. She was sitting with her legs apart while this sick perversion of an adult was "listening" to her talk, but his focus was not on her face. As he leaned forward, resting his arms on his legs, it became apparent what his eyes were focused on, which caused my stomach to turn. I just knew something wasn't right, and it was becoming more obvious. When they left, the oldest girl put her siblings in the truck's front seat and was ready to climb in when the mentor got out of the truck and removed the younger two so the twelve-year-old could sit by him.

"That's it. I've seen enough. Celeste, that guy is doing something to that girl."

"Are you sure? How do you know?" I was 1000% sure he was a pervert. It was that gut feeling I get when something isn't right, and I'm seldom, if ever, wrong. I had written down the license plate number and the truck's description. I gave it to Celeste to pass along to her daughter, who worked as a dispatcher for the Lockston Police Department. Upon further investigation by the police and Child Protective Services, this "mentor's" emotional hold on that twelve-year-old now made sense.

He had been raping her for two years.

72. Keep on Truck'n

Celeste

Everyone does their best to avoid getting stuck behind a truck when traveling. It doesn't matter what the driver is transporting. No one cares. It's the fact that a truck (semi or otherwise) will slow you down. I hate being unable to see ahead or the rocks from the highway flying up and hitting my windshield, cracking it. I wish some roads were strictly for trucks, avoiding the inconveniences they provide. Truth be known, truck drivers get a bad rap, especially the over-the-road (OTR) drivers. Many think all these guys have to know is how to drive a truck, and you qualify. But the reality is far from it. These drivers must plan out their routes, ensuring they get from Point A to Point B on time, while also managing hours traveled, rest periods, fuel costs, repairs, toll expenses, miles covered, and using the proper placards for transporting hazardous materials. It's a complex job that requires a lot of skill and responsibility.

I always found it fascinating that someone could live out of a semi-truck for weeks while traveling the country and think nothing of it. That was my client, Fred. The unique lifestyle of truck drivers and their ability to adapt and thrive on the road has always intrigued me. Fred was referred to me about six years ago through another client. Word of mouth has always been the best advertisement for me.

Fred always took the last appointment of the day "...cause I got things to do." He was friendly and rough around the edges, mainly when he talked. It took some getting used to. His appearance made him look older than his actual age. He was in his 50's. He was a big, burly guy with a mullet that was thinning on top. His hair was long and gray. Scraggly with dreadlocks. He would see me every three weeks. I tried to keep conversations professional, preventing him from sharing his "colorful" take on things. I would ask where the road took him since the last time he was in, which was usually a safe topic.

"They had me start in Oklahoma, then head east to Tennessee. I went through the Carolinas, hit By God West Virginia, then Indiana, Iowa, Nebraska, and Wyoming. It ain't been too bad of a drive, giv'n fall, 'specially in the east."

"I know what you mean. I love fall. It's my favorite season. Too bad it is short-lived." Fred seemed tamer on this visit. He was probably exhausted from driving all over the country. I was exhausted with the thought of making that trip. But you could tell he enjoyed his job.

As I mentioned earlier, Fred would stop every three weeks when he was back in town. Given the length of his hair, I knew it would not be a 15-minute appointment. For starters, Fred never washed his hair at home. That is because Fred didn't have running water in his house. One time, I asked him about that.

"Don't need it and don't want it. Take showers at the truck stop. Save me a lot of money that way." Heck, even *Little House on the Prairie* had running water. Talk about being frugal. I had so many questions but opted out of continuing that conversation.

His dreadlocks needed some serious attention. I started to brush them out when the "colorful" side overran the tamer side of Fred as he started laughing. "Don't make that knot my b**ch!" *Okay, Fred, I hadn't planned on it.* I wasn't even sure what he meant and didn't care to find out.

"Don't worry, I won't." I didn't know what else to say. Fred never used that statement again, for which I was thankful. He did, however, come up with some other one-liners that day, especially when I had commented that he seemed to be hustling all the time.

"Yeah, they pay me to hustle. I feel like a hooker without a pimp." He was the only one laughing. I just chalked it up to another one of his Fredisms. I never knew what was coming out of his mouth that could offend others or myself.

That is why Fred will always have the last appointment of the day.

73. I Did Not Go to School for This

Gabby

Some of my favorite clients are older people. One especially was Ethel, one of my regulars for years, getting her usual shampoo, set, and color. At 75 years of age, she had a boisterous and fun-loving personality with a matter-of-fact attitude, which was the opposite of her frail appearance. Her long red hair framed her thin face. The years had been good to her, but her health was starting to take a toll on her, but that did not deter her from staying positive. She always greeted me with a big "Hello" and a smile. It was rare when she called me by my first name, which she happened to do on this particular day. She usually referred to me as Honey.

"How's Gabby today?"

"I'm doing fine, Ethel, and you?"

"Oh, Honey, I'm thankful every day I wake up." At that age, I would feel the same way. Ethel always left me a little wiser at the end of the day, imparting weekly words of wisdom. When she started a sentence with, "You know Honey…," a teachable moment was forthcoming. The lesson for today was a quote by Dr. Robert Schuller: "Tough times never last, but tough people do."

Little did I know this quote would have such a profound

impact on me. As I gently positioned Ethel at the shampoo bowl and began to wash her hair, she spoke up.

"Why are you getting me wet? You're sprinkling me."

"No, I'm not, Ethel." I'm always careful with my clients, so I didn't know where she got the idea that I was sprinkling her. Determined to get the excess water off, Ethel placed her hands under the cape and in a downward sweeping motion, removed the water, which was red-blood red. Blood was spreading rapidly throughout her floral top. Grabbing towels, I immediately applied pressure to her chest. More blood gushed out with every beat of her heart, flowing onto the floor.

"CALL 911! I need more towels!" It seemed like forever until the EMTs arrived. It was only four minutes.

"What did you do?"

"Nothing. I laid her back in the bowl and started shampooing her hair."

While tending to Ethel, the EMT commented, "Her arterial line broke. Those usually don't break. That must have been what had happened."

Ethel was in and out of consciousness. Watching them put her in the ambulance, I couldn't help but burst into tears. Was she going to be all right? Was this going to be the last time I saw her? Go figure, of all the things they taught us in cosmetology school, how to handle an arterial line that bursts was not on the State Boards.

I often wondered what happened to Ethel. I even went as far as to cautiously check the Lockston Times obituaries, praying I never saw her name. Several months had passed since the incident. Thoughts of Ethel and her words of wisdom often crossed my mind. I missed hearing that sweet voice and her saying, "Hello, Honey."

"I said hello, Honey." I looked up and couldn't believe my eyes.

"ETHEL! You're here!" Ethel's son had brought her in to see me. She was in a wheelchair. I excused myself from my client, and my eyes instantly welled up with tears as I embraced her gently.

"I thought I'd never see you again. How are you feeling?"

"I'm fine. You saved my life! They had called the priest in to give me my last rites. But I was not giving in to them. I still needed my hair done!"

"Oh, Ethel, you still have your sense of humor. I'm so glad you're all right. I was so worried about you, and I didn't know how to contact anyone to find out how you were doing."

"By the way, this is my son, Nicholas."

"Thank you so much for helping my mother that day. She speaks so highly of you."

"I'm just thankful she's all right."

"Honey, when can you do my hair?"

"I had a cancellation for tomorrow at 1:00. Would that work?"

"Yes, I believe so."

"Ethel, seeing you today has been the best gift I could ever receive. In return, my gift to you tomorrow is that your appointment is on the house!"

Tough times never last, but tough people like Ethel certainly do.

74. When Laundry Detergent Causes Blisters

Lexi

When I think of all my clients over the years and what made them stand out, there are too many to reflect upon. But, if I broke it down into categories, such as their personalities, medical conditions, physical appearance, kids, or their naïveté, now I have a visual. In the area of gullibility, Gladys stands out above them all.

She was about 55 years old and had a short Sally Field haircut from back in the day. You never saw her without her blue eye shadow and pink lipstick. She looked very matronly in her mom-jeans that had the elastic waistband. She wore printed floral shirts that you would expect someone in their 80s to wear. She was a throwback to the late 60s. I don't know how else to describe her without sounding mean, but she was just weird. Few people make me uncomfortable. Gladys was one of them. As I washed her hair, she did not hold back on how it made her feel. I felt like I needed to offer her a cigarette by the time I was done.

"Oh, that's it. That feels so good. Yes, that's the way I like it." Her moaning in between her comments didn't help. I had to watch that my silent thoughts to God weren't verbalized. *Help me, Jesus, to get through this appointment as quickly as possible. She is creeping me out.* It didn't help when she emphasized the one time how much she liked me. I promptly changed the subject.

As matronly as Gladys appeared, her husband, Albert, was the opposite in looks. He had an average build and height, brown hair, and blue eyes—nice-looking. He worked in the IT department at the hospital in Lockston. Opposites do attract. You would never put these two together if asked to pick a partner for each.

Their neighbor girl's reputation preceded her. She was very "popular" among the boys at her school. Barely underage, she caught Albert's attention. We all knew about those two. It seemed like everyone knew about those two except for Gladys.

On this day, Gladys was not enjoying me shampooing her hair as much as she had in the past. The first sign something was bothering her was the moaning had ceased, followed by only one comment. "This feels so good." Towel-drying her hair, I asked, "So, how's it going?"

"Oh, it's not been good."

"What's going on?"

"My husband might have been having an affair with the neighbor's young daughter."

"Oh, I'm sorry." *Finally, Gladys, did you figure out what we've known for months?*

"Oh, it's not that. My husband has some other problems."

"What's the matter?"

"He's got blisters on his penis."

"Ouch, that has to be uncomfortable."

"Yeah. Albert went to the doctor. She said to put a salve

on it. He wears a white sock to bed every night. He's allergic to our laundry detergent."

What? I could not believe what I was hearing. I'm not a family physician nor an allergist, but I'm pretty sure the little ho next door gave Gladys's husband an STD, not that he didn't deserve it. Now Gladys thinks he's allergic to laundry detergent. I had nothing else to say as Gladys continued.

"Now I have to figure out what laundry detergent is safe when I do his clothes. You'd think they would have put a warning label on the box."

Could you be that naïve, Gladys? I guess so.

75. The Irony of It All

Arianna

As a hairstylist, you touch lives in a way that makes people feel good about themselves. In return, you feel good that you helped them. Years ago, Lockston started this event called 'Hair for You' at the Cultural Center. Stylists would volunteer their time to cut hair for people experiencing homelessness. Given the number of people attending, it was a one-day event that required 15 stylists.

Matthew had asked for volunteers representing My Preference Hair Studio, so I volunteered with Lexi and Matthew. It was amazing to walk in and see the setup. They had a nail station, wax station, and massage station. They had barbers and, of course, stylists. We didn't have shampoo bowls, so we used spray bottles and just got through it. Of course, an abundance of food was on hand for people experiencing homelessness to have a meal, along with book bags filled with essential items for men, women, and children.

My first customer was Francesca. She was short with a round body, and was heavy-set. She was an Italian lady with very dark hair. Most people think of people experiencing homelessness as being dirty. Francesca was very clean. In fact, 90% of the people who came through that day were clean. She and her husband, Peter, were homeless at one point. They were both recovering alcoholics and addicts. They were living in an apartment complex called 'First Steps.' It was a step above a homeless shelter, where individuals got help getting back on their feet and becoming productive citizens. As Francesca sat in my chair, she appeared somewhat reserved. I introduced myself, greeting her warmly, and asked what she would like done today. Her smile quickly became a grin from ear to ear, sharing, "I can't wait to get my hair cut."

"Oh? What are you getting your hair all done up for?" She was like a little kid, filled with so much excitement I thought she would burst. As she started to tell me about her journey, she shared that she and Peter had a child. Due to their addictions, they lost parental rights to their daughter. She would have supervised visitations, but as her daughter became a teenager, the visits became fewer, and she wanted nothing to do with Francesca or Peter by the time her daughter turned 21.

"Well, it's been 13 years since I've seen her. We were estranged all this time." Her eyes welled up with tears. "I'm going to see her this weekend." Now, my eyes had welled up.

"And guess what?" I have an 11-year-old grandson whom I've never met. I am so excited to meet him. I always wanted to be a grandma!" Hearing her story, I made sure I took extra time with her. Today was a special day for Francesca all the way around. When I was finished with her, she looked in the mirror and said, "Oh my God, I'm so beautiful." She walked around the Cultural Center with a confidence that eluded her when she first walked in.

***

It had been three years since I had seen Francesca when she walked into the studio. She had gotten on her feet and now was helping others with addictions. Talk about coming full circle. Did the job pay well? No, but it was enough to sustain her. She wasn't in it for the money. She was so proud of what she had accomplished, and so was I. She was now one of my regulars. She and her daughter were closer than ever.

They would talk on the phone at least three times a week. They even went out to lunch together.

Two years had passed at this point. Francesca would drop in periodically. I hadn't seen her for a few months when she showed up at the studio. I had a client, so Lexi took Francesca. As Francesca walked past my station, I greeted her with a hug.

"Francesca, it's so good to see you. I've missed seeing you. How are you doing?"

"Not so good. It's been a rough year." *Oh no, she's relapsed.*

"It has? What happened?"

"You remember I reconnected with my daughter and grandson. Well, a drunk driver killed her a couple of months ago."

"What! Oh, Francesca, I am so sorry." My eyes were filling up with tears.

"Isn't it ironic? I stopped drinking and got my daughter back, only to have her taken away from me again, permanently. Except this time, by a drunk driver. It's only by the grace of God that I have pulled through and never relapsed."

"How is your grandson doing?"

"It's been hard. He and his mother were very close. Her husband is allowing us to be involved with our grandson. Pete and I are so thankful."

"You know, Francesca, the most beautiful thing was that you got to reconnect with your daughter before anything happened. You have those beautiful memories to help you get through those tough days."

I had no idea how much more challenging the days ahead would be for Francesca. Due to her excessive drinking years ago, she has a long-term issue with her vascular system and osteopenia. It has affected her bones and hips. She uses a walker to get around but doesn't let it slow her down.

She relies on God to give her strength daily. Francesca, you're an inspiration to all who know you.

76. Keeping Me Abreast

Gabby

Cami, our receptionist, was out sick, so we were all taking turns staffing the desk and answering the phone. It felt good to sit down and relax, even though it would only be for thirty minutes. It was nice to greet clients of the other stylists I usually don't get to chat with, getting caught up on their families, jobs, etc. We were busy as usual. Sitting at the desk and looking around at the entire waiting area that was full, was a nice problem to have, not to mention job security. I never thought playing receptionist on this day would be etched in my mind forever, but it was when Melissa walked into the studio.

I hadn't seen her in years, and it was good to see her. She was probably around 67 years old by now. Her perm was fuzzy and curly, and she wore thick glasses. Her blush was everywhere, with a little bit on her cheeks. Her lipstick didn't look any better. I don't believe she wore her glasses when applying it. Would lip liner have helped? I doubt it.

"Melissa, how are you? Gosh, it's been ages."

"Yes, I know. Good to see you."

"So, how are you doing?"

"I'm doing well. My husband passed away a couple of years ago."

"Oh, Melissa, I had no idea. I'm so sorry."

"Thank you. It was rough at first. Being married for 40 years, you get used to someone always being around the house." Melissa was talking loud enough that everyone in the studio could hear her. I forgot about that part of her.

"I had insurance money to do whatever I wanted with it. I always told my husband when he died, I was going to get new boobs."

"Boots?"

"No, boobs."

"Oh, nice." What else was I supposed to say? I didn't have to come up with anything else because Melissa took the conversation to a new level.

"I got them done, but they didn't feel right. They got red marks." I believed her and had no reason to doubt her, but she felt she needed to convince me, but not with her words. She lifted her shirt to show me and everyone else her boobs.

Oh, how I wished she would have gotten boots instead.

"Do you think they still look okay?"

"Melissa, put your top down! You can't do that here." Of course, everyone was shocked by her actions, which didn't faze Melissa one iota. Truth be known, her breasts didn't look like they were fixed. I felt terrible for her.

Somebody took her money and ran, probably to purchase new boots.

77. Shake a Leg

Celeste

Matthew was a stickler regarding the studio needing to be spotless. He demanded that it look like it did the first day we opened My Preference Hair Studio. We always kept our stations clean, but he would go above and beyond. Floors were waxed at least twice a year. Yes, it did look like we had just opened the studio, even though it was eleven years ago.

I've always enjoyed working with older people. They have so many life lessons to impart to us. Listening to them talk about when they were young, I realized that their life may have been more complicated, but it was also simpler. No electronics to occupy their time. Only human beings. What a concept. I had a client, Olive, who was the sweetest elderly woman. She was in her early 70's. Fine, thin hair dyed dark. Very dark. It was always tinted. She would get a roller set every two weeks. She loved to laugh. We would talk about everything under the sun. She would giggle and smile the entire time. What a joy to be around. Unfortunately, her granddaughter lived with her, which was not a good choice. Olive was under the impression it was a good idea to have her granddaughter live with her so she could help Olive. Instead, it was more like Olive raising her granddaughter, who had an attitude and would be verbally abusive towards Olive. I would tell Olive, "Every time you allow her to talk to you that way, the message sent is that it's okay to treat you like that. It's not!"

Olive had a laid-back personality, not letting much get to her. But her granddaughter was the one person who liked to push the envelope. That said, we made sure Olive had a lot of love when she was in the studio. I would always take the extra time with her. It made her feel special, and I could tell she enjoyed it.

We talked about everything except politics and religion. Laughter was inevitable with every visit. Listening to Olive talk about her first date when she was 16, I could not contain my laughter. We all thought we were in love at that age, and this would be the one. Continuing to listen to Olive's story as I cut her hair, I turned her chair around. Unbeknownst to me, Olive had one leg tucked behind the chair that suddenly came off and slid across the freshly waxed floors, past Cami sitting at the receptionist's desk while coming to a complete stop against the potted plant. I looked at her prosthetic leg, lying there waiting to be picked up. I wanted to laugh, but that would be rude, so I did it in my mind. I walked over, picked up Olive's leg, and handed it to her, apologizing that I should have looked before turning the chair. I was embarrassed for her. Taking it all in stride, Olive was undaunted by the whole event.

"Oh honey, it's fine. It's no big deal." To Olive, it wasn't. She reattached her leg and continued the conversation that had abruptly stopped a few minutes earlier. Olive eventually ended up in a nursing home, passing away years later.

Since that day, I only turn a chair around after checking where my clients' legs are positioned, especially if prosthetic legs are involved.

78. The Cream of the Crop

Matthew

Growing up, I was the middle child. You know, the one that gets the short end of the stick. You're not firstborn, and you're not the baby. You are the tweener. I had my brother's hand-me-downs. My sister, being the baby, was the princess in the family. I didn't feel slighted when it came to love, but I had to be creative to be noticed when it came to getting attention. That was why I was the one usually in the most trouble. I often used humor to get me through those awkward middle and high school years, only to be reminded by my teachers, "You're certainly not like your brother." *Thank God, I never wanted to be.* Yes, I was a people pleaser but could also be rebellious. A lot of the time, I felt left out growing up. The middle child has to be creative when fitting in. That can be to his advantage or disadvantage, depending on the day. Today, it was neither. Instead, it was a bonding moment between me and a six-year-old.

I had just finished my client when Bobby and his mother walked in. You could tell by the look on his mother's face Bobby was giving her a run for her money that day. Bobby was six years old, with brown hair and big brown eyes. He was usually good for me, but he's a kid. He's allowed to have an off day. I had hoped it would have been before he walked into the studio, getting it out of his system.

No matter what his mother Stella suggested, Bobby responded, "No!" She remained calm, never yelling at him, which was impressive. Greeting her and Bobby as they walked over to my station, she made the comment that was a trigger for me.

"Oh, don't mind him. He's the middle child. He's been having an issue with people telling him that all the time." *Yeah, I've been there and heard that. So why don't you keep reminding him, especially when you're out in public?*

As Bobby settled into my chair, I realized I had a unique opportunity to share some wisdom with him. I began, "Bobby, do you know what it means to be a middle child?"

Quietly, he responded, "Yeah, I'm the middle child."

"Well, that makes YOU special."

"How?"

"You eat Oreo cookies, don't you?"

"Yes."

"Well, what's your favorite part?"

"The cream."

"There you go. The middle child is the cream between two Oreo cookies." Bobby's face lit up, changing his whole demeanor. You could see the confidence fill his soul as he walked out of the studio proudly declaring to his mother, "I am the cream between two Oreo cookies."

His mother called me later to thank me and told me that scenario had helped Bobby so much. Hopefully, it trumped the negative thoughts planted about being the middle child.

Today was one of those days when I had the privilege to make a difference in someone's life, beyond their appearance. It's moments like these that remind me how blessed I am to be in this industry, where I can use my experience to guide and inspire others.

79. You Have the Wrong Number

Isabella

I am not only a licensed hairstylist, but I am also a licensed massage therapist. Once a week, I put aside my talents with hair to do massage therapy, usually on Monday evenings. Matthew is always in on Mondays, so I'm comfortable working on clients while he's in the office or somewhere on the premises.

It was a Friday night, and I received a phone call from a gentleman named Derrick right before I wrapped up my day at work. "Hey, I heard you guys do massages."

"Yes, I'm the one that does them. It's not just for relaxation. I do massage therapy that helps reduce tension and improve circulation. It also promotes the healing of soft tissue injuries. Is that something that interests you?" As we talked, he inquired about pricing, etc. He sounded legitimate, unlike the few perverts that had shown up before. Another reason why I always made sure Matthew was here when I had a client. I knew Matthew had to leave early this coming Monday, and I would be in the studio by myself at the last hour Derrick was scheduled. But as I mentioned, Derrick sounded legit during our conversation until I was ready to hang up.

"I just want you to know you have a sexy voice." *Okay, now*

I'm feeling uncomfortable. It was the way he said it that gave me chills. I didn't know what else to say except, "Oh!"

All day Saturday, I couldn't get Derrick out of my mind. I kept hearing his voice play over and over in my head. On Sunday, I was telling my husband that I was scared. I just didn't have a good feeling about this. I don't know this guy. Matthew wasn't going to be there. My husband would have waited at the studio while I had the appointment, but he had to work that night. I kept going back and forth, justifying my rationale for canceling. But I also kept thinking, "What if he turned out to be a decent guy and he was just being nice, in a twisted way?" Finally, as usual, my husband spoke up, being the voice of reason. "If you are getting that uncomfortable feeling, you need to cancel. You don't need the money that bad." I never cancel on my clients, but I was willing to make the exception this time. I finally got the nerve to call.

A woman answered, "Hello."

"Hi, this is Isabella from My Preference Hair Studio. I wanted to tell Derrick the massage appointment he had booked for Monday needs to be canceled."

"He's having a massage? I think you have the wrong number."

"This is the number he gave me." The conversation between me and the woman shifted to her conversing loudly with Derrick, questioning his motives. In typical denial fashion, Derrick retaliated.

"I don't know an Isabella, and I didn't schedule a massage."

"Derrick, how did she get this number? And she even knew your name." He had no convincing response, only more lies. Once they both had taken a breath, I quickly interjected.

"Ma'am."

"Yes."

"Please tell Derrick this is probably not the type of massage business he had in mind. He's looking for more of a 24-hour, happy-ending service. This is a professional and medical service." His wife was screaming at him while she was listening to me. It was a different kind of multitasking. Finally, I ended the call.

"You have a great day."

I felt a burden lifted off of my shoulders. Unlike Derrick, who, from the sound of things, was going to be in the market again looking for a massage. Only this time to relieve the tension and stress he felt after his wife hung up the phone.

80. Blind as a Bat

Lexi

I wear contacts most of the time, and sometimes my glasses. When I picked out my glasses, I made sure they were a style I would be comfortable with, unlike the cat glasses I wore when I was younger, which made me look like I was in special education. Thanks, Mom.

Nowadays, kids have many styles available, sparing them from the humiliation I experienced. Even as a senior citizen, you have designer frames that make you look chic. That was my client, Claire. She was 87, almost six feet tall and wore very nice clothes. She was a classy dresser who had the sweetest old soul. She had the skinniest legs I had ever seen on a woman her age. But what stood out about Claire was her glasses.

She wore these Coke bottle glasses with a magnifying glass attached to them. She would use the magnifying glass while perusing the magazines in the studio. Her focus would be on any picture with men in underwear or Speedos, zooming in on all the essential parts. She was funny, and we always had a good laugh when Claire was in the studio.

The last time Claire was in, she left a memorable impression on several of us. Being the classy dresser she was, she took a break on this day. Claire was wearing a white shirt that was practically see-through. God love her, with her eyesight as bad as it was, when she took that last look in the mirror before leaving the house, she probably didn't see her boobs hanging out from the bottom of her bra. How do you tell someone to shove their boobs back into their bra without embarrassing them? I couldn't do it. I also cannot unsee it to this day.

Claire asked to use the restroom. I had just finished with my client, so I sat down and took a moment, waiting for Claire to come out of the bathroom. I waited and waited and waited. Now, I was getting a little concerned. I was just about to knock on the restroom door to ensure she was okay when the door opened. I silently breathed a sigh of relief. Claire also took a deep breath.

"Claire, I was getting concerned. Are you okay?"

"Oh, I had a problem. I overate last night. I had too much chocolate." *Sometimes, I need to mind my own business.*

As she sat down in the chair, I asked her what was new. "Well, I got a bit of poison ivy. I was working in my flower bed and didn't see it, so I must have come in contact with it. The itching has been driving me up a wall."

"Oh, Claire, so sorry to hear this. Poison ivy is the pits. That constant sensation of scratching can drive anyone mad. Did you go to the doctor's?"

"Oh yes. He gave me medication. In fact, can you grab my purse over there? I need to take my pills."

"Sure." I'm searching through her purse but not seeing any pill bottles.

"Claire, are you sure you put them in here?"

"Yes, I'm positive. They're little, tiny pills in a bottle." Now I'm taking out her wallet, a package of tissues, a fingernail file, an envelope that needed to be mailed, her brush, keys, phone, etc. All of a sudden, another client in the studio came over to me and asked what I was doing.

"Oh, I'm looking for Claire's pills. She swears they're in

here, but I think she forgot to put them in her purse."

"Maybe she did, but that's *my* purse!"

"What! I am so sorry. She told me this was her purse." Her purse was the same color and was near the purse I was going through. Thanks to Claire's excellent eyesight, I took inventory of this client's purse while being embarrassed and apologetic. Thank goodness the client understood. I finally located Claire's pills in her purse.

In typical Claire fashion, she took it all in stride.

81. What Just Happened?

Arianna

I had 15 years under my belt and built a substantial clientele base. Usually, when I get a new client, it's by word of mouth, or there's a connection with a client I already have. So when this customer walked in and sat in the waiting area, I was curious if she had an appointment, having never seen her before.

"Hello, can I help you?"

"No, I'll just sit here." It was unusual. Odd, yet I felt like there was more to her than she let on. I still had about 45 minutes left with my client, Nora, so we continued talking as this mystery guest sat and watched me finish Nora's hair. I was done with Nora and greeted this woman, asking, "Is there anything I can help you with? Were you waiting for someone?"

"I was watching you cut hair and listening to you talk to your client. I want you to cut my hair." I did not see that coming. She continued to tell me that she had surgery for a brain tumor, which left a bald spot on her right side. She wanted to camouflage the bald spot and trim her hair up. Her name was Abigail.

She was average in height, in her 50s, with mousey brown fine hair. She wore it in a shoulder-length bob. She appeared quiet yet reserved. She loved what I had done with her and continued to book with me every 4-6 weeks. I just kept trimming her hair up to grow the length out. At this point, I had been doing her hair for six months, and it was finally a one-length bob.

It was Christmas time, and I was booked solid. On this day, I was running a half hour behind. Abigail showed up half an hour early, meaning she would have to sit longer. Everyone was in a good mood, sharing their plans for Christmas, the gifts they had purchased, the cookies they had made, etc. I was finally ready for Abigail. As we discussed what she wanted done, which was her usual wash, trim, and blowout, I tried to start the conversation regarding Christmas.

"So, what are you doing for Christmas?"

"I don't want to talk about it. It's private." Okay, that was a first for me. Unless the client were Jewish, I usually wouldn't ask about their plans for Christmas. After Abigail's response, there was little left to talk about.

As she scheduled her appointment for January, she made it clear how she felt about our time together. "I'm not happy with you today. I don't feel like it was my time, so I'm not giving you a tip!"

"I'm sorry you were unhappy with your appointment today. Let me know if I can do anything to make it right." Later that evening, I called Abigail and left a voicemail. "Hi, Abigail. It's Arianna. I just wanted to tell you I'm so sorry you were not pleased with your visit today. If there is anything I can do to make it up to you, please let me know. Have a good evening." I never heard from her until about three weeks later via text messages.

I have a big event coming up. I need you to tweak my hair.

I'm sorry, I have no openings.

All the times we've worked together, I can't believe you can't make this work. You are so unprofessional. You don't care about your clients. You just care about making money. I've never had a stylist be as rude as you've been with me.

I wish I could help. I am so sorry, but my

schedule is jam-packed. I have no openings

at this time. Otherwise, I'd gladly fit you in.

You're just saying that to cover your ass.

At this point, I was so upset. I did everything to accommodate Abigail and did not appreciate her attacking me in a text. I always strive to be professional with my clients, and for her to attack my integrity was unconscionable. I showed Celeste the text since she has always been the voice of reason.

"You need to fire her!" I was thinking the same thing. But I didn't want to be too hasty about it, so, I sent Abigail a text.

Our relationship isn't working out anymore, and you need to find another salon.

Abigail never responded. Phew! I didn't want to deal with more hateful texts, and I felt like a burden had been lifted off of my shoulders.

It was February, and despite the frigid temps outside, I was having a good day at work. Usually, when I'm with a client, that is my entire focus. I rarely concern myself with who walks into the studio, except for this one time when I looked up and saw Abigail standing there. Suddenly, the burden was heavy on my shoulders.

"Hi, Abigail. I thought we were cancelled since I never heard back from you."

"We are. I wanted to talk with you." She proceeded to talk loudly at me, not with me, in front of the entire studio.

"I can't believe you run a business like this. I have more

class in my little pinky than in your whole body. You act like you care about your customers, but that's all a front. You only care about the money you can take from them!"

I stood there speechless, unable to formulate a response. My mind was racing. No matter how appropriate my response would have been, it would have only escalated the problem. Abigail was so loud that Matthew could hear her in his office. Curious, he came out to see what the commotion was all about. Hearing Abigail berate Arianna was not happening in his studio.

"That's enough. You need to leave now!" Matthew is no-nonsense when it comes to people being disrespectful. He is very direct and to the point.

"I'm not leaving. You and everyone in here have no class. You run a poor business. I don't even know how you stay in business." As he guided her to the door, noting he would call the police if she returned, I held the door open for her. Since the last time Abigail was in, I had changed my hairstyle, wearing it now in a pixie, and changed the hair color to platinum. I received many compliments on it, except from Abigail, as she was leaving.

"And by the way, your hair looks like s**t!"

Matthew and I just looked at each other. "What just happened?" Everything happened so fast, catching me off guard. I was still trying to process it all. Matthew called the police, explaining we had an irate customer and to be on alert that she might return or do something to the place.

The thought did cross my mind: What if the personality change was due to her tumor returning? I guess I'll never know.

82. If I Had to Do All Over

Celeste

Alcohol was his first love, putting intimacy and me on the back burner. Timing was of the essence, and I needed Tom to want me by the weekend. I had to have sex with him, acting as if I enjoyed it, hoping all along he would be able to climax. I even picked out something extremely seductive from Victoria's Secret. Knowing it would take more than the outfit to hold his attention, I did things to him reluctantly that I hadn't done in four years.

That's how desperate I was to get him in bed.

***

I couldn't believe I was listening to Julie talk like this. She had been coming to me for six years. Over the years, we shared many things, but never anything this personal. She was in her forties, medium build with blonde hair, sporting a short-layered bob. At first glance, she appeared to be attractive. Up close, one could see the loneliness and sadness in her eyes. On this day, Julie came in for a cut and style. We started with the usual chatter, catching up on what the other had been doing since we talked last. The conversation slowly became one-sided. I was talking, and Julie was listening, responding with an "Uh huh" or a faint smile, acknowledging she heard me. She was very preoccupied with her thoughts. I thought it was something I said or maybe the way I was cutting her hair. It was neither. I could tell she wanted to talk on the last couple of visits but only opened up about what was on her mind on this day.

"Oh Celeste, have you ever wished you could live your life over? Maybe do things differently?"

"Yes and no. I definitely would not marry my ex. But then again, I wouldn't have my daughter. Having her without him in the picture would have been the ideal situation. But that didn't happen. I'm okay with my life as it is now. Am I happy being a single mom? No. When the time is right, the right guy will come along. I've heard it's when you least expect it. It'll happen. How about you? What would you change?"

"Everything! I don't know. When I met Tom, we were madly in love with each other. Then, I got pregnant early in our marriage. That was unexpected. We had only been married two years. Don't get me wrong. I'm glad we had Michael. But things seemed to go downhill after he was born. We had moved into a larger home. It was expensive but nice. The neighbors were the kind that always got together for parties. We loved socializing, and alcohol was a never-ending presence at these gatherings. During the times we all got together, I had the unfortunate pleasure of watching my husband slowly but surely become an alcoholic right before my eyes.

"He loved his alcohol. No, he cherished it. I remember the days when he used to cherish me. It got to the point that we weren't even having sex."

"That's sad. Do you two still love each other?"

"We coexist. Um, Celeste, I need to tell you something that I've never shared with anyone before. Ever!"

"Okay. What is it?"

"Well, Jason, my youngest…

"Yeah."

"Well, he isn't Tom's." *Oh, how I had hoped she was going to say something else.*

"You're kidding." That may not have been the most appropriate response, but I was at a loss for words.

"No, I'm dead serious. There was nothing between Tom and me for some time. My boss always showed an interest in me by complimenting me on my outfits, asking about Michael, and telling me what a good job I had done. I didn't have to seek his attention; it came naturally. Tom was giving his undivided attention to the bottle."

I didn't know what to say, so I said nothing, intently listening while Julie continued talking.

"There were many times I was so disgusted with Tom and his drinking from the night before that by the time I got to work the next morning, it was just refreshing to talk to someone who didn't reek of alcohol and slur his words. My boss was a very kind and considerate person. Often, I silently wished Tom was more like him. More often than not, I wished my boss was my husband, envying his wife. Before I knew it, we were going to lunch together, and one thing led to another. The weekends were becoming more challenging to enjoy at home. While most people dread Monday mornings, I couldn't wait for them."

"Are you still seeing your boss?"

"Oh no. It ended when he found out that I was pregnant with his child. Tom had no reason to believe it wasn't his after the one night of intense sex that still turns my stomach when I think about it. I left the company for a better-paying job, or that's what I told everyone. My boss wanted nothing to do with the added responsibility. I was hurt and depressed. Jason is now in his twenties, and I've harbored the guilt of knowing his real father while I watched him interact with someone he thought was his father."

"Julie, I just can't believe it. It had to be hard to keep this secret all these years." Hoping she couldn't see in the mirror, the look of disbelief on my face, I could see tears slowing streaming down her cheeks. It all made sense now. When I recall Julia's conversations about family over the years, she always talked about Michael, seldom mentioning Jason. Michael was tall, good-looking, and stylish. Jason was short and shouldered many insecurities. Wiping away her tears, Julie looked at me with regret.

"I will never forget the day I was told I was pregnant. What's worse is that Jason reminds me so much of his biological father that it's not even funny. I look at him and am reminded of what should have never been. Boy, I wish I could live my life over. One thing for certain: I would *never* work at an insurance company again!"

Every time Julie came in for her appointment, I understood the reason behind the sadness and loneliness in her eyes. Then, one day, several years later, when she walked into the salon, I noticed something different about her, but I couldn't tell what had changed. As we started talking, she wanted to tell me something. I set the stage by asking, "How are things going? Anything new?"

"I don't know if you heard, but Tom died."

"Oh Julie, I'm so sorry. No, I hadn't. When?

"Three days ago. The obituary should be in the paper today. He died of cirrhosis of the liver. Shocker, huh?"

"How are the boys doing?"

"I think it's mixed emotions for them. Tom's drinking affected every relationship, especially with his immediate family. Quite honestly, I am relieved. I feel like I can finally move on with my life."

Fortunately for Julie, Tom never learned the truth about Jason. Unfortunately for Jason, he was left to mourn what he thought was the loss of his biological father, oblivious that his birth father was still alive, wanting nothing to do with him.

Yes, Julie, you can move on but will carry the guilt for the rest of your life

83. A Promise I Wish I'd Never Kept

Lexi

Abby had been coming to me for about ten years. I always enjoyed our visits. She was easy to talk with, with a quiet demeanor, yet so personable. When she first started coming to me, Abby shared she had just broken up with her boyfriend of two years after she found out he was cheating on her. I told her it was his loss; at least she found out before marrying him. Abby had been so devasted by the last relationship that she hadn't dated anyone or had the desire to date. Thanks to social media and mutual friends, Dave came into the picture. They had met at the local restaurant/bar and hit it off from the start. He was a truck driver; she was an elementary school teacher. Abby had long blonde hair and was average in the looks department. She came from money but never flaunted it. She was careful not to share it with Dave initially.

"Lexi, he is so polite. I'm used to opening the car door myself. Instead, he holds it open for me. I'm used to no one caring about my opinion. When we discuss a topic, he'll ask my opinion. When he says he'll call, he does. He is a man of his word. I'm not used to this kind of treatment."

"I'm really happy for you. It's about time you had someone who appreciates you for who you are instead of trying to mold you into someone you're not."

Abby dated Dave for four years. During that time, she casually mentioned things he would do, which appeared to be a red flag in their relationship. Still, she didn't seem bothered by it. I didn't want to give my opinion unless solicited. My job was to cut her hair and listen.

Abby's mother liked Dave from the start. Who wouldn't? He was tall and slender, with brown hair, brown eyes, and a great smile. If a guy were going to impress his girlfriend's mother, it would be with flowers, offering to help clean up the dishes after a meal, replying, "Yes ma'am, no ma'am," or any other social graces out there, unless you were Dave. Abby mentioned Dave enjoyed his alcohol, like her mother, who was an alcoholic. He would bring Abby's mother alcohol when he stopped over to see Abby. A bond that will not be broken among alcoholics. At times, Abby felt like the third wheel. She had diabetes and would have a drink once in a while but was determined to stay away from it as much as possible, seeing how it was destroying her mother. Abby mentioned that before her mother died, she had told Abby, "You need to marry Dave. He's a good guy." She did and soon regretted it.

She noticed a pattern with Dave and his jobs. He would purposely get hurt to get money from the system. Given Abby's financial status, repeating this pattern at various jobs did not bother him because he knew Abby would pick up the financial slack. It was always his way or the highway if he didn't like a supervisor's decision. He seemed to always lose his job, but it was never his fault to hear Dave tell the story.

I started cutting his hair after they married. Honestly, I dreaded seeing his name on the books. He and Abby would schedule appointments back-to-back. He was always the loudest in the studio, always putting on a show. It was as if what Dave had to say was important, and everyone should listen, especially when he was on his phone and had it on speaker. He also didn't hesitate to embarrass Abby in front of us.

"Lexi, I don't think there's any hairstyle out there you can do to improve her looks. Sorry, Abby." He was the only one laughing. "Hey Lexi, have you ever seen anyone's hair scream for help like Abby's?" He was such a jerk.

"I don't have a problem with her hair, Dave. Never have." I thought of letting him have it, but better judgment prevailed. Looking at Abby and seeing how beaten down she was, I knew if I got on Dave's wrong side, he might forbid Abby from returning. I didn't want to lose her, so I shut my mouth.

I would always make sure I cut his hair first to get him out of my hair, no pun intended. Dave would sit in the car and wait for Abby to get done. That is when Abby would open up, telling me how Dave would publicly embarrass her.

"We could be eating out, and our waitress would ask if we needed anything else. Dave would reply, 'Yeah, my wife needs to learn how to put makeup on. I noticed you know how. Can you help her?'" Once again, Dave was the only one laughing.

If the public humiliation wasn't enough, Abby also endured verbal abuse. She once shared with me an argument they had over something stupid when he unleashed a plethora of toxic statements. "You have no idea how good you have it. As smart as teachers are supposed to be, you're pretty stupid." "Being married to you, I understand why your mother drank so much!"

"Lexi, he never was like that when we dated. Well, I never looked at it as verbal abuse. It didn't happen that often. It seemed like once we were married, he changed, and it got worse. He always found an excuse not to work, whether he got injured or 'they were stupid idiots,' or he didn't like the job. I never expected my life to turn out like this."

I couldn't stay silent anymore. "Suggestion, Abby?"

"Sure."

"You deserve better. You are smart. You have the means to leave Dave. Sometimes, it's lonelier being with someone than being single. He has been toxic towards you for some time. As long as you let him talk to you that way, all you're doing is permitting him to continue this unhealthy relationship."

"You're right. I'm just scared of being on my own. But I know I'll be okay financially. Dave doesn't know it, but I have a secret account with money put aside if something like this happens. I've had that gnawing feeling that I needed to do that."

After five years of marriage, Abby divorced Dave. It was a win for me, as well. Dave found someone else to cut his hair and listen to his lines of bull.

84. Runs in the Family

Matthew

Relationships are complicated, whether you're married or not. When you're older, it becomes problematic when one partner decides to step out on the other after years of marriage. Such was the case with Cynthia and Kevin.

Cynthia had been coming to me for years. She is one of my closest clients. Cynthia has two grown adult sons. She was 62 with blonde highlights and wedged hair. She was very attractive. At first impression, she is one sophisticated lady. Always well groomed, her clothes tailored to fit. Kevin was average in the looks department and a farmer. I don't know if I would have matched those two, but they've been together for forty-four years.

Cynthia has shared everything with me. I asked Cynthia how she and Kevin were doing. I expected to hear about an upcoming trip or how things on the farm were going. Instead, she went out of her comfort zone and mine to share. "I'm buying bikini underwear and wearing more negligées to spice things up in our marriage."

"Oh, I'm sure Kevin is liking that." I didn't know what else to say.

"Well, ever since I found out he was having an affair with someone in her 40s, I knew I needed to step it up."

"Oh, I'm sorry to hear that. I had no idea you guys were having trouble."

"In all honesty, I needed to show him more attention. I'm not making excuses for his infidelity, but I was just as much to blame. We both realized we had taken advantage of each other, not appreciating the other one as much as we should."

"Oh honey, I'm glad you two could work it out. In this day and age, I've heard getting divorced when you're older is hard. You want that special someone to grow old with you."

"I realize that, and so does Kevin, thank God."

***

Cynthia and Kevin had a son named Beau. He was 35, 5 feet 10 inches tall, average-weight, and quite nerdy-looking. Beau had fair skin and blonde hair. He was married to Ginny, who was a year younger than him. At 5 feet 5 inches, Ginny had a slender build. Her thick red hair was shaped in a diagonal cut that dominated her petite facial features.

Ginny and Beau were clients of mine. Having a husband and wife for clients can be a blessing and a curse. The blessing is listening to those with healthy relationships and taking mental notes. The curse is when it gets crowded with a third party, and you know about it.

I noticed Beau's appearance changing over the next couple of months. He started having me color his hair. He was looking bulkier, thanks to muscle-building vitamins. As a regional manager for Microsoft, his job took him away from Ginny and their two girls several times a month. Ginny felt like she never got a break from being a mother and having adult time with Beau. Beau didn't mind the travel but cherished sleeping in his bed over hotel ones. At least that's what he told Ginny.

Ginny informed me that she found out Beau was having an affair with a coworker. He usually had his phone everywhere he went, even when showering, "...in case work calls." But in his haste on a Sunday night to prepare for

Monday's departure, he forgot to take it into the bathroom. He had received a text. Ginny couldn't resist, suspecting there may be someone else.

Did you make dinner reservations for Thursday, or do you want me to do it? Looking forward to it.

She knew it! As expected, a huge argument ensued once Beau finished his shower. The next time Ginny came in, she updated me on their situation. I didn't have to ask. I did not want to get in the middle of this one. I'm thinking, "Like father, like son."

"Matthew was willing to leave our two little girls and me to be with HER and her two little girls. What do you think about that?" Great, this is precisely what I didn't want to happen. I had to stay neutral, hoping Ginny could problem-solve this one. "I have no idea, Ginny. It's unfortunate for everyone."

At his next appointment, Beau opened up about what was going on between the two of them. I was thankful he didn't ask for my opinion. My heart ached for him when I heard how he truly felt about Ginny. "All I want from her is to know I'm still her knight in shining armor. I'm still her man. That she still finds me attractive. I don't hear that from her anymore. I can't tell you the last time I heard anything close to that from her."

Wow! Now it's time to put on my mediator hat. I understood what Beau was saying. Men need affirmations as well. The next time Ginny was in, she didn't waste any time discussing Beau. I could hear the mixed feelings of hurt and anger in her voice. "Ginny, suggestion?"

"Sure."

"Maybe consider giving him more attention. Positive attention, instead of him looking elsewhere for it."

"I am NOT doing that! It's out of the question."

"But if it could help him, it could help both of you in the end."

"There is no way I'm doing that. He's just like his father. He gets what he deserves."

Update: Beau stopped his affair with his coworker. He and Ginny are still married. He never cheated on her again but is miserable. Ginny is happy doing her own thing.

85. You'll Pay One Way or Another

Isabella

I don't mind helping others with their problems when they ask, and I also don't mind fixing someone else's mistakes regarding hair. Just be honest with me when I ask about your hair. Don't blame others. Take some responsibility.

Darcy was in her late forties. The first time I met her, my impression of her was unfavorable. It's always someone's fault, no matter the subject. She would pop into the studio every three weeks to share how someone had ruined her hair which was full of highlights, and trashed. She would ask how much it would be to fix her hair, and I would quote her a price for the corrected color. It was pricey.

"Well, I've been to two or three different salons, and you know I don't have a lot of money."

"Okay. This is the price to get your hair looking better. It's up to you. Just let me know." I wasn't giving her a discount, knowing what needed to be done. I also wasn't falling for the line, "I don't have a lot of money," especially when she was holding a Coach purse. She had made her decision.

"Okay, I can come in and do it." So she came in, and I did the corrective color on her. Not to sound arrogant, but I did a great job. It was beautiful. She looked amazing. She handed me her charge card. "Your card only has $23 on it."

"Well, that's all I have. I'll come back tomorrow with the rest."

"No, you can't do that."

"Well, I don't have any money with me." I could not believe she was pulling this stunt.

"You leave your driver's license with me, and when you come back to pay me, you'll get it back."

"I can't trust anybody with my driver's license."

"And I can't trust you when you told me you had the money for this, and we did the service. Your hair looks healthier and better; this salon didn't mess it up! I can't trust you to come back here because you lied about having the money, yet you knew you only had $23 on your card."

"Well, I'm leaving." *Over my dead body.*

"You'll give me your license. You're not leaving. I'm not playing with you. You have to pay for my services. If you don't, I will call the police to report that you left without paying for services rendered. I will have you arrested for theft of services."

"Fine! Call my boyfriend."

"Would you call him, and I'll talk to him on the phone? He'll have to send a text to my phone from his number stating that it's him. He will also need to give approval to use his credit card over the phone." The boyfriend did. I got paid. The entire process was like pulling teeth.

"You know, Darcy, we've corrected problems with hair on other clients, and they learned from those mistakes. You keep making a mess of things. This is going to be the best day of your life. This is the day you get to find another salon that will deal with you because you won't be bringing your services back here, and I will go back to having paying clients."

It turned out to be my best day, knowing I never had to deal with Darcy again.

86. When Cancer Turns Into Diabetes

Arianna

The one thing I can't handle is watching those St. Jude commercials. They get me every time. Those poor kids that have cancer and what they have gone through. Then you hear the parents talk, and I can barely hold back the tears. I have to change the channel. If I had three wishes, the first would be a cure for childhood cancer.

That said, I hadn't seen Tabatha in years. She used to be a client of mine. I often wondered what had happened to her. She was a bit on the wild side but always nice and respectful. I didn't initially recognize her when she walked into the studio the Friday before Mother's Day. I was pleasantly surprised and shocked when I realized it was Tabitha-the years had not been kind to her. I knew she liked to dress a little risqué when she was in her twenties. Now, at the age of 42, she dressed like a hoochie mama. She spared no expense when it came to the makeup and perfume. She wore a lacey sleeveless top, allowing her to flaunt her cleavage proudly. Her short skirt showcased her long-tanned legs. The stiletto heels only added to her height of 5 feet 7 inches. Tabitha constantly tested the waters no matter the situation. It was like an adrenal rush to see how much she could get away with.

"Hey Tabitha! How are you? Long time no see."

"Hi Arianna, I'm good."

"Can I help you?" I couldn't imagine what would bring her back to the studio after all these years.

"Can I put this jar in here?" It was a glass jar with a picture of her son attached to it. I didn't even know she had a son. He was cute. He looked about 11 years old—brown hair and hazel eyes.

"What's going on?"

"My son has cancer. They're telling me it's terminal, but I'm not giving up on him. He's my only child. He's at the Children's Hospital in Denver and is receiving treatments. I'm trying to collect money because I'm out of work. It's been hard holding down a job with me spending so much time at the hospital with him. The money collected would pay for gas and parking up there. At least I can stay overnight in the room with him, thank God."

"Oh, Tabitha, I am so sorry to hear this. I had no idea." I felt terrible. No child should have to go through that hell, and no parent should have to watch their child go through it.

"Would you be willing to donate anything?" I thought about writing a $500 check right then and there and marking it as a donation from My Preference Hair Studio.

"Before I donate, I need to talk to my manager, Matthew. Give me till next Wednesday, and I should have a check for you. Call me on Tuesday, and I'll tell you when we can get together."

"Okay, I will. Thank you so much."

After Tabitha left, Lexi and Celeste told me I had better check her out to ensure she was legitimate. "Really, guys? I feel terrible that her son is terminal. You can tell it's taken a toll on her. I can't imagine how hard it has been for her to swallow her pride and ask for donations. I can't call the hospital and ask if they have a patient faking cancer. Plus, with HIPAA, they'd never say if he was a patient."

Once again, Celeste being the voice of reason, I knew she wouldn't say anything unless it didn't feel right. "Look, you have a heart of gold, and that's very admirable. All we're saying is before next Wednesday, you must ask around. If she's legit, then you're a saint for donating. If you donate and she's not, you're a sucker."

Tabitha called on Tuesday around noon. I told her to come in on Wednesday at 12:45. Two other clients would be in the studio. The one was going to be tanning, and the other one was going to be in the back getting a manicure. It was the best time to talk with her. I knew someone who worked at Barber Elementary, where Tabitha's son, Dino, attended. On Tuesday morning, I called the school counselor, Mary Kay. I had done her daughter's hair for prom. I knew she would know if anybody knew how Dino was doing.

"Hi, Mary Kay, it's Arianna from My Preference Hair Studio. Do you have a minute?"

"Sure, how are you doing?"

"I'm fine, but I need to ask you something. I need to get clarification on Dino Rizzoli's health status. Do you know his mother, Tabitha?"

"Yes, why?"

"Well, she was in the studio last Friday with a jar with Dino's picture, asking for donations because his cancer is terminal, and he's in the hospital."

"WHAT?" Don't give her a donation!" Mary Kay's response surprised me.

"Why not? I was going to write a check. It wasn't cash."

"Dino does not have cancer. He has diabetes. He's not terminal, and he certainly is not in the hospital. Tabitha doesn't even have custody of him. He lives with Tabitha's mother. Tabitha has a boyfriend who just got out of prison. He's on drugs. She's on drugs. We provide vouchers for clothes for kids who are from low-income families. She's always here wanting to turn the vouchers in for cash." Oh, brother, Celeste was right. I would never hear the end of this if I had given Tabitha a donation.

I had already blocked off time on that Tuesday afternoon to run errands. The errands could wait. Now, I was on a mission. I went around to as many businesses as possible in our area, warning them not to donate to Tabitha's cause because she was a fraud.

On Wednesday, she came in as sweet as could be to me— sickening sweet. "Hi honey, how are you?"

"I'm fine." Didn't ask how she was doing? I didn't care at this point.

"I'm having a bad day." *And it's about to get worse.*

"Why are you having a bad day?"

"Somebody called the sheriff and went around to all these businesses and said I was a scammer."

"Oh, I did that." She kept talking, not hearing what I said.

"This is terrible. I'm not a scammer. I need money to go to the hospital to see my boy." Lexi was videotaping, so Tabitha couldn't say we did anything to her. At this point, I would not put it past Tabitha to make up a story. She was pretty good at being very convincing. So was her boyfriend. They had pulled up in a car with thirty-day tags on it. So they must have scammed somebody.

"I can't believe someone would call me a scammer. I've never scammed anyone in my life."

"Why would you pimp your son out and bring me this jar, asking for money for a child you're not raising."

"Oh, you're wrong. Dino does have cancer." She wouldn't let up.

"I have done my investigation, and I know what you're doing is a scam. You're pimping your child out to make money for drugs. I refuse to be a part of your sick, twisted plot." We went back and forth, not in an argumentative way. She maintained her composure, knowing I was on to her. Tabitha could no longer hide behind her jar of lies. Reality had set in and she was visibly getting nervous, creating distance between us.

"I want my jar back!"

"Not a chance. You won't get it back, and you won't be taking it somewhere else. You can forget it. By the way, do you see that door over there?"

"Yeah."

"Don't let it hit you in the ass when you leave. Don't ever put your toes to the front door of this studio again. I don't want you back here. You mess with kids. You and I have nothing to do with each other from this point on. Children are a gift from God, and you are trying to pimp out your son, who is not even in your custody."

Tabitha left grumbling. I'm pretty sure I heard f-bombs as she walked out. I was shocked they didn't try to do something to me or the studio.

I never saw her again in town and have no idea what happened to her, but I've often wondered how Dino was doing.

87. God Sent Me an Angel

Lexi

We've all hit rough financial patches in our lives, be it when all of the appliances break down at once or you came up short of making a credit card or car payment and needed to borrow money. When I lived in Doylestown, Pa., I was fortunate to have a successful salon before moving to Lockston. Early in my career, money was tight, I'm not going to lie, but it eventually worked out.

Some of my clients have had it tough, as well. Listening to them complain about not having enough money, and the money they did have went towards paying bills. I certainly could relate. You learn to be frugal even when you're not trying.

Anna was very frugal with her money. She was in her 70s, on the heavier side, with short grey hair that was fine. She had been coming to me for about a year. Although Anna was frugal, she always tipped well. I felt so bad for her. She was a lovely lady who had developed Parkinson's disease. In the short time she had been coming to me, I watched month after month as this disease took its toll on her. Her speech became slurred, and understanding what she was saying became more challenging. A year later, conversations were kept to a minimum, preventing undue stress for Anna.

She had filed for disability. She also had to do a spend down for Medicaid, finding creative ways to spend her money. This prompted her to ask how much it would cost for a year's worth of manicures, pedicures, haircuts, etc. I never had a request like that, but I finally came up with a figure. The next time Anna came in, she brought her checkbook. She asked me what amount I had come up with, and I told her, given my best estimate. Remember I mentioned earlier how we all have fallen on hard times financially at some point in our lives? I never said anything to Anna, but my hard times occurred throughout the year when Anna came to me. The fact is, I never said anything to anyone in the studio. I was getting ready to file for bankruptcy, risking losing my home. It didn't dawn on me until I got home that night to look at Anna's check. Then, I realized it was for the exact amount I needed to save my home. Down to the last penny! She was my angel. Thank you, Lord, for sending me Anna.

I wished I could have returned the favor in some way. Anna had heard about surgery for Parkinson's that would decrease the tremors but also put her at high risk for complications. No one could talk her out of it. She was determined to have the surgery. During surgery, she had a stroke. She came to but ended up in a nursing home, dying shortly after.

I will always cherish the time I had with Anna. She persevered through her Parkinson's, determined it would not get the best of her. In a sense, it did.

I miss you dearly, Anna.

88. When You Can't Take Anymore

Gabby

Working in New York City before moving to Lockston in 2000 was an eye-opening experience. I saw it all. There were some things I had seen that I wished I hadn't. There were also bright spots, especially at Christmas time, with Rockefeller Center's Christmas tree lighting and the city adorned with beautiful decorations. Or in the summertime with the summer concerts provided by the morning news shows of NBC, ABC, and CBS.

Of course, the time of year didn't matter; the clients always had an abundance of stories. But in this case, it wasn't the clients who had something to share. It was me.

In our NY salon, we had a nail technician, Jessica, who had two daughters opposite each other. Both were well-liked in high school. One had masculine features and mannerisms, was gay, and had a great sense of humor. The other daughter, Kara, was an all-around American girl. She could sing like an angel, which led to her always getting the lead in high school musicals. No doubt, if American Idol or The Voice were around back then, she would have made it onto either of those shows. She graduated valedictorian in her class. She had a lot going for her. If there was ever a perfect child, it was Kara.

Kara was brilliant on all levels for her age, except for one: Dating. She seemed to struggle with having a healthy relationship with a guy. Kara had hooked up with this nineteen-year-old bad boy, who got her pregnant at 18. Shortly after she had her son, Colby, she turned 19 and decided to celebrate her birthday with her boyfriend at a party. The gift: it was heroin. That was the night that would change Kara's life forever. In the following weeks, Jessica told me she was becoming very concerned about Kara. There was a noticeable change in Kara's behavior. Kara and Jessica always got along. Now, they were fighting. At one point, Kara had stolen money from her. Jessica figured it went towards drugs, though Kara tried to convince her mother it was to buy diapers for the baby.

Within six weeks, Kara was committed more to heroin than caring for Colby. Jessica knew if she didn't do something, Kara would end up dead. Kara was placed in rehab in Massachusetts, while her boyfriend went to rehab in Maryland. Jessica made it clear to Kara that she would not get Colby back unless Kara was clean and stayed clean. Otherwise, Colby would live with Jessica forever. Kara successfully finished rehab and regained possession of Colby. She was doing wonderfully. She spent that year at home making up for lost time with him. Her mother was so proud of her. Her boyfriend had successfully completed his stint in rehab, which bode well for their relationship.

A year had passed, and Kara wanted to return to the workforce. She got hired as a waitress at one of the restaurants. Things were finally looking up for Kara. She was getting established in her job, bringing home a steady paycheck, and getting a lot of praise from the customers and her boss. Her boyfriend had now become her fiancé, and they were planning a wedding. Colby was going to have his mother and father together. Kara's life had finally turned the corner.

Her boss noticed Kara's work ethic and that Kara was the waitress most requested by customers. It got to the point where Kara had to turn customers away because she was at her maximum limit with tables, apologizing profusely. At one point, her boss called her into his office to sing her praises and to let her know he was pleased to have her on staff. As she was leaving, he walked her to the door, placing his hand on her back and rubbing it up and down. She initially didn't think too much of it but found it strange.

Over the next couple of weeks, her boss became more comfortable with sexually harassing Kara, leaving Kara to feel very threatened. She had confided in Jessica about what was going on. She chose not to tell her fiancé out of fear that he might take matters into his own hands. Jessica told Kara she did not have to endure that abuse, strongly encouraging her to quit and reminding Kara that her reputation as a waitress would lead to a better job. Kara couldn't sleep as thoughts of her boss and his actions played repeatedly in her mind. She needed to escape this nightmare that was tormenting her. After another uncomfortable day at work, Kara returned home to Colby, who was a toddler at this point. No matter what kind of day she had, he always greeted her with a smile and arms raised to be picked up. After reading Colby a bedtime story and putting him to bed, Kara became anxious about returning to work the next day. She couldn't take another day with that pervert. Her mind went to a place it hadn't been in over a year.

She called her dealer.

He came over and shot her up with heroin. Going by the weight Kara was when he provided heroin to her over a year ago, it didn't matter to him that she was thinner now. He already had his money. She appeared calm and relaxed, escaping the thoughts that plagued her.

Jessica had this strong feeling she needed to go to Kara.

Something didn't feel right. Kara's fiancé had tried calling Kara several times. No answer. He called Jessica, and they met over at Kara's apartment. Entering the apartment, Kara's fiancé frantically called out for her. Jessica looked in Colby's room to make sure he was okay, as he was sleeping. Kara was lying on the bathroom floor, dying. Immediately, CPR was administered by Kara's fiancé while Jessica called 911. It was a total of 45 minutes of CPR, to no avail. Kara had died.

If only Narcan were available back then, Kara would still have been with us.

Further drug testing determined the heroin was laced with fentanyl. The police could track down the drug dealer via Kara's phone. Cartier Jacques, better known as CJ, was arrested. Nineteen people had died that weekend from the same batch that killed Kara, thanks to CJ.

***

It had been a couple of months, and Jessica still needed time off, which was understandable. I answered the phone one day at work only to hear on the other end, "Is Jessica working?"

"No, she's not. Is there something I could help you with?"

"I'd like to get my haircut." I had an opening that Thursday, so I scheduled Maddie for 10:00 a.m. It never dawned on me that she was asking for Jessica, our nail tech, but instead ended up with an appointment for her hair. Or did she think Jessica did hair?

Maddie showed up on time. First impressions are essential in a stylist's world. As I was doing Maddie's hair, she mentioned Kara, which seemed to be the main topic of conversation around town, especially since Kara had made the front page of the New York Times and was in the news on television.

"That girl Kara, I heard she was a mess. She had issues and was a frequent user. This wasn't her first rodeo."

I would not allow her to talk about Jessica's daughter that way.

"I know Kara had turned her life around and was holding down a job, taking care of her son, and going to get married."

"Yeah but look what she did. She ended up messing herself up." *Was there no* stopping *Maddie from bashing Kara?*

"Your last name is Jacques, right? By chance, would you be related to Cartier Jacques, the one they connected to Kara's death and 19 others?"

"Ya, that's my son. He's in prison. I lost him to prison. I'll never have a holiday with him or celebrate his birthday. When he calls, it's only for a few minutes. I miss him so much. I don't think I'll ever get over him having to go to prison. That prison life is not good. I feel so bad for him."

Thank goodness I was done with her hair. I just wanted to kill her. How could she be that selfish?

Jessica had been mourning Kara's death, and so had the rest of us in the salon, and this woman purposely came in to pull this crap. I had had enough.

"Maddie, you knew what you were doing when you scheduled the appointment. Of all the salons in New York City, you had to pick this one. How dare you come in here and disrespect Jessica's daughter. You've upset me and succeeded. You'll never do it again. Do not *ever* step foot in this salon again."

She never did.

***

If you or anyone you know is struggling with drug abuse, contact the Substance Abuse & Mental Health Services Administration at 1-800-662-HELP (4357) or visit the website: www.samhsa.gov. This national helpline offers free and low-cost services. Or text your zip code to 435748 (HELP4U) for a list of treatment centers in your area.

89. Still a Virgin

Celeste

I had a client who was expecting her first child. She was over the moon. She did have that glow about her. She and her husband had been trying for a long time, and when they had given up and accepted that they should adopt, she became pregnant. Her demeanor was the opposite of that of the coworker I had at the salon in Grand Island, NE, of which I was now the manager.

Lisa was fresh out of cosmetology school when I hired her. She was very quiet, appearing backward, but had a happy-go-lucky attitude. Her family were Pentecostal. From what I could gather, her parents disregarded any aches or pains, even if it required a doctor's attention, as long as the kids were still breathing. They never went to the doctor. They believed any healing would be done through prayer. I'm all about prayer when you need it, but God also gave man the mind to be a physician for a reason.

Shortly after Lisa started working for me, I noticed a baby bump. I didn't say anything. I was waiting for her to say something to me. Every week that passed, she was getting bigger and bigger. Finally, I couldn't stand it anymore, and I asked.

"Lisa, are you pregnant?"

"No."

"Honey, are you sure? Your belly keeps growing."

"I swear I'm not. I know for sure. I'm still a virgin." As time passed, her stomach was protruding, becoming more prominent. Now, the clients were talking about it. Even when she was doing their hair, her stomach rubbed against them, and they commented, "Oh, she's definitely pregnant." I was getting concerned. I loved this girl like a daughter. I could tell she was scared to say anything or admit anything. No doubt she was scared to tell her parents.

Finally, Lisa had no choice but to fess up. She had shown up in a pair of dress overalls on this day. She did not even make it through the first half hour and was lying on the salon floor on her back in excruciating pain. I was beyond concerned.

"Angel, honey, you gotta come clean. I know you're pregnant."

Crying at this point, Lisa was loudly protesting, "I'm not pregnant! I'm not pregnant!" She was out of breath and exhausted in the short time she was lying on the floor.

"Honey, we can't ignore this." Lisa wanted to argue with me, but I didn't have the time. I called her sister who came and got her. Her sister had to convince her mother that Lisa needed to see the doctor.

Lisa got in to see Dr. Greko and was admitted to the hospital for surgery. I was so upset. I talked to Lisa the night before surgery as I was sitting out on my porch. I told her I would be there in the morning to see her before she went to surgery. She was crying and terrified. I tried to calm her down. While I was talking to her, a praying mantis appeared on my porch stoop. I hadn't seen a praying mantis in years. I thought, "Okay, God, you just sent me a sign. It's going to be alright." I shared that with Lisa, hoping to reassure her that God was in control and that he was not leaving her. I was still very nervous for her. Lots of prayers were going up. We were a praying salon. Churches in the area were praying for

Lisa. How could God not answer our prayers? My thoughts fluctuated between it was going to be okay and being terrified that we were going to lose her-so much for totally trusting God.

I arrived at the hospital the following morning. Her parents, brother, and sister were already there. Time was getting close for Lisa to go to the OR. We gathered in a circle to pray as Dr. Greko entered the room. "Do you mind if I join you?" How many doctors would ask to be in a prayer circle? That was my second sign everything was going to be okay. After we prayed, Dr. Greko talked with us.

"I want you to know the surgery will take four to six hours. If it takes longer, then I'm running into problems." I grabbed that doctor's arm as the family returned to the waiting room.

"I don't know what you have to do, but she wants to have kids. Please do whatever it takes."

"I'll do what I can." My heart sank.

I couldn't sit still. I kept pacing back and forth, watching the clock. We waited and waited and waited. It was past the six-hour mark. I couldn't take much more. I couldn't lose her. All of a sudden, the doctor approached us. He wasn't smiling.

God, I'm not ready to give her to you.

"Lisa is in recovery now. She had an ovarian cyst that had attached to her organs. It weighed 24 pounds. The good news is I was able to save one of her ovaries."

Tears streamed down my face as I thanked Dr. Greko and silently thanked God for saving Lisa's life. Later that evening, I was sitting on the porch. The praying mantis never left my porch until I got home from the hospital that night.

Coincidence, I think not.

Lisa returned to work as healthy as could be. Results from her surgery showed the cyst was not cancerous. Years later, she married and had two healthy kids—all thanks to Dr. Greko.

275

90. I Only Do the Top Part

Matthew

As stylists, we can get some unusual requests. Mine have ranged from a celebrity wanting my scissors to cut the dead skin off her foot to clients asking for sexual favors. As strange as those might sound, nothing could top Josephine's request in all my years of doing hair.

Josephine had moved to Lockston to live with her niece after retiring from a factory in the Midwest where she was a foreman. Her parents were from Sora, Italy, and immigrated here in the 1930s. Living in Manhattan until she was in her twenties, Josephine decided to spread her wings and move to Kansas City, Missouri. After she retired, she moved to Lockston to live with her niece, whom she was very close to. Her niece was a client of mine, and that's how I got the referral.

Josephine was 93, a very spirited 93-year-old. She was Italian and spoke with that Italian New York accent. She was only 4 feet 10 inches tall but packed a punch-verbally. Josephine minced no words, and everyone in the studio knew her business. She had never heard of "use your indoor voice" growing up. Everyone always outtalked the other one. I experienced this firsthand when I tried to have a conversation with her over the years. I finally gave up and just listened.

Josephine had short black hair. I always did rollers with her every week. Staff couldn't wait to hear what she had to say, week after week. She talked about her mother, who had passed years ago, singing her praises every chance she got. When she wasn't talking about her mother, she was sharing about her 40 years in the steel factory.

"I worka da steel factory. I owned all these girls. I was da boss of all these girls, and I told them what to do. They roughneck girls, and I made sure they listened to me because, you know, they respected me because I was their leader. They just did what I told them to do, and I never had anybody go astray. You know whatta mean?" Josephine did not take a breath the whole time. Even if I wanted to ask for clarification, I knew waiting until she was done was best.

"Josephine, did you ever have to fire anyone?"

"You listen to me. I no fire. They quit if they no do what I said. They know I mean business. They know if they no like the way I do business, they can go find 'nother job. No use me for a reference."

Okay, we got past the 40 years at the factory, and now she was discussing anything that came to mind. When I had her at the shampoo bowl, she was still talking. I'm not even sure about what. I would throw in an "Uh huh" and "Really?" to appease her. She would tell me how to wash her hair in between her stories.

"Get da soap in my ears, behind them. Clean 'em real good. Escrub harder."

She was very demanding, no matter what I was doing. She couldn't let that foreman mentality go. At this point, I put the sink sprayer closer to the inside of her ears and around her eyes to shut her up purposefully. When I was done, I would Dutch rub her head (rubbing knuckles into her scalp), only to hear her say, "Oh, thatta feels good." I give up.

Josephine made the number one spot on the Most Unusual Client Request list. Sitting in my chair, she told me that she had been sleeping on her couch. It was very old, to the point that you could see the springs through the fabric. Did I mention Josephine was also very frugal?

"Josephine, that can't be good for your back. Why don't you sleep in your bed?"

"Oh no. It's no comfortable. Da couch is better. And I no feeling good lately. All I drink is a chicken broth. That's all I can eat. I no keep food down. My doctor said I shoulda do those enemas in my rear. I tried, but every time I put in applicator, she shoots 'cross da room. I don't know what I do wrong. Can you give me an enema?"

"Oh honey, I can't go down there. I just do the top."

"Oh, you gotta help me. You have to do it. Can't you put some gloves on and go down there?"

"Josephine, I can't do that. I only do the top part. I don't do the bottom. In medical terms, it's out of my scope of practice. That's not something hairstylists do with their clients."

"Oh, please, please do it. I no have no one else to help me."

"What about your niece?"

"She says she getsa grossed out and refuses."

"I'm sorry, but I don't know what else to tell you except maybe call your doctor and talk to him." It wasn't until Josephine left that I thought of my sister, who is a nurse. I called her for suggestions. She told me to have Josephine lay on her stomach and give herself the enema. I passed the information on to Josephine.

The following week, Josephine showed up for her appointment, all excited. "Guessa, what? I did it! It worked. Oh, I feel so much better. Thank you so much for helping me. Thank you. Thank you."

Thank you, Josephine, for such a memorable request.

91. Thanks, But No Thanks for the Referral

Isabella

I enjoy my married couples as clients. I especially appreciate those who have been together since high school or college. That was Trent and Alicia. They were childhood sweethearts. They had gone to the same school since kindergarten, all the way to and including college. They ended up getting married and having two children. Both of their children were in college. It was just a natural progression of their relationship.

Alicia had brown hair cut short and styled like Dorothy Hamill's. She was very tall. Trent was just as tall, with brown hair and hazel-colored eyes. My first impression was that he was voted Best-Looking in high school.

I had been doing their hair for years, including their children, and I always looked forward to them coming in. They did an excellent job raising their kids, who were polite, social, and had a great sense of humor. They acquired those traits from both parents.

I had a new client come in the other day. Her name was Sherry. She mentioned she knew Alicia and Trent.

Note to self: Thank Alicia the next time she's in for the referral.

Sherry was polite. She is attractive, with long blonde hair, blue eyes, and a thin build. During this appointment, Trent stopped by. I was surprised to see him. The only time he is here is when he needs a haircut.

"Hey Trent, what brings you in today?"

"I'm just stopping by to pay for Sherry's haircut."

"Oh. Okay. We're almost done. Just give me five more minutes." *Note to self: Don't thank Alicia for the referral. It was Trent.*

I was finished with Sherry when Trent pulled me off to the side.

"Listen, don't say anything to Alicia, and make sure you don't schedule Alicia and Sherry simultaneously. Understood?"

"Sure." I was in shock! I couldn't believe Trent, someone I thought I knew, was stepping out on Alicia.

Everyone knew about Trent's betrayal except Alicia and me. Each time she came in, I would ask what was new, and she would respond with a smile, telling me everything was fine, oblivious to the truth. My heart ached for her. She was so kind, so trusting.

When Sherry came in, she couldn't stop talking about Trent and everything they were doing, including their trips. It made me sick to my stomach. It got to the point where I was getting stressed over it. Trent asked me not to say anything if Alicia asked me about Sherry and him. I told him I would not lie for him. That wasn't my style. He couldn't understand why I wouldn't do it. Personally, I think it was a rush for him to be doing two women. It was like he was controlling both of them, calling the shots. I decided I had enough. It was getting too much regarding scheduling, knowing more than I needed to about this lovers' triangle. Sherry got upset with me because her availability didn't work out with my schedule. Disassociating myself from this nightmare, waiting to become a reality, I made up excuses as to why my schedule could no longer accommodate them.

For the first time in months, I felt a burden lifted off of my shoulders, knowing I had done the right thing, and it felt good.

92. It Really is a Small World

Gabby

I am not one to push my political or religious views onto others. I mainly don't discuss those two topics with clients unless they bring them up. Even then, I try to stay neutral. So, when I was working in the Big Apple, I had a melting pot of clients ranging from straight to gay and everything in between. It was the gay clientele that had the most interesting stories. Once I moved to Lockston and met Matthew's friend Lucas, a hairstylist, I knew he would be one interesting storyteller.

Lucas was as flamboyant as they come when it came to hairstylists. His attention to detail with clothes was always spot on, giving off a very GQ vibe. He was thin, 5´11´´ with brown hair, caramel highlights, and green eyes. He would fill in for Matthew from time to time over the years. This was one of those times forever etched in my mind. Matthew was out for six weeks due to surgery and wanted to ensure his customers didn't go elsewhere. Most of them were familiar with Lucas and enjoyed him as much as he enjoyed them. He brought a lot of energy to the studio. Lucas had a great sense of humor and always had stories to share with staff and clients. But nothing could have prepared me for what we witnessed on this day.

It was Tuesday, Lucas's first day with us. Before our day started, he told me about his weekend, which made mine sound like a total bust. Lucas never hesitated to describe his escapades with other men in detail. He would show me pictures of the flavor of the month whenever he saw me. I knew, one way or another, it was going to be a long six weeks, but I also knew I wouldn't be bored. Lucas was chomping at the bit to tell me about his weekend.

"I went to this gay bar on Saturday, I know, shocker. This good-looking guy walks in with these girls. My gaydar was going wild. There was no way any of them was his girlfriend. So I walked my cute little self over and introduced myself before anyone else approached him. It turned out he was with one of his female friends who was having a bachelorette party, and they all wanted to go to a gay bar, having never been and asked him to accompany them. By the time the evening was over, we all had a good time, especially Tay and me. You know what I mean."

"I get the point. You don't have to go into any more details." Thank God he didn't.

"So, how was your weekend, darlin?" I'm not sure that Lucas was that interested in hearing about it. He was just being polite.

"Who cares? It can't compare to yours. I just relaxed, went to Zumba, came home, and finished reading a book I started last week. Boring, I know." It was time to open up the studio. Lucas hadn't met Cami, our receptionist hired since the last time he was in, so I did the intros. In typical Lucas fashion, he started assessing her fashion sense, followed by compliments.

"Oh, gurl, I like those earrings and bracelets. Those are my favorite colors." Lucas posed to point out his teal-colored Ralph Lauren polo shirt with the purple embroidered polo player. Cami responded, "They're my favorites as well. It was nice meeting you." Cutting short the pleasantries Cami checked the answering machine for messages, unlocked the studio doors, and was ready to start her day.

It was getting close to lunchtime. It was one of those unusual days that I had time to enjoy my lunch. Well, I thought I could until Lucas came running back to the breakroom with excitement in his voice. I jumped, almost spilling the iced tea that I was drinking.

"Oh my gosh, you're not going to believe this. Tay is walking towards the studio with flowers. I didn't even know he knew where I worked. I can't believe it. I'm so excited, but I'm trying to stay calm."

"Yeah, I can tell."

"I know. I'm freaking out. I'll stay back here until Cami comes and gets me. Oh, but you have to see him. He's gorgeous."

"Can I at least enjoy my lunch you interrupted?"

"No. What if Tay drops them off because he doesn't know I'm here."

"Then you need to get out there!"

"You're right, but you have to come with me." Taking several deep breaths, Lucas turned around and started walking towards the studio. I followed, almost running into him, as he stopped dead in his tracks. Right before our eyes, we witnessed Tay giving Cami the flowers as she gave him a thank-you kiss. The Tay Lucas met this past weekend was Taylor during the week, Cami's fiancé. I couldn't believe Cami was marrying someone who was bisexual. She never mentioned it before. I'm pretty sure she didn't know.

Lucas was beside himself. "Gawd, what am I going to do? Do I tell Cami? All indications Saturday night, I never got the vibe he was bisexual." Now Lucas was torn between letting go of Tay and accepting Taylor as Cami's fiancé. Several weeks had passed before Taylor walked in one day to take Cami to lunch, making eye contact with Lucas for the first time since their "encounter." Lucas never said a word to Tay(lor), putting his focus back on his client.

Lucas had decided to wait until his last day at the studio to mention something to Cami. I wasn't sure if Cami knew this other side of Taylor, but she acted like the fling between Lucas and Taylor never happened. Lucas had already informed Matthew of what happened since the other stylists knew. Matthew could not believe it. He felt terrible for Cami. We all did. She was so innocent and naïve. She ended up marrying Taylor.

Now, every time Taylor walked into the studio to see Cami, it was a reminder of the double life Taylor was living, and Cami refused to accept.

93. ULTERIOR MOTIVE

Arianna

Going to the dentist as a kid can be fun and scary at the same time. I always enjoyed going. I had been going ever since I was little. You could say ever since I had teeth in my mouth. I remember the bubble gum toothpaste they would use to clean my teeth. I just wanted them to squirt the whole tube in my mouth. Our family dentist, Dr. Filamore, was good with kids. Unlike some of my friends, I always looked forward to my dental appointments when I was younger, especially when the time came to pick out a toy from the treasure box. To this day, I still get compliments on my teeth, especially now that I'm an adult.

That said, I was unsure how I would continue receiving dental care since I was no longer on my parents' insurance, having aged out and starting my career as a hairstylist. My mother mentioned my concern to Dr. Filamore.

"Tell Arianna I will give her a discount to clean her teeth. I don't want her to get behind on her cleaning."

So I set up an appointment. While I was there, Dr. Filamore knew I did hair, mentioning, "I'm going to start coming to you to get my haircut." Okay, in my mind, I'm thinking that's another paying customer to add to the list. I was working at another salon in Lockston at the time.

So, Dr. Filamore shows up for his appointment. He was in his 50's. By today's standards, he strongly resembled

Smithers on *The Simpsons*, from head to toe. But he was a nice guy. After I finished cutting his hair, he paid me but didn't leave.

"If you don't mind, I'll just sit here and wait for you to get off work so we can get something to eat."

"No, no, no. You don't have to wait. I'm going to be a while."

"That's okay. I cleared my schedule. I don't have anything planned." Okay, how weird is this? The last thing I want to do is go to dinner with a 50-year-old. At this point, he was making everyone uncomfortable. Finally, I said, "You know I'd like an iced tea."

"Oh, I can get that for you." When he came back, I was gone. He kept calling the salon the following week.

"I just want you to know I'm going on an Alaskan cruise, so if you don't hear from me for a few days, that's why. I'd like to see you when I get back." Of course, I told him that wasn't going to work. He kept calling the salon. He wouldn't take "No" for an answer. I told my parents, but they didn't believe me.

"He's married Arianna. You're reading too much into it." Typical response. I knew I should have never said anything.

Avoiding his calls, he finally got the hint. I made sure I could afford to go to another dentist ASAP. I never had contact again with Smithers. I mean Dr. Filamore.

94. Water Under the Bridge

Lexi

When I think back to my salon days in Doylestown, PA, the clients who stood out were memorable in one way or another: the good, the bad, and the ugly. But the ones I cherished were my connections with high school classmates. Well, most of them.

Once they entered the salon, we talked about teachers, boy crushes, football players, band and choir members, cheerleaders, and the cafeteria food that was not your mom's home cooking. And that was just from junior high. All the memories of junior high that many of us tried to forget. Just when you thought it couldn't get worse, WHAM! The junior high bully, Emily, was in the house. Loud, obnoxious, rough around the edges, and downright mean to those less fortunate. Depending on the day and her mood determined the intensity of Emily's bullying. Of course, she was already physically developed more than the other girls in our class and had started her period. We all knew when it was "that time of the month." There weren't enough hiding spots in our school of 225 students to protect us. God forbid if you called her Emmy. One of the guys in our eighth-grade class commented to her, ending the sentence with, "...Emmy would agree with me." It was the last time that name came out of his mouth.

Emily was the middle child of three children. Her mother was tough on her. Her grandmother was her only reprieve. Of course, I didn't know this when she was scaring the crap out of me. She was kind of like the forgotten child. Maybe that's why she acted up—making up for the attention she never received at home.

As freshmen, we moved on to high school, which was pretty intimidating. Not only did the school look bigger, but so did the upperclassmen. But that did not deter Emily. Her bullying had transitioned from junior high to senior high without skipping a beat. It was nothing to see a random fight break out in the halls during my four years of high school. The one common denominator: Emily was involved.

One time, I was walking down the street, and out of nowhere, Emily and another girl jumped out of a car and tried to fight me. I was only five feet tall and weighed 100 pounds. I did not engage with them at all. They left me alone.

Fast-forward 18 years, and Emily sent me a friend request on Facebook. Next thing you know, she likes the pictures I've posted, and I like hers. Emily saw that I was a hairstylist and wanted to schedule an appointment. I figured I had matured; hopefully, she had, and the past was in the past.

I recognized her as soon as she walked into the salon. She was still rough-looking and taller with a bigger boned frame. When she started coming to me, she was going through a divorce. I was going through a breakup, which led to our bonding. I would have never thought in a million years that we would end up friends years later. Emily works for a trucking company, handling logistics and dispatch. She married a few years later, and I did her hair for the wedding. Truth be known, I love the person she has become. Though I'm in Lockston now, we still keep in touch via social media.

What did she say when I brought up how she treated me in high school? Nothing. Because I never brought it up, and neither did she. It was water under the bridge, where it belonged.

95. You Get an "F" for Looks

Celeste

My husband and I had done some upgrades at our home over the last couple of years, and this year, it was time to do some serious upgrades with the deck and patio. After three estimates, we accepted the renovations would be more than anticipated. Still, given this was our forever home, we bit the bullet and went forth with the project. That also involved seeking a loan, which I loathed, but we had no choice. We decided to go with the bank we've had since we moved to Lockston.

We knew Clyde, the Senior Client Advisor at First Savings and Loan. I only learned once we were doing business with him that he was also a professor at night at the School of Business at the University of Lockston. He is very intelligent.

As we were filling out the application, he noticed where I worked. "Isn't that the same studio Matthew Siveky manages?"

"It is. Do you know him?"

"Heavens, yes, we go way back. Tell him I said, 'Hello.' By the way, I've been looking for a new stylist since my current one had moved away. Are you taking new clients?" *I just applied for a loan; of course, I'm taking new clients. I need all the money I can get.*

"Yes, I am. Here's my card. Call me, and we'll set you up with an appointment."

A few weeks later, I heard from Clyde. "Hi, Celeste. This is Clyde from First Savings and Loan. How are you doing?"

"Oh yes. Hi Clyde, how are you?"

"I'm fine. I was calling to see if you had any openings sometime this week. I'd prefer it at the end of the day since I work. Do you have any evening appointments? I don't teach on Thursdays."

"I don't this week, but I could get you in next week if that would be alright."

"Yes, that would be great."

"Is six o'clock okay?"

"Yes, perfect. I would like to have my hair and makeup done."

"Excuse me?"

"I would like my hair and makeup done, and then if you could take a couple of photos of me in dresses, I'd appreciate it." There was silence on my end. I didn't know how to respond. Photos? Makeup? Why did I give him my card?

"Hello? Are you still there?"

"Yeah, I'm here. I was double-checking my schedule." *Celeste, you know better than to lie, but how do I get out of this one?*

Stalling for time, I asked, "How many outfits are involved?"

"I don't know, six or seven. I have several trunks in a storage unit. I need to go through them and decide. I could call you back if you'd like to confirm it?"

After further discussion with Clyde, he mentioned that his wife of 35 years does not know he's a cross-dresser. He also wanted to make sure I understood he wasn't gay. He just liked to cross-dress. Knowing I would be going behind his wife's back didn't make it any better. I am not sure that I'm comfortable doing this. I don't care that I need the money. I told him I would call him back. I needed to check on some things.

I contacted our makeup artist, Whitney, first to see if she would do Clyde's makeup, and she said, "Yes." Then I asked if she knew anyone else who would do his hair and be interested in doing the photos he wanted. I told her it would need to be on a Thursday at 6:00 p.m., preferably.

As luck would have it, Whitney pulled through and had a friend who was a stylist at another salon and did photography on the side. *Thank you, Lord.* I called Clyde back the next day and told him I had no problem doing his hair and makeup, but I couldn't do it in good conscience because his wife didn't know what he was doing. I told him I referred him to someone else, and they could do everything he wanted, including an evening appointment. He was greatly appreciative. Boy, talk about dodging a bullet. I'm just glad our loan was already approved.

Clyde had his appointment and was eager to share his photos with me. Picture this, no pun intended. You have a 60-year-old man of average height and weight, gray hair, and nerdy looks. Slap makeup and a wig on him, and now you have a 60-year-old man trying to look like a woman. A terrible-looking woman in frumpy dresses, to be exact. If you have ever seen the movie *Some Like It Hot* with Marilyn Monroe and the scene when Tony Curtis and Jack Lemmon are on the train dressed as women, that was what Clyde looked like, except worse. I heard he even struggled with walking in heels.

I'm sorry, Prof. Clyde, but I must give you an "F" in the looks department. You might consider sticking to banking.

96. No One Ever Told Me I Was Beautiful

Matthew

Back in the day, I was overweight. I'm talking 175 pounds overweight. I knew I was already out of control and needed to get my act together. I decided to go with a personal trainer since Matthew's ways weren't working. I watched what I was eating but didn't deprive myself if I wanted something sweet. I just had to take smaller portions. I learned it was a mindset I had to change before changing anything else. It got to the point where my taste buds and waistline were changing. After two years of self-discipline and a phenomenal support system, I lost the extra baggage and have kept it off for seventeen years. It is true people treat you differently when you're overweight, and not in a nice way. That said, ever since I went on that weight loss journey, I became even more sensitive to my clients' appearances, especially those who were overweight, which brings to mind Pam.

No matter your size, when someone sits in my chair, I look at you and think, "What is their best asset? Is it their eyes, their smile, the shape of their face, etc."

With Pam, I couldn't help but notice her eyes and beautifully arched eyebrows that complimented her skin. Every time she came in, I told her she had the most beautiful peaches and cream skin, and green eyes I had ever seen. It was flawless. I could sense she was insecure about her looks and weight of 350 lbs. With a 5´6´´ frame, she was big. There was no sugarcoating it. She had a great personality hiding behind her insecurities. She liked doing funky colors with her hair and wanted whatever was cool and trendy at the time. Pam shared with me that she always felt like she was in her sister's shadow, who was younger, skinny, very active, and always received numerous awards. Always in the spotlight. Pam felt like the forsaken one. I never missed an opportunity to compliment her, with hopes she would start to feel somewhat better about herself.

A couple of months had passed, with Pam coming in for her usual trendy requests every three months. I thought she looked a little thinner, but I didn't want to say anything. It was hard to tell since Pam was still wearing oversized clothing. I let her know she still had those beautiful green eyes and the peaches and cream skin working for her.

Several months had passed since I had seen Pam, and over a year since she first started coming to me. We were crazy busy on this particular day. I was able to squeeze in a much-needed 10-minute break before Cami came back and told me my 1:00 was here. I walked out to the waiting area, looked around, didn't see my 1:00, and figured Cami confused her with another client. As I turned around and headed back to the breakroom, I heard someone call my name.

"Matthew!" I recognized the voice but not the person at first.

"Pam! Oh my gosh, I didn't recognize you. You look great!"

"I'm going to take that as a compliment," laughing as she walked over to my chair.

"Girl, you look amazing. What have you done?"

"Thanks. I've been losing weight gradually and naturally. I've lost 100 pounds, and I'm still going."

"One hundred pounds? You go, girl! I am so proud of you." It was the first time I saw Pam in appropriate clothes for her size. Her appointments were scheduled closer together, and every time she came in, she was getting smaller and smaller. I shared my personal story of being overweight with her and felt like we had a bonding moment. The other stylists noticed Pam's weight loss and complimented her, which only contributed to building her self-esteem. I could not be prouder of her. You never know how the simplest gestures can have such a monumental effect on a person. I had no idea how monumental it was until another year had passed, and I received a beautiful card from Pam with a letter enclosed:

Dear Matthew,

Thank you for making me feel so beautiful from the first day I met you and ever since then. No one had ever told me that I was beautiful. Growing up I always felt left out and less important than my sister. I was being made fun of in school because of my weight, which didn't help. I was the ugly, forgotten child. You saw beyond my weight. Driving home one day after my appointment with you two years ago, I looked in the rear-view mirror and saw someone with beautiful hair who looked beautiful from the neck up; hearing your voice tell me often how pretty my face and eyes were meant more to me then you'll ever know. At that moment, I decided to do something from the neck down. I turned the car around and went straight to Weight Watchers. I am now at the milestone of losing 200 pounds, and it is all because of you. Thank you for seeing the inner Pam I had tucked away all my life, hiding behind food and insecurities, too many to list. Here's to the new Pam and the stylist who made

Wow! I never saw that coming. I still get teary-eyed when I read it. It's a reminder of how important the smallest act of kindness is and how the smallest act of kindness can change a person's life forever. Once Pam lost 210 pounds, she had loose skin that needed removal. I was able to help her find a surgeon who did body contouring and removed the excess fat.

Pam has been coming to me for 19 years. She has kept off her weight and has helped others who have struggled with similar issues.

What an inspiration, Pam, you are to all of us.

97. I'm Not a Psychiatrist, But...

Gabby

It doesn't matter what part of the country you work in as a stylist. It's known that hairstylists are the unofficial therapists, counselors, psychologists, and doctors with their clients. Now I can add a psychiatrist to the list regarding Candace, aka Candy. After an appointment with her, one of us was certifiable. When I worked in New York City, I knew it was only a matter of time before I had a nut job like Candy.

Candy was 36 years old, very clean-looking, short, and curvy with large breasts. She never wore makeup or made eye contact when talking with me. She bought her clothes at Goodwill and would always show up wearing a sports bra with an off-the-shoulder sweatshirt, kind of like Alex from the movie *Flashdance*.

My first clue that she was a little paranoid was the hair extensions she would buy at Lyleth's Beauty Supply because she didn't trust what I would order. Her broken-off hair was a mousy brown. Instead of coloring it, she would purchase these 12-inch tape end extensions in gawd awful colors like orange, pink, black, and blonde, wanting me to put them all together. I would do it, making Candy look so cool. She loved it, and I love the results of her paying me. It was a win-win.

The next indication I had that Candy might be more than

just a little paranoid was when she was in the studio telling me people could see into her life. They watched what she was doing and knew what she was eating, who she was having sex with, or when she was pleasuring herself. They even knew where she was shopping. Candy was convinced the State of New York was watching her. She would not elaborate on who "they" were. Still, she mentioned she had to give her daughter up "...because they were going to sell my daughter into sex trafficking if I didn't."

Candy was a stripper, which explained why she always scheduled her appointments for late afternoon. She was beyond proud to be selected for the Gals for Pals calendar. The majority of the women chosen were trashy strippers. There was no other way to say it politely. They, indeed, weren't your Playboy models. Candy was making good money as a stripper, and in her world, life was good until life's uncertainties happened.

Her mother fell ill, placing her in a nursing home. During this time, Candy was accused of taking her mother's money. Her mother passed away, which was the catalyst for Candy's schizophrenia. *Yes, that was my diagnosis of Candy, and I'm sticking to it.* She always talked about retaping her mother's last hour of life. Candy referred to it as her mother's death hour. She convinced herself the State of New York was making a retape of her mother's death. I think my medical diagnosis of Candy from a hairstylist's point of view was pretty accurate. I can also officially add "whack-a-doo" to the list. I gathered that the retapes Candy talked about referred to replaying the memory of her mother's death.

Candy never brought her phone into the salon. Otherwise, "they" would know where she was. I was her safe place, which was a little unsettling. I felt sorry for her. She would make friends, and they would eventually turn on her because they were watching her from home, in her mind. Candy also had this rigorous diet where she only ate fish and vegetables. If she ate a hot dog, "they" would know or think she was an evil person.

I hadn't seen Candy for months. She decided to go to Myrtle Beach to get away from it all. Instead, she ended up pregnant. She came back to Lockston to have her baby. After she had her baby, she was convinced the babysitter she originally had with her first daughter was now "seeing into Candy," along with others, seeing everything Candy was doing.

I always have a jar of Starlight Mints in wrappers on the counter. Candy would eat all the mints while in the studio because she was afraid "they" would be watching her eat at home.

Candy always showed up early and paid with cash. She tipped well. Sometimes, she would pay me in ones. I would go to the bank and have $450 in ones to deposit. It was embarrassing. I always apologized to the teller.

It was rare Candy would cancel. If she had a bad night or didn't have the cash to pay for services, I would get a text saying so. There were times Candy would text me incessantly. I had to choose wisely which texts to respond to out of concern she could turn on me. I was always very concerned about her. I felt like I was the only one she trusted, so she felt safe at the salon.

Her daughter, who was in high school, would come in with Candy. What a hot mess. Then again, look at her mother. The daughter was very emo, had several facial piercings, and wore these terrible black wigs. No, the apple didn't fall far from the tree. I often think of Candy and wonder, after all these years, if she's still convinced "they" are watching her. I'm sure she is.

I'm just thankful she's never associated me with "them."

98. Today is Not About You

Isabella

A bride's day is supposed to be a once-in-a-lifetime dream come true. It's nice when you know the bride and the person she's marrying and have that gut feeling it is meant to be. Clarise's day had arrived, and she and her bridal party of six bridesmaids were in to get their hair done. Clarise had stunning features, from the big brown eyes to the perfectly shaped eyebrows to excellent bone structure, making it easy to decide early on how I would style her hair. She could be a model for a bridal magazine. She was that beautiful.

Clarise wanted her bridesmaids to have a slicked-back look with a ponytail, like in the Robert Palmer video, "Addicted to Love." Easy enough. All of the bridesmaids had long hair except for one who had a ponytail added. Lexi and Celeste were helping me that day. As usual, our makeup artist, Whitney, did an excellent job with all the girls. I was thankful for their assistance. I hadn't realized until working on the last bridesmaid, Monica, that I had picked the short straw. Everything was going smoothly, in fact, better than expected, until Monica started having a meltdown over the hairstyle selected by the bride. Between Monica breaking out in hives and hyperventilating, she was able to verbalize as she was crying, "I don't like it. I can't wear my hair like this. It looks terrible. This isn't me."

I could not believe what I was witnessing. Of course, Monica caught the attention of the rest of the bridal party. The look on Clarise's face was a combination of shock, panic, and anger. They all knew ahead of time and agreed on the look. For Monica to wait until today to do an about-face on this was unconscionable. Now I'm in panic mode. The limo was outside waiting. The bridal party was done, except for Monica, who now needed her makeup redone, and that was not happening. Whitney had already left.

Sorry, Monica, it's called natural consequences.

I could do only so many versions of the slicked-back look, and none of them were up to Monica's satisfaction. I'm sweating bullets trying to please her, knowing everyone was standing around watching this fiasco unfold, when I finally had had enough.

"Monica, are you married?"

"Yes, I am."

"Well, you had your day. Let Clarise have hers. This day is not about you. Just wear the damn ponytail. Take the pictures and take it out when you get to the reception!" I believe the bridal party broke out into applause in their minds. Clarise looked at me and mouthed, "Thank you."

Monica had nothing left to say or cry about. She put her ego in check, paid the fee, and I gladly opened the door for her when she left.

I would have loved to have seen those pictures, especially of Monica. How did her makeup look and were her hives visible in the photos?

99. I Can Do One Better

Arianna

It is so true that when they say age is a state of mind. I laugh when I hear people getting depressed because they hit a milestone in their lives, like turning 40, 50, 60, etc. Can you imagine going through life without an age attached to your being? We may act younger, not knowing any better—just a thought.

I remember growing up with *Winnie the Pooh and Friends*. It wasn't until I was older that I realized there are a lot of Eeyores in this world. You know the ones I'm talking about. The down-in-the-mouth, nothing ever goes right, poor me attitude. We need more Winnie the Poohs. Very positive, upbeat, always looking on the bright side. Those are the kind of friends you want in your circle. The ones that lift you up, not drag you down.

Alice was my Winnie the Pooh. She was amazing, cute as cute could be. She was optimistic about life in general, taking things in stride and never worrying. Reminding me, "It always works itself out." Pure joy to be around. I learned so much from her about life, especially the older you become. Not bad for someone who was a centenarian. Yes, Alice was 103. She just got her first set of hearing aids at 100. She used a walker to get around and never needed glasses. Alice didn't drive, so her daughter would bring her. I always rolled out the red carpet for Alice. I would order pizza. She liked a particular coffee. I would have it for her along with the chocolates Alice enjoyed. She was sharp as a tack. One day, my sister came in and sat down while I finished up with Alice, and Alice recognized her, "Oh, there's your sister." Wow, impressive, Alice. Alice would always ask me about my daughter, mother, and family. She was so genuine. No one believed she was 103. She has a rich life, filled with love, laughter, and a positive outlook that kept her going strong even in her late years.

Alice always wore a wet blonde bob, curled under, and parted to the side. She would have a clip-on bow that went on the side. One day, I told her, "Alice, your hair is so pretty, I don't understand why you just don't let it go white." Alice didn't miss a beat.

"Well, if I let my hair go white, it looks like I already left this world." How can you debate with the voice of reason? Blonde it will stay.

Mildred was the Eeyore in the studio. She was 93 years old. She happened to be in the studio while Alice was there on this particular day. Alice was sitting there processing (i.e., hair was chemically treated) when I told Mildred, "This lady is older than you," as I pointed to Alice, thinking it would be cute to have them start a friendship. Mildred walked over and got within one inch of Alice's face due to her poor eyesight, and the competition began.

Mildred: Sorry, I have to get so close. My eyesight is terrible.

Alice: That's fine. I don't wear glasses.

Mildred: Oh, Alice, I'm 93, and I have a bad heart.

Alice: I'm 103, and my heart is fine.

Mildred: Well, I have arthritis.

Alice: My fingers hurt sometimes, so I rub them, and it's okay.

Alice: Do you have children?

Mildred: Yes, but my son doesn't talk to me. It's all because our religious beliefs are different.

Alice: Oh, I'm sorry to hear that. My little Robby is coming home from California. I can't wait to see him.

Little Robby was 83 and looked older than his mother. In fact, he looked like he could have been Alice's father. That was one gene that skipped little Robby.

Mildred: My hearing aids always give me trouble. I don't like them.

Alice: I just got mine two years ago. I've been blessed so far. They haven't given me any problems.

What was I thinking when I put Alice and Mildred together? I'll tell you. At 93 and 103 years of age, it's not like you have many friends. These two could be good for each other. Alice, with her unwavering positivity, could be a beacon of hope for Mildred. She was strong enough that she would not let Mildred get her down. She would be an encourager if only Mildred would give her a chance.

That never happened. At least I tried.

100. When They Have Money, They Own You

Lexi

I make a comfortable living as a hairstylist, and I always have, even when I had my salon back in Doylestown, Pa. Did I grow up with a silver spoon in my mouth? Absolutely not. However, I learned how to budget and be frugal with my money. It served me well when I made the move to Lockston. I always admired those who were well off. I wish I would have had their financial sense early on in my career. Then again, I always said the good Lord gave me what I needed financially, not what I wanted.

Moving to Lockston 18 years ago, I quickly learned the sections of town that had money and the stories behind them. I have wealthy clients, most of whom you would never know had money. They would come dressed nicely but weren't flaunting their designer shoes, purses, jewelry, and clothes. But my client Elise didn't have to flaunt anything. She was the type that you couldn't help but notice when she walked into the studio. She stood out above everyone.

Elise was in her 60s and looked amazing. She had brunette hair with balayage highlights. Very thin. She always had her nails and face done. As much money as she had and how she looked, I knew she had to have plastic surgery. Elise wouldn't admit it, but she didn't realize I could see the scars on the side of her face. They were clearly visible from my perspective. I'm not complaining. She never told me. She also had Botox with all the fillers. In all honesty, Elise was a dream client. She was usually nice and not demanding, to a certain point. She would get the total package with me, including hair extensions. Elise tipped very well. When she wasn't in Lockston, she would frequent her home in Beverly Hills or her rustic home on the lake in Deep Creek, Maryland. The latter was her and her husband's escape from the hustle and bustle of city life. Money was no object to Elise, having nothing but the best.

Elise was a giving person. She would buy me and my parents gifts. In addition to the gifts, she mentioned the donations made to local charities by her and her husband. I felt privileged that Elise selected me out of all the hairstylists, but I also felt a commitment like none other.

One Saturday, Elise showed up for her appointment. She had rescheduled for a color. As we finalized what I would do on this day, she said something about extensions. "You are also doing my extensions, correct?"

"No, I only have you scheduled for a color. I don't have the time to do extensions."

"Well, when I rescheduled, I thought it was obvious I would need them done. You have to do it." Elise had now broken into tears, crying. Standing there watching her get emotional, I'm speechless, caught between a rock and a hard place. My mind was racing, second-guessing the decision I was about to make. All I kept thinking about were the other clients I had scheduled that day and how this would throw everyone off, which I despised. Putting it in perspective, technically, I worked for Elise. She pays me very well, and I always do what she asks. At that moment, I realized Elise had an emotional hold on me via guilt. I needed to comply with her requests no matter how busy I got or risked losing her business. Plus, I knew she had a lot of connections who would hear what had happened.

I moved the rest of my appointments that day to focus on Elise. She tipped me very well, sensing the inconvenience she had caused. I was upset, knowing my other clients were not pleased, though they said they understood. They were just being kind. Since that day, whenever I schedule Elise, I always repeat what I will be doing on her next appointment to ensure we're on the same page, followed with, "This is the time I have you locked in, given what I'm going to do." Of course, I can be flexible to a certain point but not to where my other clients pay the price. Whether one has money or not, boundaries need to be established.

Note to self: Always set boundaries with every client, regardless of their financial status. Be aware of people who spend a lot of money on your services and throw in gifts throughout the year. They think they own you.

101. Do You Hear What I Don't

Celeste

I usually don't have difficulty understanding my clients, especially the elderly. But when it comes to someone with a severe speech impediment due to being deaf since birth, that can be a challenge. I am just thankful Colorado had Relay Colorado, which helps those who are deaf or have speech disabilities communicate effectively with others when talking on the phone. The device has been a godsend, connecting those with auditory impairments to the hearing world. That was the same device Arianna's client, Lydia, who was deaf, used when scheduling appointments. Whenever Lydia was in the studio, she would use hand gestures, which were very interesting and, at times, bordering on X-rated.

Lydia was in her 60s, cute, and very tall. She had a curly mullet that was cut, not all the way around her ears but halfway up her ears. Lydia would come in about three times a year to get a cut and perm. In her way, Lydia would tell Arianna she wanted to look beautiful for her boyfriend, followed by hand gestures insinuating about their sex life that were for adult eyes only. She couldn't talk but could read lips and liked when told she was beautiful. It was admirable how well Lydia did in the "hearing world." She has stayed gainfully employed, was able to rent an apartment, and lived independently.

I had a client in my chair that I was doing when Lydia walked towards us from the shampoo bowl. As she walked in front of us, she let out the loudest fart. It sounded like a tuba holding a note for four counts, followed by staccato farts, as she walked to her chair to sit down. The look on Arianna's face was priceless. I could not contain myself as I burst out laughing. I knew Lydia couldn't hear me, and I waited until she passed by me before I lost it. My client did the same, followed with, "What the heck was that? Can't she hear that?"

I enlightened my client by telling her, "Actually, she can't. She's deaf." We realized she may have the sensation of releasing gas but didn't know that it made sounds. Boy, did it ever make sounds. I looked at Arianna; now she was trying not to laugh, especially after seeing us crack up.

I was just thankful they were odorless farts.

102. Foot in Mouth

Arianna

Before I came to My Preference Hair Studio, I had worked at a smaller salon in Lockston. When Matthew hired me, I felt confident that most of my clients would follow me, and they did. I can also say with 100% confidence that I was glad I did not have to see some clients who weren't mine anymore.

I was new in the industry and still building up my clientele, so I wasn't very busy and would help work the front desk and answer the phone. I always enjoyed meeting people, so this was a good place to be, except when Leo walked in. Leo could pass for Lurch's cousin if you remember Lurch in *The Addams Family*. Ugly! Leo was the CEO of a healthcare facility in the next town over, but he lived in Lockston. He stood out in a crowd. You always knew when Leo was around. His cologne would waft through the door before he would. I swear he was wearing Arrogance by Leo. He acted like we were supposed to be honored that he had arrived. Leo had a thing for my boss, Yvette, making sure she always cut his hair. He was just slimy. His comments bordered on perversion. He was downright disgusting.

Well, this one Monday, late afternoon, it was just Yvette and me in the salon. Yvette was with her customer, Tara. Tara was very proper, matronly, and friendly with personable characteristics you would expect of a teacher, which she happened to be. I was staffing the front desk when the phone rang. I answered it, only to hear Leo's voice on the other end. *Gawd, why couldn't I have been in the bathroom when the phone rang?*

"Hi, is my hot and dangerous, sexy, little blonde stylist working? I want to schedule an appointment with that doll." *Insert finger in mouth and gag.*

"She's with a customer. Can I help you with an appointment?" He proceeded to tell me when he would like to come in, etc. I got off the phone with my skin crawling and the thoughts of Leo coming in. Projectile word vomit came out. I couldn't help it.

"OH MY GOD!" Yvette looked at me in shock. I did not hold back once I got on a roll. "That was Leo. He was so disgusting on the phone. 'Is my hot and sexy blonde working?' What a pervert. I can't believe he thinks that is something a woman wants to hear. He is just creepy. I don't like him. He is sick!"

As I ran off with my mouth, Yvette stood behind Tara, pointing at Tara. *What in the world is Yvette doing? I don't get it.* Finally, Yvette mouthed, "This is his wife." OH, now I get it. I wanted to crawl under the desk. Tara never said a word. She did not even look up at me as I walked past her, nor I at her, donning my fifty shades of embarrassment.

After that day, Tara never came in when I was working, which worked for me. I also learned the importance of not talking trash in front of a client.

They might know who you're talking about, or worse yet, they might be married to that person.

103. I Got One Over on Her

Isabella

When I lived in Florida, Mount Dora, to be exact, we were always known for our quaint little town. The salon I worked in was well-known in the area. I had a decent amount of clients. I was cutting hair but also able to do manicures. It was a nice change of pace from standing on my feet all day. Manicures were always on Thursdays. I figured by then, I was ready to get off my feet.

My clients were a joy to be around. Well, most of them, except for one or two. Antonella was definitely in the top two. She was in her 40s, Italian, and very nice to me. But she wasn't nice to everyone. A lot of people didn't like her. She had a shady side to her, but I never pried into her business. I figured the less I knew, the better.

What is the best way to describe Antonella? You've heard of telegrams and telegraphs, but there is also tele-Antonella. She was into everyone's business. She knew who was sleeping with whom, who was pregnant, who got fired or promoted, and the list goes on. I never had to read the newspaper the week she was coming in. I knew she would have all the dirt and the behind-the-scenes info to catch me up. Today was no different.

"Did you hear about that dentist who got caught with one

of his patients by his wife? She had stopped by the office unannounced." Before I could answer one way or another, Antonella was off and running with the details. I barely had a chance to comment, "No, I hadn't heard," and she was on to the next bit of gossip.

"What about those two kids that carjacked that elderly woman's car and severely beat her?" Even if I would have said, "I heard," it didn't matter. Antonella was going to spew out every last detail. When she finally stopped long enough to breathe, I decided to get one over on her.

In our small town, we had two car washes. Right outside of Mount Dora, there was this big, elaborate car wash being built. "Have you seen what's happening outside of our town?"

"No, what?"

"Oh my gosh, I don't know whose brain wasn't working when they thought about this, but somebody is building a huge, fancy car wash. We don't need another car wash. We already have two of them. Why in the world would they do that? Of all the things the residents in the area could benefit from, three car washes certainly were not the way to go. Who in their right mind thought, 'We need to build a bigger car wash?' How dumb could you be?" Once I got wound up, I could only stop long enough to take a breath before I continued on my soapbox. I was having an adrenaline rush with the thoughts that I finally knew something Antonella didn't, and I had to seize the moment. Boy, did it feel good. After sharing my thoughts, I respectfully asked Antonella what her thoughts were about it.

"My father, Anthony, that's his business. He's the brains behind it. He always wanted to build one." *Open mouth, insert foot and chew.* There was nothing left to say at this point, and I was beyond embarrassed.

The good news is that Antonella showed me grace and continued to come to me to get her hair done. The bad news is Antonella will never forget how I bashed her father's business.

The next time I bring up a subject involving someone, I'll ask Antonella first if she knows the person and follow her lead.

So much for trying to one-up her.

104. What a Gentleman... Not

Gabby

Does anyone remember back in the day when a guy would open a door for a woman entering any building or hold a car door open for her? I've heard chivalry is not dead. Maybe not, but it's on its last breath. I'm sure there are men in this world who know how to treat a lady. The bulk of them are with the baby boomers. As I mentioned, I've been blessed many times over with my husband. He still opens the doors for me, whether entering a building or getting into a car. He'll joke and say, "Here, let me get the door for you. People are watching. It makes me look good." I just love that man.

As usual, my Wednesday was booked solid, except for a 15-minute break around 4:00 p.m. Thank goodness for energy bars. By then, I will need one or two, maybe three? I had just finished my 10:00 appointment when Cami approached to see if I had any openings this afternoon. She told me a gentleman was on the phone wanting to schedule an appointment for his wife, but it had to be after 2:00 today. I told her I was booked but had an opening on Friday at 1:30 if he wanted to schedule it then. If not, I suggested Cami check with Celeste, who was in the back. She might be able to help.

Fortunately for this husband, Celeste could take his wife

today, but it must be at noon. As Cami delivered the message, the caller responded, "Thank you, but I know my wife won't be happy about the time. She stressed she wanted the appointment in the afternoon. I guess we don't have a choice." *No, you don't. Take it or leave it.*

The following is what took place, told by Celeste.

***

I've been blessed with the gift of perception. I can tell by looking at a couple whether they are a good fit for each other. Watching what Isabella went through with the one couple whose husband kept stalking Isabella over his wife's improprieties, made me appreciate my clients who are couples even more. The clients I have now, for the most part, have decent relationships with their spouses. I'm glad.

My noon appointment arrived on time. As I introduced myself while greeting the couple, the reception was cold. I was not getting a good read on their marriage or them. They did not look like a happy couple. I know couples can have their days when they aren't in sync. Truth be known, this couple looked out of sync all the way around. They didn't look like they belonged together at all. He was chubby, 5´7´´, in a suit jacket that could not hide his round stomach, covered by his dress shirt, with no tie. He was in his 60s.

On the other hand, his wife, Deann, was about 45 and attractive, with no makeup and soft brown hair past her shoulders. She was wearing a T-shirt and jeans. They were a very odd couple.

I discussed with Deann what she wanted me to do, but she never had a chance to finish telling me before her husband took over the conversation. "Do what you need to do to make it soft and curly. It needs to last for three days. We have a big affair in Denver." Hmmm. I don't recall reading about any significant events this weekend. I'm usually up on those

319

things and often go to Denver. I could have missed an event going on. I was still curious about what event was taking three days, but I didn't want to sound too eager to ask.

Little communication took place during the appointment, which left me wondering if Deann was abused by her husband, either verbally or physically. I didn't see any bruises on her, but her quiet persona left me to question the type of relationship they had. Her husband stayed for most of the appointment, looking up intermittently from the newspaper to ensure Deann's hair was styled how he wanted it. There was no way I was asking him for his approval. I was already doing both of them a favor by taking Deann today. Towards the end, her husband stepped out of the studio. I couldn't let the moment pass and had to ask.

"So, that's your husband?"

"No. Just a friend." I knew it. He did not look like her type, and I thought maybe he was her sugar daddy.

"You're going to Denver this weekend. The weather is supposed to be good."

"It doesn't matter to me. We have an event to attend, and it's indoors." She didn't elaborate, and I didn't ask. I didn't have to. I finally figured it out.

Her friend returned to pay for Deann's appointment, with a nice tip included. It all made sense now why her friend was adamant about Deann needing an appointment after 2:00 p.m. She was up through the night "working" and needed her sleep.

105. Country Boy Meets City Cougar

Lexi

Faith and I have been friends ever since cosmetology school back in PA. We would always look forward to vacationing in Lockston. I knew it was just a matter of time before I called Lockston my home. It took Faith a little longer to come out west. She finally did after she ended a four-year relationship with her boyfriend. She now manages a salon five miles outside of Lockston. We go to each other to have our hair done. We always make sure we're the last appointments because, well, you know, we have a lot of catching up to do. Be it clients, Faith's new beau, if there's one that month, family gossip, etc., the list continues to grow.

Faith grabbed the attention of men and women alike. She easily could have been a swimsuit model with her slender 5′6′′ frame that females envied and men desired. Her long, balayage blonde hair with a brown base complimented her brown eyes. Her social life was off the charts, and she was always in demand to do something with someone. That is why we cherished our appointments.

Faith hadn't been seeing anyone serious since she moved to Lockston. I always lived vicariously through her. When she walked into the studio that night, she had that Cheshire cat smile and couldn't contain it. I knew, looking at her, this was going to be good. "Okay, out with it. What's his name?"

Laughing, Faith responded, "What? Why do you think there's someone?"

"Hello, I know you, and I know that smile. It's not because you came across a great sale at Macy's." As Faith sat down, I put the cape on her and didn't ask what she wanted done today. Instead, I demanded to know what she was dying to tell me. "Start talking."

"Well, I was watching the World Series at the Blue Pine Bar 'n Grill, and this guy caught my attention. I purposely stood by him at the bar to order my drink. He was in my way, and I said, "Excuse me. I need to order my drink.""

"He said, "Sure, what can I tell the bartender you would like?""

"Kahlua and Cream." Then he paid for my drink. I thanked him, and he introduced himself. His name is Casey. He's German and proud of his German heritage. He's a cowboy. A first for me. He is 6-foot, with light brown hair. He was not my usual type. You know I like dark-haired guys. He has a little facial hair but is clean-cut. No tattoos. He reminds me of a county singer. He always wears a cowboy hat and boots. He's rugged-looking and good-looking. He reminds me of someone you'd see on a Western TV show. He lives on a farm."

"Wow, he sounds handsome. This is so unlike you. He must be something else."

"He is. Before the night was over, I gave him my card and told him to call me if he ever needed a haircut."

"Oh, you smooth operator. You know you could have cared less about his hair."

"Shut up. I do." *I couldn't hold back the grin on my face.* "Casey called me about a week later and scheduled an appointment. He was so nice and polite. After his appointment, I asked if he wanted to schedule another appointment. He responded, 'Yes, but to take you to dinner.' He said that he was interested in getting to know me and was attracted to me."

"Awe, how sweet. Let me guess. You said 'yes?'"

"Yes. Casey was so charming. I couldn't resist. He picked me up in his jacked-up truck, which was so tall that it hit the tree branches by my home. The neighbors knew when he was visiting because his truck was so loud."

"A far cry from the Lexus SUV you had back east. Where did you go to eat?"

"He took me to Texas Roadhouse. He was charming. When he paid for the bill, he had this stitched leather wallet. He is country through and through."

"I can't believe you are dating one of your clients. That's very risky."

"I've never done that before. I thought about it numerous times, knowing this could backfire. I can't help myself. He is not someone I'm used to being with. I really like him. He is so well-mannered. When we go out to eat, he removes his cowboy hat. If he runs into someone he knows and they introduce him to their spouse, he tips his hat and responds, 'It's a pleasure to meet you, ma'am.'"

"Oh, Faith, he sounds like a great guy." It's been a long time since I saw Faith this happy. It sounded like he could be the one. She was so devastated by the last relationship she vowed it would take years to get over it. Her ex, who shall remain nameless, and Faith had dated for four years. They talked about engagement one month, and her world exploded the following month. He traveled for business, and Faith thought she would surprise him by meeting him at the hotel, making it a little getaway at the end of the week. She showed up the night before he was to check out, around 9:30 p.m. She told the front desk she was meeting her husband but forgot the room number. The clerk told her the room and provided Faith with a key. If he weren't in the room, she would slip into something sexy and wait for his arrival. Instead, she entered the room to find him in bed with his coworker, who was a male. Moving out to Lockston was the best thing Faith could have done, leaving all that garbage behind. Now, I see life in her eyes when she talks about Casey. She couldn't stop talking about him.

"Did you know cowboys have their own language? The other night, he was at my house for dinner. I asked him if he wanted more wine. He said, 'Just a freckle.' I'm wondering what the heck a freckle has to do with a refill. Then, he gave me a lesson in Cowboy Talk 101. He always compliments me on my clothes. He once said, 'You sure know how to rag proper.' Excuse me? It meant dressing well. Who knew? Another time, he mentioned hair in the butter, and we weren't even eating. I found out it meant a delicate situation. Casey did make me a little nervous when he told me about two of his friends he spends time with, using the phrase 'crawl his hump.' It was a trigger for me, which he didn't know then. I found out it meant to start a fight. Phew, that was close. I've learned so much about cowboys. Also, I have a new respect for them and the responsibilities that come with that lifestyle."

I'm listening to Faith talk this entire time, and I can't believe this is the same person from back in the day in Doylestown. This new side of Faith was one of joy and excitement. She found someone who appeared to appreciate her. I was honestly happy for her. I'm thankful she decided to move to Lockston when she did, as hard as that decision was for her. "Hey, by the way, you never said how old he was?"

"Well, he's younger than me. He's 25."

"WHAT! That's 17 years younger than you. You're a cougar!"

"I never looked at it that way, but you're right. I'll take that. No one else is around when he comes in for his appointment at the end of the day. I'll finish his appointment with me, and then we have scheduled appointments with each other. You know what I mean?"

"Wait, are you telling me you guys do it in the salon?"

"All I'm saying is that I close the blinds, the Open sign shuts off, and you can let your imagination run wild from there."

***

Update: Faith and Casey's affair lasted on and off for seven years until they both agreed that, with the age difference, it wouldn't work. Faith said it was sad, but they had a lot of fun throughout the years, creating memories. Casey married a teacher, and Faith is still single.

106. Till Death Do Us Part

Celeste

Growing up in Grand Island, NE, I remember, when I was young, how excited I was to go over to my friend Sharon's house to play. She always had the coolest toys. Her parents were well off, and Sharon wanted for nothing. She had a playhouse outside that held many tea parties with our stuffed animals. Although playing at Sharon's house was fun, and I looked forward to it, it came with a price. Her mother, Madeline, was mean. Sometimes, she would yell at Sharon, causing Sharon to burst into tears. Heck, I wanted to cry. She scared me. There were other times Madeline would yell or hit Sharon's two older sisters, who grew up continuing not to be fond of Madeline. Sharon's father was not exempted from Madeline's wrath when he came home from work. Looking back on the situation, Sharon's father probably thought often, "Why didn't I work over?" Sharon and I remained friends through high school. After graduation, Sharon went on to college for nursing, and I entered the world of cosmetology.

As a stylist, you must be dedicated to your job and clients. If not, you will only last a short time in the profession. The hard part is when you have a challenging client, and you have to suck it up and bite your tongue. It is times like those I keep reminding myself, *Celeste, if you didn't do such a good job with your clients, they wouldn't return. You have no one to blame but yourself.*

Twenty years later, I received a phone call out of the blue at work. It was Madeline. "Hi Celeste, it's Madeline, Sharon's mother."

"Oh, hi. How are you?"

"Can you come over to my home? I need you to touch up my hair. I am going someplace later tonight?" If I were a betting person, I would have never thought after all these years that I would have heard from Madeline. She had her own stylist but would call me to touch up her hair. It was mostly her bangs. I would get a call once a week. A few times, it was up to three times a week to come over. I wouldn't be there long at all, plus it was on my way home. She paid me for my time but not for my frustrations. Her focus was on her bangs, wanting them a certain way. I would do them like she wanted, but Madeline would take the brush and say, "No, I need it to be more like this," sweeping the bangs off to the side more. There was no pleasing her, yet she seemed pleased with me because she kept calling me back to do her hair.

Being an adult, I wasn't scared of her anymore, but the memories that raced through my head like a video on fast-forward weren't always pleasant when I walked into Madeline's home. I do recall Madeline always wore a housecoat. She would get dressed, run her errands, then return home and change into her housecoat for the rest of the day. To this day, when I see a housecoat, I think of Madeline.

Madeline had taken ill and was in the hospital. She was nearing the end of her life. Believe it or not, her husband paid me to come to the hospital to do Madeline's hair. Although Madeline had become physically weaker, she was still strong verbally, reminding me, "Get my bangs right. Make sure you get my bangs right." I just went along with whatever she wanted. That's the way it was the ten years of fixing her bangs.

Madeline passed away at the age of 74. Fortunately, I was not asked to do her hair after she passed. I would have declined. There was no way I was taking the chance of her returning and haunting me because I didn't get her bangs right. It was almost ten years of phone calls from Madeline asking me to make house calls that abruptly ended. That was going to be a psychological adjustment for me. My car was programmed to stop at Madeline's home every week.

Standing before the casket, I told her husband, "I think Madeline's hair looks nice, especially her bangs. They did a good job. I think she would be happy."

Laughing, he responded, "Oh, you know she still wouldn't be happy, especially with the bangs."

Madeline was known throughout the years for not being very kind to people. I realized now that I was one of the very few she was nice to, knowing no one else would take the time to come to her home. As frustrating as it was to fix her bangs, she told me several times, "You do a pretty good job."

Thanks, Madeline.

107. Looks are Deceiving

Isabella

When I worked in Mount Dora, Florida, we would get some unusual people wanting their hair cut. I tried very hard not to judge. You never know the road they have traveled that brought them to this point in life or brought them to you, which brings me to Sadie.

She was in her early 40s, but life had not been kind to her. Sadie had one arm. The other arm ended at the elbow with what looked like a little hook about three inches from her elbow. It was some kind of appendage that would move up and down. Very strange. She walked with a slight limp. I don't know if one leg was shorter than the other, resulting in her using a cane. When she wasn't using her cane, she would hang it on her appendage. Sadie usually wore big, fluffy dresses. Sometimes, you would see her in polyester pants and shirts like an older woman would wear. You always saw Sadie with a cap. She had one that looked like a fisherman's cap, and the other looked like a puffy ball cap, except it had a brim that went all the way around. Sometimes, she would wear makeup, sometimes not.

I would do her hair once a week, usually on Saturdays, and Sadie was always pleased with how it turned out. She would make a point of coming in daily to visit or talk with the other clients. She would talk stupid crap and make up conversations irrelevant to her visit. "What do you think about that restaurant?" "Have you tried that new grocery store in town?" "Boy, this weather is something else." "I heard on the news there was a bomb threat at a high school up north." *Sadie, you need to stop talking.*

Sadie also made a point of using the restroom. Once, she flooded the bathroom and wanted us to replace the stamps in her purse that got wet when it was on the floor.

That's a hard "No!" Sorry Sadie, you need to purchase more stamps.

I had this gut feeling something wasn't right with Sadie. I kept telling the other stylists there was something wrong with Sadie. They all would respond, "She's just a little bit crazy and needed someplace to go. She's not hurting anything. You're reading too much into it." Okay, maybe I was, but I didn't think so. I felt there was more to Sadie's story than we knew.

The one thing I found strange was that I could hear tapping and banging on the walls every time Sadie used the restroom. That is not normal when you go to the bathroom. The first time I heard it, I was concerned. I knocked on the door and asked Sadie if everything was okay. She replied, "I'm fine." I didn't bother her after that, but it was still strange. I figured it must have been her bathroom ritual. I don't know what else to call it. It went on for a week, from Saturday to Saturday.

It was Sunday morning, and I realized I had left my eyeglasses at work. I needed to leave earlier than usual to get them before meeting friends for breakfast. Pulling up to the salon, I saw cops everywhere with their cruiser lights on. What the heck was going on? I exited my SUV and headed for the salon when an officer stopped me.

"Ma'am, you can't go in there. This is a crime scene."

"Crime scene? Did someone get murdered?"

"No, breaking and entering. Whoever it was, they thought everything out. They hit every business in this plaza." All the businesses, including our salon, were connected. Sadie was the culprit. Well, part of a gang or a chain of people that robbed us clean. She had gone to each business and used their restrooms, and by tapping on the walls, she could figure out the areas on the walls to break through without hitting the pipes. This group of thieves broke through every wall, tunneling from business to business in the middle of the night. Sadie had frequented the yogurt shop several times in the past week, noticing the vault in the floor of the yogurt shop. Police reported the vault was pulled out of the floor and the money stolen. These guys (and girls) wasted no time ripping all of us off. I'll never forget that feeling of helplessness standing outside the salon. I also never retrieved my glasses that day.

I knew something was peculiar about Sadie. I just had that gut feeling.

108. Thoughts to Ponder

After reading *Salon Confidential,* I hope you will have a new appreciation for hairstylists and what they go through daily. They are the chameleons of the profession. The ability to play a different role with each client, such as a therapist, counselor, doctor, psychologist, etc., while simultaneously focusing on making you look good is a true talent. The depth of their emotional support for their clients knows no bounds.

Every day, hairstylists come to work with their professional emotional tank filled, ready for you to share what's on your mind, even when their personal emotional tank may be empty. They show up for work, whether they feel good or not, demonstrating their unwavering dedication to their craft and to you, their client.

Please be understanding whenever they contact you to tell you they are sick and need to reschedule. It's not to upset you. It's a necessary step they take to protect both of you. Understanding their needs in such situations is crucial.

Speaking of canceling appointments, make sure you know their cancellation and no-show policy so there are no surprises on your end when they charge you for the time you failed to contact them in a timely fashion. Keeping your appointment is crucial because they include your costs in their budget for the month. Yes, life happens, and stylists get that, but be mindful that they make no money when you don't show up and their chair is unoccupied until their next appointment, which could be two hours out.

It's imperative to always arrive on time. When you're late, it not only disrupts the stylist's schedule but also shows a lack of respect for their time. Remember, their time is just as valuable as yours. Respect it.

Stylists make their jobs look easy because they're good at what they do. Many people think you can become a hairstylist if you know how to use scissors and a blow dryer. Not so fast. With a cosmetology license comes the knowledge of you knowing your client's bone structure (anatomy), chemical processes, perming, manicure, pedicure, makeup, and facials, to name a few. Plus, hundreds of hours of training before you're on your own. When these future stylists have achieved academic overload, instructors throw in for kicks and giggles the laws they must abide by in their states.

Stylists enjoy trying new looks with their clients. This can only be achieved when you bring in a photo or pull the picture up on your phone to show them. Stylists prefer you avoid hand-drawn illustrations that look like a Picasso drawing. Otherwise, it will look like Picasso is your stylist.

Above all, *please* remember always to tip your stylist. Show them that you appreciate the time they took to make you look and feel better while boosting your morale and building your confidence.

Hairs to you! ☺

Susan